CULT TV

THE ...

DETECTIVES

CULT TV

THE ...
DETECTIVES

JON E. LEWIS AND PENNY STEMPEL

PAVILION

First published in Great Britain in 1999 by
PAVILION BOOKS LIMITED
London House, Great Eastern Wharf
Parkgate Road, London SW11 4NQ

Text © Jon E. Lewis and Penny Stempel
Design and layout © Pavilion Books Ltd

Designed by Nigel Partridge

A CIP catalogue record for this book is available from the
British Library.

ISBN 1 86205 311 1

Set in Futura
Printed in Singapore by Imago

2 4 6 8 10 9 7 5 3 1

This book can be ordered direct from the publisher.
Please contact the Marketing Department.
But try your bookshop first.

CONTENTS

KEY TO ENTRY CREDITS

1 **7** **2** **3** **4** **8** **5** **9** **6**

BANACEK

USA 1972–4 16 x 90m, 1 x 120m col NBC.

Universal Television. UK tx 1975–7 ITV.

10 ▶ **CR** *Richard Levinson, William Link.*

EXEC PR *George Eckstein.* **PR** *Howie Horowitz.*

DR *Lou Antonio, Herschel Daughterty, Daryl Duke, Theodore J Flicker, Richard T Heffron, Bernard L Kowalski, George McCowan, Bernard McEveety, Andrew McLaglen, Jimmy Sangster, Jack Smight.*

WR *Mort Fine, Theodore J Flicker, Stephen Kandel, Richard Levinson, William Link, Harold Livingston, Stephen Lord, David Moessinger, Paul Playdon, Robert Presnell Jr, Del Reisman Roberts, Star*

1 Country of origin

2 Year(s) of transmission

3 Number of episodes

4 Programme length

5 Colour or black and white

6 Transmission channel in country of origin

7 Production company/companies

8 Transmission date(s) in secondary country

9 Transmission channel in secondary country

10 **CR** creator(s), **EXEC PR** executive producer(s), **PR** producer(s), **DR** director(s), **WR** writer(s), **MUS** composer(s)

INTRODUCTION

Freeze! Ever since the first TV transmitters were pointed to heaven, detective shows have made for some of the most arresting programming to appear on the tube. From vintage classics like *Adam 12* and *Highway Patrol* through to contemporary objects of desire such as *Law and Order* and *Homicide: Life on the Street*, mystery shows have garnered audiences of loyal millions. More perhaps than any other TV genre, the detective show has endured the passing decades. Why? Well, it's elementary, my dear Watson. In an age of rising crime, detective shows provide a fictional reassurance that evil is booked, Danno, and sent to the penitentiary. On TV, at least, no crime goes undetected, no criminals go unpunished.

If the basic MO of crime TV never alters, however, the reel detectives who do the catching have come – and gone – in a long parade of differing identities: spinster sleuth, cultured cop, tough-guy PI, cerebral amateur, paraplegic ex-detective chief, sexy woman cop ... the list is almost endless. But not entirely reasonless. If a magnifying glass is held up to the history of detectives on the small screen, definite fashions can be seen. The 1950s were the era of the straight-arrow cop, exemplified by

Joe Friday in *Dragnet*, Dan Matthews in *Highway Patrol*, George Dixon in *Dixon of Dock Green*, all of whom reflected the basic conservatism of that age. A shift in public attitudes in the late Sixties and early Seventies ushered in a parade of minority and women detectives – *Shaft* (a black PI), Pepper Anderson in *Police Woman*, *Banacek* (Polish-American), and *Longstreet* (blind). Not to mention the *The Mod Squad*, comprising cops who were ... hippies, and Ironside, a white wheelchair-bound police captain forced to rely on a woman, a sensitive liberal male and a black van driver to get justice done. The Seventies also saw the arrival of the door-slamming, tyre-squealing brigade, trail-blazed by *Starsky and Hutch* in the USA and *The Professionals* and *The Sweeney* in Britain, whose macho antics, if risible, implicitly recognised that crime-busting was oft times a violent job and that the catchers themselves became brutalized in the process. Indeed from the Seventies through to the present, the most significant change – but perhaps least noticed – in reel detection has been to put the detectives themselves under the spotlight, to peruse their private and personal lives voyeuristically. Witness Chris Cagney's alcoholism in *Cagney and Lacey*, John Kelly's angst-ridden relationship with Mob-compromised officer Jenny Licalsi in *NYPD Blue*, the creeping homo-erotic attraction between Pembleton and Bayliss in *Homicide: Life on the Street*. Modern detectives still get the bad guys. It's just that they suffer while doing so.

If there is one TV genre that will never go out of fashion, it's crime TV. It has heroes to fit every TV age and a raison d'être which provides comfort amid the endless horrors of real life crime. And, while every TV viewer has his or her favourite detective show, thanks to the time-warp programming of cable/satellite stations and the nostalgia of terrestrial TV, almost all the 700 crime programmes ever made are available on a small screen near someone now. The TV 'tec fan has never had it so good – except for the need for an authoritative guide.

Cult TV: The Detectives is the first guide to those detective TV shows which really matter – the shows which have truly handcuffed the viewer to the screen. There are case files on 200 such cult shows, with critical analysis, fascinating facts, classic episodes, and catchphrases. Plus full cast and crew credits, including episode directors, not least because so many Hollywood helmsmen have come up through the mill of detective TV (Robert Altman and Michael Mann among them), together with awards and video availability. The full range of detective shows is covered: action dramas (*Starsky and Hutch*, *The Professionals*), cerebral whodunnits (*Inspector Morse*), American private eye shows (*Cannon*, *Magnum*), and police dramas (*Dragnet*, *The Streets of San Francisco*). There is also a slot or two for the camp (*Green Hornet*), the off-beat (*Millennium*), and the strangely bewitching schlock (*Hart to Hart*, Michelle Pfeiffer's *BAD Cats*).

And, hey, let's be careful out there.

ADAM—12

USA 1968–75 175 x 30m col NBC. Mark VII/Adam–12 Productions/Universal Studios Television/MCA Productions.

CR *Robert Cinader, Jack Webb.* **PR** *Robert Cinader, Jim Doherty, Herman Saunders, Tom Williams.* **DR** *Various, including Dennis Donelly, Harry Morgan, Jack Webb, Lawrence Doheny, Hollingsworth Morse, Alan Crosland Jr, Phil Rawlinson.* **WR** *Various, including Jack Webb, Preston Wood, Robert Holt, Stephen J Cannell, Leo V Gordon.* **MUS** *Frank Comstock.*
CAST *Off Peter 'Pete' Molloy (Martin Milner) Off James 'Jim' A Reed (Kent McCord) Sgt MacDonald (William Boyett) Dispatcher (Shaaron Claridge) Off Brinkman (Claude Johnson) Off Wells (Gary Crosby) Sgt Jerry Miller (Jack Hogan) Off Jerry Walters (William Stevens) Off Woods (Fred Stromsoe).* **VIDEO** *Columbia House.*

Long-running US police series about the day-to-day work of two LAPD officers who rode a patrol car call-signed 'Adam–12'. Martin Milner played senior officer Pete Malloy (badge 744), Kent McCord probationary rookie cop Jim Reed (badge 2430). It came from Jack Webb's Mark VII company and, like his famed, earlier >*Dragnet*, was an exercise in low-key cop TV with cases running the realistic gamut from speeding violations to homicide. By the end of the run Reed had been promoted to officer and Malloy to

Policeman 3, with the duo upgrading their vehicular hardware from a 1967 Plymouth Belvedere to a 1972 AMC Matador. The show – which made the top ten of the Nielsens in 1971 – spawned a pale direct descendant, *Adam 12* (1989–90, 52 x 30m col, syndicated, with Peter Parros and Ethan Wayne in the leads), and left its tyre mark on numerous others. Not least the mobile buddy–buddy show >*CHiPS*.
GUEST CAST: Cloris Leachman, Mickey Dolenz, Robert Fuller, James B Sikking.

Kent McCord (left) and Martin Milner in cop-car classic Adam-12.

 *Elementary, my dear Watson. Jeremy Brett (right) in the definitive* The Adventures of Sherlock Holmes.

THE ADVENTURES OF SHERLOCK HOLMES

UK 1984–6 13 x 60m col ITV. A Granada Television Network Production. US tx 1985–6 WGBH.

PR *Michael Cox.* **DR** *Paul Annett, John Bruce, Alan Grint, David Carson.* **WR** *Alexander Baron, Anthony Skene, Jeremy Paul, Alan Plater, Alfred Shaughnessy, Paul Finney, Bill Craig, Derek Marlowe, Richard Harris, John Hawkesworth.*
MUS *Patrick Gowers.*
CAST *Sherlock Holmes (Jeremy Brett) Dr Watson (David Burke) Mrs Hudson (Rosalie Williams) Inspector Lestrade (Colin Jeavons).* **VIDEO** *Granada.*

'Elementary, my dear Watson.' Modelled closely on the mood and style of the original Victorian Strand Magazine stories (illustrated by Sidney Paget), old Etonian Jeremy

12

Brett's interpretation of Holmes is generally agreed to be definitive: a man of awesome genius, but also prone to something akin to melancholia and madness under the influence of his cocaine habit. The series also played it narratively straight from the page, against the comic bent of the famous Basil Rathbone films (with their bumbling Watson and outrageous, anachronistic Nazis). Handsomely mounted, with a Baker Street set specially created at Granada's Manchester studios (next to that of sudster *Coronation Street*), the show inaugurated a trend for historical detective series such as >*Miss Marple* and >*Agatha Christie's Poirot*. Scriptwriters included Alan Plater.

Holmes' Adventures came to a finale in 1985, with the pipe-smoking sleuth plunging to his death at the Reichenbach Falls (*'The Final Problem'*); however, he was resurrected from the dead in *The Return of Sherlock Holmes* (1986, 11 x 60m col), in which the role of Dr Watson was played by Edward Hardwicke (son of thespian Sir Cedric). Hardwicke kept the part of Holmes' companion for a 120-minute version of *The Hound of the Baskervilles* (1988, col), *The Casebook of Sherlock Holmes* (1991, 6 x 60m col), *The Master Blackmailer* (1992, 1 x 120m col), *The Last Vampyre* (1993, 1 x 120m col), *The Eligible Bachelor* (1993, 1 x 120m col) and the valedictory *The Memoirs of Sherlock Holmes* (1994, 6 x 60m col). Jeremy Brett – whose real name was Peter Huggins – died in 1995 of a heart attack. He had been the 117th actor to play Holmes.

The Adventures were: *A Scandal in Bohemia/ The Dancing Men/The Naval Treaty/The Solitary Cyclist/The Crooked Man/The Speckled Band/ The Blue Carbuncle/The Copper Beeches/The Greek Interpreter/The Norwood Builder/The Resident Patient/The Red-Headed League/The Final Problem.*

GUEST CAST: Eric Porter (as Professor Moriarty), Charles Craig (as Mycroft Holmes), Gayle Hunnicutt, Gareth Thomas, Jeremy Kemp, Natasha Richardson, Lisa Daniely, Joss Ackland.

AGATHA CHRISTIE'S POIROT

UK 1989–97 3 x 120m, 53 x 60m col ITV. London Weekend Production/Carnival Films. US tx 1990–7 WGBH Boston.

EXEC PR *Nick Elliott, Linda Agran, Sarah Wilson.* **PR** *Brian Eastman.* **DR** *Various, including Edward Bennett, Renny Rye, Andrew Grieve, Richard Spence, Ross Devenish, Brian Farnham, Andrew Piddington.* **WR** *Various, including Clive Exton, T R Bowen, Anthony Horowitz, David Renwick, Andrew Marshall, David Reid, Michael Baker, Stephen Wakelam, Russell Murray, Rod Beacham.* **MUS** *Christopher Gunning.*

CAST *Hercule Poirot (David Suchet) Captain Hastings (Hugh Fraser) Inspector Japp (Philip Jackson) Miss Lemon (Pauline Moran).*

'Observe, 'astings ...' Agatha Christie's fastidious Belgian sleuth with the 'leetle grey cells', first met in the Queen of Crime's début novel, *The Mysterious Affair at Styles* (1920), was portrayed on the screen by, among others, Albert Finney and Peter Ustinov, before David Suchet (brother of newscaster John) brought the character to TV in the definitive screen interpretation. The confines of the tube suited well the detective's meticulous modus operandi, while Suchet was gesture and appearance perfect in his withering put-downs of Poirot's nice-but-dim sidekick Hastings and of his out-intelligenced Scotland Yard foil, Inspector Japp (who routinely arrested all the wrong people). Scrupulous in its period mid-Thirties settings (usually British upper-class, with the occasional venture to the Med) and lavishly produced, the series sold to over 40 countries, often as the abbreviated *Poirot*, with later specials airing in the USA before the UK.

The TV cases, all adapted from Christie's 33 novels and 56 short stories featuring Poirot, were: *The Adventures of the Clapham Cook/Murder in the Mews/The Adventure of Johnnie Waverly/Four and Twenty Blackbirds/The Third Floor Flat/Triangle at Rhodes/Problem at Sea/The Incredible Theft/The King of Clubs/The Dream/Peril at End House/The Veiled Lady/The Lost Mine/The Cornish Mystery/The Disappearance of Mr Davenheim/Double Sin/The Adventure of the Cheap Flat/The Kidnapped Prime Minister/The Adventure of the Western Star/The Mysterious Affair at Styles/How Does Your Garden Grow?/The Million Dollar Bond Robbery/The Plymouth Express/Wasp's Nest/The Tragedy at Marsdon Manoir/The Double Clue/The Mystery of the Spanish Chest/The Theft of the Royal Ruby/The Affair at the Victory Ball/The Mystery of Hunter's Lodge/The ABC Murders I/The ABC Murders II/Death in the Clouds I/Death in the Clouds II/One, Two, Buckle My Shoe I/One, Two, Buckle My Shoe II/The Adventure of the Egyptian Tomb/The Underdog/The Yellow Iris/The Case of the Missing Will/The Adventure of the Italian Nobleman/The Chocolate Box/Dead Man's Mirror/Jewel Robbery at the Grand Metropolitan/Hercule Poirot's Christmas I/Hercule Poirot's Christmas II/Hickory Dickory Dock I/Hickory Dickory Dock II/Murder on the Links I/Murder on the Links II/Dumb Witness I/Dumb Witness II/Lord Edgware Dies/The Murder of Roger Ackroyd.*

GUEST CAST: Josie Lawrence, John Stride, Joely Richardson, Frances Barber, Nigel Le Vaillant, Stephanie Cole, Sorcha Cusack.

AMERICAN GOTHIC

USA 1995 22 x 60m col CBS. CBS Television/Renaissance Pictures.
CR Shaun Cassidy. **EXEC PR** Sam Raimi. **PR** Shaun Cassidy, David Eick, Edward Ledding. **DR** Lou Antonio, Mike Binder, Jim Charleston, James A

14

Contner, Mel Damski, James Frawley, Bruce Seth Green, Michael Katleman, Elodie Keene, Michael Lange, Doug Lefler, Nick Marck, Michael Nankin, Peter O'Fallon, Oz Scott. **WR** *Shaun Cassidy, Robert Palm, Steve de Jarnett, Stephen Gaghan, Michael R Perry.* **MUS** *Joseph LoDuca.* **CAST** *Sheriff Lucas Buck (Gary Cole) Caleb Temple (Lucas Black) Selena Coombs (Brenda Bakke) Merlyn Temple (Sarah Paulson) Gail Emory (Paige Turco) Dr Matt Crower (Jake Weber) Deputy Ben Healy (Nick Searcy) Dr Portis Fields (1996) (Michael Genevie) Dr Billy Peale (John Mese).*

Deep in the heart of South Carolina lay a small town called Trinity. And behind Trinity SC's picture-perfect exterior all was not as it seemed. Or was it …? Laden with spiritual and supernatural overtones (from the town's name on), throbbing with mystery, part horror, part drama, part thriller, *American Gothic* gripped a passionate cultish audience from the moment it hit their screens and kept them on the edge of their armchairs.

Who was Sheriff Lucas Buck and what was his hold over the citizens of this town? Why was he so obsessed with a young man called Caleb Temple? Was Caleb really the Sheriff's son, as Lucas claimed? Was Caleb's sister Merlyn truly an angel back from the dead to protect him, and if so from what? What was siren school marm Selena Coombs' real relationship with Lucas Buck, and why had Caleb's cousin Gail suddenly shown up in Trinity?

A steaming cauldron of Tennessee Williams-esque sex, repression and intrigue knowingly stirred by executive producer Sam Raimi *(Evil Dead)* and creator Shaun Cassidy (brother of >*David Cassidy – Man Undercover,* and formerly the star of juvenile sleuth show *The Hardy Boys/Nancy Drew Mysteries,* 1977–8, 46 x 60m col, ABC), a large part of *American Gothic's* hold was exerted by its anti-hero Lucas Buck. Devilish, droll and utterly fascinating, Buck had a touch of Clint Eastwood's avenging angel about him and his creator described him thus: 'The devil and some angel mated and he was the result.' Influences on the show were *Frontline,* a movie about a witch-hunt in a small town in South Carolina, and *The Godfather,* from which some scenes were intentionally lifted wholesale (notably in episode 'The Resurrector'). And clearly *American Gothic* took its place in a post->*Twin Peaks* televisual landscape.

The show suffered in the making from a change of team at the top of CBS – the new regime pushing for more mainstream, moral product. But it managed to remain murky, difficult and dangerous, with a range from difficult to dark and a fan base so loyal that they mounted a massive campaign to bring it back.

The episodes were: *Pilot/A Tree Grows in*

Trinity/Eye of the Beholder/Damned If You Don't/
Dead to the World/Meet the Beetles/Strong Arm
of the Law/Rebirth/Resurrector/Inhumanitas/The
Plague Sower/Doctor Death Takes a Holiday/The
Beast Within/To Hell and Back/Learning to
Crawl/Triangle /The Buck Stops Here/Requiem/
Potato Boy (unaired)/Ring of Fire (unaired)/
Echoes of Your Last Goodbye (unaired)/Strangler
(unaired).

GUEST CAST: Sonny Shroyer, Ted Raimi.

ARCHER

USA 1975 1 x 120, 6 x 60m col NBC. A
Paramount Television Production.

EXEC PR David Carp. **PR** Jack Miller, Leonard B
Kaufman. **DR** Gary Nelson, Paul Stanley, Edward
Abroms, John Llewellyn Moxey, Arnold Laven, Jack
Arnold. **WR** David P Harman, Jim Byrnes, Leigh
Brackett, David Karp, Harold Livingston, Anthony
Lawrence & Wallace Ware. **MUS** Jerry Goldsmith.
CAST Lew Archer (Peter Graves (pilot)/Brian Keith)
Lieutenant Barney Brighton (John P Ryan).

Although one of the Mr Bigs of American
crime writing, Ross Macdonald long failed
to translate his peeper novels to the screen.
Something about the psychological deepness of
his Californian private investigator hero, Lew
Archer, his need to penetrate the mystery of souls,
made Macdonald virtually unfilmable. Paul
Newman had a go in a brace of movies, in
1966 and 1975, but implicitly acknowledged the
difficulty by changing Archer's name to Harper.

And then came this NBC series, which found
trouble in the first can. A pilot was made with
Peter Graves (from *Mission: Impossible*), but for
the series the network insisted on Brian Keith,
better known as a comedy face and western star.
Aware that his sunny screen aura was wrong for
the job, Keith was persuaded by the money.
Meanwhile, the screenwriters turned out a series
of routine whodunnits which owed nothing to
Macdonald save the gumshoe's moniker. Archer
wasn't made. It was committed, like a felony.

The episodes were: *The Turkish Connection/
The Arsonist/The Body Beautiful/Shades of Blue/
The Vanished Man/Blood Money.*

GUEST CAST: Sorrell Booke.

ARREST AND TRIAL

USA 1963–4 30 x 90m bw ABC. A Revue
Studios Production for Universal. UK tx 1964
BBC.

EXEC PR Frank P Rosenberg. **DR** Various, including
Lewis Milestone, Jack Smight, Ralph Senensky.
Elliott Silverstein **WR** Various, including Larry
Cohen. **MUS** Franz Waxman.
CAST Det Sgt Nick Anderson (Ben Gazzara) Atty
John Egan (Chuck Connors) Mitchell Harris (Don
Galloway) Jake Shakespeare (Joe Higgins) Det Lt
Carl Bone (Noah Keen) Asst Dep DA Barry Pine
(John Kerr) Dep DA Jerry Miller (John Larch).

16

Innovative, if short-lived, crime show. The first 45 minutes traced the efforts of Detective Sergeant Nick Anderson of Los Angeles PD in catching the episode's villain; the second 45 minutes witnessed the attempt of lawyer John Egan (Chuck Connors, formerly of >The Rifleman) to get him or her found not guilty. A & T's joining of crime caper and courtroom melodrama has been widely imitated since, not least by >Law and Order and >Murder One.

GUEST CAST: Roddy McDowall, John McIntire.

B.A.D. CATS

USA 1980 6 x 60m col ABC. A Spelling-Cramer Production. UK tx 1980 ITV.
EXEC PR Aaron Spelling, Douglas S Cramer.
PR Everett Chambers. **DR** Bernard Kowalski.
MUS Barry De Vorzon, Mundell Lowe, Andrew Kulberg.
CAST Ocee James (Steven Hanks) Nick Donovan (Asher Brauner) Samantha Jensen (Michelle Pfeiffer) Capt Skip Nathan (Vic Morrow) Rodney Washington (Jimmie Walker) Ma (restaurant owner) (LaWanda Page).

Unlikely to be the show Michelle Pfeiffer puts at the top of her CV. A squealing tyres cop actioner out of the >Starsky and Hutch school, B.A.D. Cats featured the officers of the contrivedly titled 'Burglary, Auto Detail, Commercial Auto Thefts' (Badcats – geddit?)

division of the LAPD, whose ace-driving, rule-bending cops Ocee James and Nick Donovan provided the main thrills'n'spills. Pfeiffer, in one of her earliest roles, played beautiful cop Samantha Jensen, while TV screen veteran Vic Morrow (Combat) took the part of sclerotic detail commander Captain Nathan. Jimmie Walker ('JJ' in Good Times) was the obligatory – and racist – comic black turn, here a former thief turned repo man, Rodney Washington.

❉ Chuck Connors and Ben Gazzara played a lawyer and cop duo in Arrest and Trial, an innovative crime show first broadcast in 1963.

Alas, *B.A.D. Cats* was so lamentably juvenile, so narratively slight that it was cancelled after a mere six episodes, an early death that caused the producer to complain that $40,000 worth of cars, bought for pyrotechnical screen smash-ups, were left unused. Those surviving the wreckage included Pfeiffer and exec producer Aaron Spelling.

GUEST CAST: George Murdock, Lance Henriksen (as Timothy).

BANACEK

USA 1972–4 16 x 90m, 1 x 120m col NBC. Universal Television. UK tx 1975–7 ITV.

CR *Richard Levinson, William Link.*

EXEC PR *George Eckstein.* **PR** *Howie Horowitz.*

DR *Lou Antonio, Herschel Daughterty, Daryl Duke, Theodore J Flicker, Richard T Heffron, Bernard L Kowalski, George McCowan, Bernard McEveety, Andrew McLaglen, Jimmy Sangster, Jack Smight.*

WR *Mort Fine, Theodore J Flicker, Stephen Kandel, Richard Levinson, William Link, Harold Livingston, Stephen Lord, David Moessinger, Paul Playdon, Robert Presnell Jr, Del Reisman, Stanley Roberts, Stanley Ralph Ross, Jimmy Sangster, Lee Stanley, George Sheldon Smith, Jack Turley, Robert Van Scoyk, Richard Bluel.* **MUS** *Billy Goldenburg.*

CAST *Thomas Banacek (George Peppard) Jay Drury (Ralph Manza) Felix Mulholland (Murray Matheson) Carlie Kirkland (Christine Belford).*

P.I. show Banacek, *starring George Peppard, received an award for its positive portrayal of a Polish-American.*

Shrewd Polish-American investigator Thomas Banacek enjoyed a lucrative line of work: he recovered stolen goods for the Boston Insurance Company, collected ten per cent commission on the recovered items, and never went after anything cheap. Not that he needed the money. He rode around high society in a chauffeur-driven limo (his cars numbered a 1973 Fleetwood Cadillac and a 1941 Packard Darrin)

18

and lived in the exclusive Beacon Hill section of Boston. He had impeccable taste in clothes, wine and women, and among his several providential gifts was an effortless ability to solve apparently insoluble cases (eg, in 'Let's Hear It for a Living Legend', the disappearance of a footballer before a packed stadium).

Mostly a solo operator, Banacek (played by George Peppard, later to lead the *A-Team*) did get occasional help from native New Yorker Jay Drury, who drove his limo, and upmarket friend Felix Mulholland, proprietor of Mulholland's Rare Book and Print Shop. The other series regular was rival investigator Carlie Kirkland, who – naturally – fell for Banacek's charms. At the end of each episode the mystified viewer was put out of armchair sleuthing misery, when Banacek revealed how he had cracked the case.

The show's gimmick was ethnic. Polish proverbs were sprinkled through the show, and Banacek's cool, achieving character, who was able to make it in the USA without abandoning his roots, won the series an award from the Polish-American Congress for positive portrayal of Polish Americans. (Creators Richard Levinson and William Link had a long history of tackling racism on TV, beginning with their scripts for oater *Johnny Ringo* in 1959.)

Banacek was one of the rotating elements of NBC's *The Wednesday Mystery Movies*. It started as a 1972 TVM (directed by Jack Smight, and also known as *Detour to Nowhere*), then moved into the Wednesday slot when previous occupants >*Columbo*, >*McCloud* and >*McMillan and Wife* were shifted to Sunday. The producer-writer team of Levinson and Link were also the power behind such other crime TV successes as >*Mannix*, >*Columbo*, >*Ellery Queen* and >*Tenafly*.

The episodes were: *Banacek* (aka *Detour to Nowhere*)/*Let's Hear It for a Living Legend*/ *Project Phoenix*/*No Sign of the Cross*/*A Million Dollars the Hard Way*/ *To Steal a King*/*Ten Thousand Dollars a Page*/*The Greatest Collection of Them All*/*The Two Million Clams of Cap'n Jack*/*No Stone Unturned*/*If Max is So Smart, Why Doesn't He Tell Us Where He Is?*/*The Three Million Dollar Piracy*/*The Vanishing Chalice*/ *Horse of a Slightly Different Colour*/*Rocket to Oblivion*/*Fly Me – If You Can Find Me*/*Now You See Me, Now You Don't*.

GUEST CAST: Marty Ingels, Conrad Janis, Linden Chiles (as semi-regular Henry DeWitt), George Murdock (as semi-regular Cavanaugh), Michael Lerner, Stefanie Powers, Broderick Crawford, Margot Kidder, Ted Cassidy, Penny Marshall, Don Collier, George Murdock, Cesar Romero, John Saxon, Pamela Hensley, Linda Evans, Victoria Principal, Stafford Repp, Byron Morrow.

BANYON

USA 1972–3 13 x 60m col NBC. A Quinn Martin Production for Warner Bros. UK tx 1975 ITV.

EXEC PR *Quinn Martin.* **PR** *Richard Allen Simmons.* **DR** *Various, including Theodore J Flicker, Robert Day, Ralph Senesky, Marvin Chomsky.* **CAST** *Miles C Banyon (Robert Forster) Peggy Revere (Joan Blondell) Lt Pete McNeil (Richard Jaeckel) Abby Graham (Julie Gregg).*

Miles C Banyon was a hard-working, straight-down-the-line private investigator. He'd handle any case that came his way, from murder to missing persons. The series novelty, in a decade when TV schedules were crowded with lone detectives working the streets, was to give its eponymous hero a period setting, viz Los Angeles in the 1930s. Banyon's girl, Abby Graham, was a nightclub singer, but he was in no hurry to settle down. His main source of support was elderly Peggy Revere (played by one-time Busby Berkeley high-kicker Joan Blondell), patroness of a secretarial school based in the same building as his office. Each week she supplied him with a different secretary for no charge, an arrangement that gave her girls thrills and experience, provided the private eye with valuable resources, and offered him and the viewer a lively procession of characters from glamour-girl to farm-girl.

The series' executive producer was Quinn Martin, a name behind a long list of solid sleuthing series: >*Cannon*, >*The Fugitive*, >*The Untouchables*, >*The FBI*, >*The New Breed*, >*Dan August*, >*The Streets of San Francisco*. Robert Forster (real name Robert Foster) went on to a somewhat lacklustre career of cops, gangsters and remakes via a spell of dubious titles – *Kinky Coaches* and the *Pom Pom Pussycats* (1980) and *Linda*, aka *Naked Super Witches of the Rio Amore*, of the same year.

GUEST CAST: Terri Garr.

BARETTA

USA 1975–8 80 x 60m col ABC. Universal TV/Roy Huggins – Public Arts Productions. UK tx 1978–9 ITV.

CR *Stephen J Cannell.* **EXEC PR** *Bernard L Kowalski, Anthony Spinner.* **PR** *Charles E Dismukes, Alan Godfrey, Robert Harris, Howie Horwitz, Robert Lewis, Jo Swerling Jr, Ed Waters.* **DR** *Reza Badiyi, Burt Brinckerhoff, Robert Douglas, Douglas Heyes, Bruce Kessler, Bernard L Kowalski, Don Medford, Chris Robinson, Vincent Sherman.* **WR** *Nick Alexander, Richard Bluel, Michael Butler, Stephen J Cannell, Paul Casey, Robert Crais, Don Carlos Dunaway, Sidney Ellis, Rift Fournier, Alan Godfrey, John Thomas James (aka Roy Huggins), Edward J Lakso, Alan J Levitt, Norman Liebman.* **MUS** *Dave Grusin, Tom Scott; theme, 'Keep Your Eye on the Sparrow' performed by Sammy Davis Jr.*

19

⊗ *Robert Blake gets to grips with another malefactor as undercover cop Baretta.*

CAST *Det Tony Baretta (Robert Blake) Insp Schiller (1975) (Dana Elcar) Lt Hal Brubaker (Edward Glover) Billy Truman (1975–8) (Tom Ewell) Rooster (Michael D Roberts) Fats Chino ('Fats' Williams).*

👁 Tony Baretta was the orphaned son of Italian immigrants. His father was a hustler, his mother was a whore. His methods were unconventional and he was out to get the gangsters who shot his girl instead of him. He lived close to the Los Angeles streets (in the rundown, one-star King Edward Hotel) and he lived alone. He didn't care for his boss's advice, but he did enjoy the company of Rooster, his streetwise pimp sidekick, and Fred, his talkative pet cockatoo.

A hard, action series – some accused it of excessive violence, despite star Robert Blake's protestations to the contrary – the show also had its softer, humorous moments. Baretta, with his trademark T-shirt, jeans, pulled-down cap and Mob-style accent ('dat' for that and 'Eye-talian' for Italian) was a lovable rogue akin to predecessor >*Columbo*. He worked out of LA's 53rd Precinct and he knew his patch like the back of his hand. When informers couldn't get him inside information he'd don any disguise – even kind old lady – to get it himself. Also at work in Precinct 53 were Baretta's boss Inspector Schiller, later replaced by Lieutenant Brubaker, and Billy Truman, a retired cop who acted as house detective at the King Edward Hotel.

Baretta started life as >*Toma* in 1973, a series starring Tony Musante and based on the adventures of a real-life cop. Musante, disenchanted, made his exit after one series. But ratings had been good enough to persuade executives to revive the show. They brought in former child-star Robert Blake as lead, changed the setting and title and ran the show in Toma's Friday niche. Initial poor ratings led to a change of slot and the show ran against – and demolished – >*Cannon* on Wednesday nights over on rival CBS.

Robert Blake – real name Michael James Vijencio Gubitosi – was a prolific small-screen actor from the age of three. Taking roles in action-adventure series, first under the name Bobby Blake, then Mickey Gubitosi, he made a smooth transition into adult roles. His real-life actress wife Sondra invented the background for Baretta's character and went on to guest star in several episodes of the series. Baretta's character fitted Blake like a glove, and he won a Golden Globe for his performance in the part (tied with Telly Savalas for >*Kojak*) in 1976. The show – which was ranked ninth in US ratings – also won an Emmy in the same year for Harry L Wolf's cinematography for the episode 'Keep Your Eye on the Sparrow'.

Producer/writer Stephen J Cannell specialised in action and adventure and later created >*The A-Team*. He polished his reputation on >*The Rockford Files*, created and produced >*Tenspeed and Brownshoe* and *The Greatest American Hero* for ABC and won an exclusive agreement with the network to produce one series a year, among them >*Hunter*, >*Wiseguy* and >*21 Jump Street*. Robert Blake failed to go on to much greater things but did star in NBC's *Hell Town* (1985–6) as Father Noah 'Hardstep' Rivers, an ex-con turned Catholic priest in a tough East Los Angeles neighbourhood.

GUEST CAST: Bruce Boxleitner, Alan Feinstein, Tommy Lee Jones, Michael Lansing, Mel Novak.

BARNABY JONES

USA 1973–80 174 x 60m col CBS. Quinn Martin Productions. UK tx 1974–80 ITV. **EXEC PR** *Quinn Martin.* **PR** *Gene Levitt, Philip Saltzman, Robert Sherman.* **DR** *Various, including Corey Allen, Marc Daniels, Robert Douglas, Michael Caffey, Walter Graumann, Lawrence Dobkin, Leslie H Martinson, Russ Mayberry, Winrich Kolbe, Virgil W Vogel.* **WR** *Various, including Larry Brody, Mort Fine, Robert Hamner, Shirl Hendryx, Stephen Kandel, Robert Pirosh, B W Sandefur.* **MUS** *Jerry Goldsmith, Bruce Broughton.*

⊗ *Former Beverly Hillbillies star Buddy Ebsen as old-ster private eye Barnaby Jones.*

CAST *Barnaby Jones (Buddy Ebsen) Betty Jones (Lee Meriwether) Jebediah Roman ('JR') Jones (Mark Shera) Lt Biddle (John Carter) Lt Joe Taylor (Vince Howard).*

👁 Buddy Ebsen overcame the typecasting (as a backwoodsman, viz in *Davy Crockett* and *Beverly Hillbillies*) of decades to star in this long-running Quinn Martin caper about a retired Los Angeles peeper who takes up the reins of the family gumshoe firm again after the new proprietor, his son, is murdered. Although the aged Barnaby Jones – for it was he – went everywhere armed with a gun, he tended to rely on smarts, psychology and forensic tests in his home lab to solve cases. He was assisted at the Jones Investigative Agency by daughter-in-law Betty (Lee Meriwether from cult sci-fi show *The Time Tunnel*), and later by Jones' young cousin, JR, a student lawyer. Also aiding and abetting nice Mr Jones was his deceptively slow and vague oldster manner which lulled the errant into a false and fatal sense of superiority.

Barnaby Jones was something of a gentle sister to Quinn Martin's >*Cannon*, with the fatman PI occasionally appearing in *BJ* episodes to give the show a ratings boost.

GUEST CAST: Jonathan Frakes, David Hedison, Terri Garr, William Shatner, Margot Kidder, Ed Begley Jr, Lou Frizzell, Ron Masak, Linda Henning, Ross Martin.

THE BARON

UK 1966–7 30 x 50m col ITV. An ITC Production. US tx 1966 ABC, syndicated.

CR *Robert S Baker, Monty Berman.* **PR** *Robert S Baker, Monty Berman.* **DR** *Robert Asher, Roy Ward Baker, Don Chaffey, Gordon Flemyng, Quentin Lawrence, Jeremy Summers, Robert Tronson, Leslie Norman, John Moxey, Cyril Frankel.* **WR** *Dennis Spooner, Terry Nation, Michael Cramoy, Brian Degas, Tony O'Grady (aka Brian Clemens), Harry H Junkin.* **MUS** *Edwin T Astley.*

CAST *John Mannering, 'The Baron' (Steve Forrest) Cordelia Winfield (Sue Lloyd) John Alexander Templeton-Green (Colin Gordon) David Marlowe (Paul Ferris).*

👁 The first incarnation of John Mannering, aka The Baron, lay between the covers of John Creasey's novels, wherein the handsome, Jensen-driving and thoroughly British hero, owner of fine antique shops in London, Paris and Washington, had turned his back on a dubious past as gentleman jewel thief and turned instead to undercover work for Scotland Yard. His small-screen namesake, however, at the behest of ATV boss Lew Grade and his push for transatlantic success, was something a little different. Played by all-American Steve Forrest (later to star as Lt Dan 'Hondo' Harrelson in ABC's crime series >*S.W.A.T.*,1975–7), Mannering became a

 *Steve Forrest as antiques dealer-cum-sleuth John Mannering – aka* The Baron.

Texan-born ranch owner, and his nickname, far from hinting at aristocratic connections, was acquired from the Baron-brand cattle he reared back home.

For this new-style jet-age antiques dealer, examining priceless *objets d'art* for his exclusive clientele played second place to his dangerous global adventures – now on behalf of British

Intelligence. His British contact was John Templeton-Green, to whom, by fortunate chance, beautiful secret agent Cordelia Winfield also reported. Soon Cordelia was drafted in as The Baron's full-time assistant and shared his every mission.

Plots, unsurprisingly, tended to feature rare antiques and jewels – in 'Diplomatic Immunity' a series of large-scale art robberies took place behind the Iron Curtain; in 'Masquerade' British

Intelligence foiled a plot to steal the Crown Jewels – although time-served storylines such as dope-smuggling rackets, evil imposters and Mafia gangsters also played their part.

The creative team behind *The Baron* was a star-studded list of the greats of British TV: creator/producers Robert Baker and Monty Berman were behind ATV's filmed adventure series >*The Saint* and >*The Persuaders!*; Terry Nation (*The Saint*, *Dr Who*, *Blake's 7*) was script supervisor for the series; and writers included Dennis Spooner and Brian Clemens (*The Avengers*, >*The Persuaders!*). Filmed at Elstree Studios and on location, this was a high-gloss action series with its tongue comfortably in its cheek. In Britain its run was extended from an intended 26 to 30 episodes, although in the US, for all Sir Lew Grade's ambitions, its run finished early.

Two TV features were produced from re-edited episodes, *Mystery Island* (1966) and *The Man in the Looking Glass* (1968).

GUEST CAST: Peter Bowles, Jeremy Brett, Patricia Haines, Robert Hardy, Philip Madoc, Lois Maxwell, Paul Maxwell, Geraldine Moffat, Lee Montague, Nosher Powell, Sylvia Syms, James Villiers, Sam Wanamaker, Peter Wyngarde.

BERGERAC

UK 1981–9 81 x 60m, 5 x 90m, 1 x 110m col BBC1. BBC TV/Seven Network.
CR *Robert Banks Stewart.* **PR** *Robert Banks Stewart, Jonathan Alwyn, George Gallaccio.*
DR *Various, including Paul Ciappessoni, Graeme Harper, Baz Taylor, Tristan de Vere Cole, Martin Campbell, Ian Toynton, Alan Grint, Colin Bucksey, Robert Tronson, Richard Standeven, Ken Grieve, Ben Bolt, Laurence Moody, Michael Rolfe.* **WR** *Various, including Robert Banks Stewart, Terence Feely, John Collee, Chris Boucher, John Milne, Brian Clemens, Robert Holmes, Rod Beacham, John Kershaw, Dennis Spooner, Bob Baker, Alistair Bell.* **MUS** *George Fenton (theme).*
CAST *Det Sgt Jim Bergerac (John Nettles) Charlie Hungerford (Terence Alexander) Det Chief Insp Barney Crozier (Sean Arnold) Deborah Hungerford (Deborah Grant) Francine (Cecile Paoli) Marianne Bellshade (Celia Imrie) Susan Young (Louise Jameson) Philippa Vale (Liza Goddard) Danielle Aubry (Thérèse Liotard) Diamante Lil (Mela White) Charlotte (Annette Badland) Det Con Goddard (Jolyon Baker) Det Con Wilson (Geoffrey Leesley).*

👁 Only created by Robert Banks Stewart after Trevor Eve refused to do another season of >*Shoestring*, this policier set on the sparkling sea'd island resort of Jersey became

one of the BBC's prime-time crime hits of the 1980s, with ratings approaching 15 million. John Nettles (previously *A Family at War* and Sandra's boyfriend in flat-share sitcom *The Liver Birds*) played divorced, ex-alcoholic, gammy-legged Detective Sergeant Jim Bergerac of the Bureau des Etrangers, a police body which dealt exclusively with crimes involving visitors to the island. By improbable but enjoyable coincidence, all Bergerac's cases entangled his ex-father-in-law

⊙ *John Nettles (centre) in* Bergerac, *Britain's version of* Hawaii Five-O.

Charlie Hungerford, a millionaire cigar-smoking businessman of roguish bent. To convey himself around the island Bergerac conspiciously avoided the plodding regulation police vehicle in favour of a 1947 Triumph TRi sports car. With his loner mode of investigation looked on with disapproval by superior Barney Crozier, a lingering tendency to hanker for the bottle, a troubled personal life (tourist guide Francine, lawyer Marianne, estate agent Susan Young were among the main squeezes), and a mumble-mouthed manner of speaking bordering on inarticulateness, Bergerac was a notably human creation (pace Eddie Shoestring), a conscious reaction to the Seventies tough-guy school of police show. On several occasions Bergerac, dangerously putting duty aside, dallied with beautiful jewel-thief Philippa Vale (Liza Goddard). And it was for the love of a woman, Danielle Aubry, that 'Je-e-em' finally quit the Bureau and moved to Provence, where he became a private eye. As with Steve McGarrett and Hawaii, so Bergerac and Jersey have become indissolubly linked, the show dramatically boosting the island's tourist industry.

Appropriately, then, on completing Bergerac, John Nettles made Jersey his home. That is, before moving back to mainland Britain and thespian service in another detective show, *The Midsomer Murders* (1998–, ITV), playing dapper Detective Chief Inspector Barnaby, whose quaintly old-fashioned rural whodunnits, based on Caroline Graham's novels, tended to involve red herrings by the shoal.

GUEST CAST: Ray Winstone, Patrick Allen, Warren Clarke, Ian Hendry, James Laurenson, Patrick Mower, Beryl Reid, Ronald Pickup, Greta Scacchi, Catherine Schell, Anthony Valentine, Joanne Whalley-Kilmer, Norman Wisdom.

BETWEEN THE LINES

UK 1992–4 29 x 50m col BBC1. BBC TV/Island World.

CR J C Wilsher. **EXEC PR** Tony Garnett. **PR** Peter Norris, Joy Lale. **DR** Various, including Roy Battersby, Charles McDargall, Alan Dossor. **WR** Various, including J C Wilsher, Dusty Hughes, Steve Trafford, Roy Heyland, Ray Brennan. **MUS** Hal Lindes (theme), Colin Thomas. **CAST** DS Tony Clark (Neil Pearson) DI Harry Naylor (Tom Georgeson) DS Maureen ('Mo') Connell (Siobhan Redmond) Chief Supt John Deakin (Tony Doyle) Commander Huxtable (David Lyon) Angela Berridge (Francesca Annis) Jenny Dean (Lesley Vickerage) DAC Dunning (John Shrapnel) DS Eddie Hargreave (Jerome Flynn) DCS David Graves (Robin Lermite) Sue Clarke (Lynda Steadman). **VIDEO** BBC.

British 'down and dirty' cop TV show, much influenced by such reality-type American policiers as >*Homicide: Life on the Street* and >*NYPD Blue*. It tracked the internal investigations into police corruption of hard-drinking Detective Superintendent Tony Clark (Neil Pearson from *Drop the Dead Donkey*) as well as his seamy and complicated external affairs with a small parade of women (hence the show being dubbed 'Between the Sheets'). Clark was assisted in the Metropolitan Complaints Investigation Bureau (CIB) by Harry Taylor and

Mo Connell, the latter one of the few sympathetically portrayed lesbians in the annals of British TV. For the third series, Clark, Taylor and Connell found themselves without the Force, working for a private security company run, ironically enough, by their corrupt former police boss, John Deakin. Alas, to remove the trio from internal affairs proved a narrative wrong turn; the characters lost their *raison d'être*, and the show its novelty.

⊘ *Neil Pearson (front) in gritty British cop show* Between the Lines.

Outside the UK *Between the Lines* was sometimes transmitted as *Inside the Line*. The executive producer was Tony Garnett, who had come up overseeing such controversial and arty small-screen products as *Cathy Come Home* and *Days of Hope*.

The episodes were: *Private Enterprise/Out of the Game/Words of Advice/Lies and Damned*

Lies/A Watch and Chain of Course/Lest Ye Be Judged/Breaking Point/The Only Good Copper/ Watching the Detectives/Nothing to Declare/ Nothing Personal/Nobody's Fireproof/The Chill Factor/New Order/Manslaughter/Crack Up/ Honourable Men/Someone Must Watch/ Manoeuvre 11/The Fifth Estate/The Great Detective/Jumping the Lights/What's the Strength of This?/Big Boys Rules I/Big Boys Rules II/ Foxtrot Oscar/A Safe Pair of Hands/A Face in the Crowd/Shoot to Kill/Close Protection/ Blooded/Unknown Soldier/Free Trade/The End User I/The End User II.

GUEST CAST: Robin Ellis, Tony Osoba, Rudolph Walker, John Hannah, Ben Chaplin, David Calder.

BEVERLY HILLS BUNTZ

USA 1987–8 12 x 30m col NBC. An NBC Production.

CR Jeffrey Lewis, David Milch. **EXEC PR** Jeffrey Lewis, David Milch.

CAST Norm Buntz (Dennis Franz) Sidney 'Sid the Snitch' Thurston (Peter Jurasik) Rebecca Giswold (Dana Wheeler-Nicholson) Lt James Pugh (Guy Boyd).

After KO-ing the loathsome Chief Daniels in the final episode of >Hill Street Blues, the irascible, barely house-trained Norm Buntz was dismissed from the service. Obliged to find new employment, he relocated to luxurious Beverly Hills, where he set up as a seedy private eye (with office to match) and was joined by his main informant from Hill Street, Sid the Snitch. Here the duo took all the worst, lowlife cases.

Such was the premise for this vehicle, tailor made by Jeffrey Lewis and David Milch for actor

◉ 'A knight in shining polyester' – Norm Buntz in Hill Street Blues spin-off, Beverly Hills Buntz.

30

Dennis Franz (born Dennis Schlachta). Yet NBC were so unsure of the fish-out-of-water concept of slimeball Buntz in fashionable LA ('Knights in shining polyester', as the ads touted Buntz and Sid's adventures) that they gave the show no less than four try-outs in different time slots, before launching a first short season. The viewers, uncertain whether they were watching a detective show or a spoof, failed to clamour for more. Franz had to wait for >*NYPD Blue*, and the virtual resurrection of his Buntz character as *Sipowicz*, for another headlining role.

THE BILL

UK 1984– 100 x 50m, 1 x 90m, 700+ x 30m col ITV. Thames TV.

CR Geoff McQueen. **EXEC PR** Various, including Lloyd Shirley, Peter Cregeen, Michael Chapman. **PR** Various, including Geraint Morris, Tony Virgo, Richard Handford, Mike Dormer, Michael Simpson. **DR** Various, including Peter Cregeen, A J Quinn, Morag Fullerton, John Woods, James Hawes, Indra Bhose, Baz Taylor. **WR** Various, including Geoff McQueen, Mike Holoway, Simon Moss, Julian Jones, J C Wilsher, Margaret Phelan. **MUS** Andy Pask, Charles Morgan (theme). **CAST** Sgt Bob Cryer (Eric Richard) DI Roy Galloway (John Salthouse) WPC June Ackland (Trudie Godwin) PC Francis 'Taffy' Edwards (Colin Blumenau) PC Reg Hollis (Jeff Stewart) PC/DC Jim Carver (Mark Wingett) Chief Supt Charles Brownlow (Peter Ellis) PC Ken Melvin (Mark Powley) WPC/WDC Viv Martell (Nula Conwell) DI/DCI Frank Burnside (Christopher Ellison) PC Dave Litten (Gary Olsen) DC Mike Dashwood (Jon Iles) DC Alfred 'Tosh' Lines (Kevin Lloyd) PC Tony Sharp (Graham Cole) DS Alistair Greig (Andrew Mackintosh) WPC Cathy Marshall (Lynne Miller) Sgt Matthew Boyde (Tony O'Callaghan) PC Dave Quinnan (Andrew Paul) DS Danny Pearce (Martin Marquez) WPC Donna Harris (Louise Harrison) DI Sally Johnson (Jaye Griffiths) PC Barry Stringer (Jonathan Dow) PC Steve Loxton (Tom Butcher) PC Adam Bostock (Carl Brincat) PC Mike James (Stephen Beckett) PC George Garfield (Huw Higgison) WPC Polly Page (Lisa Geoghan) PC Tony Stamp (Graham Cole) WDC Liz Rawton (Libby Davison) DS Ted Roach (Tony Scannell) DC John Boulton (Russell Boulter) DCI Jack Meadows (Simon Rouse) CI Derek Conway (Ben Roberts).

Modern tales of everyday coppers in London's East End. *The Bill* first patrolled the screen in 1983 as a one-off play, 'Woodentop', in Thames TV's *Storyboard*, before being launched as a one-hour weekly series, transforming into a twice-weekly half-hour series (with an earlier evening slot of 8 p.m.), and finally a thrice-weekly 30-minute show. The changes in format were at the cost of plot, and it ended up something like soap opera, though the characters' personal problems were always conspiciously worked out within the confines of the station house (a show rule forbade scenes of the officers' homes). Throughout all, realism was maintained by a free-wheeling, fly-on-the-wall camera style (borrowed by director/producer Peter Cregeen from Roger Graef's documentary *The Police*), and believably mundane storylines. In the first 500 episodes there were only two deaths among the regulars of Sun Hill station, those of PC Ken Melvin and WDC Viv Martell (Nula Conwell, the barmaid in *Only Fools and Horses*). That said, it earned several condemnations from police bodies – notably for a 1988 episode in which a teenager was hit in the face by a Sun Hill officer, the event followed by DI Frank Burnside drinking away the afternoon in a strip club – but rose through the TV ranks to become Britain's most popular police drama of its age. An ensemble cast of characters was cornerstoned by uniformed Sergeant Bob Cryer, whose old-fashioned honesty was highly reminiscent of >*Dixon of Dock Green*. The show was created by Geoff McQueen, who had previously devised the comedy drama *Big Deal* (1984–6), about a London card sharp who wanted to go straight.

GUEST CAST: Ray Winstone, Samantha Bond, Denise Van Outen, Sally Knyvette, Leslie Grantham, Craig Charles, Robert Carlyle, James Wilby, Lorcan Cranitch, Anthony Valentine, Colin Baker, Sean Bean, Gemma Craven.

B L STRYKER

USA 1989–90 12 x 120m col ABC. A TWS Production in association with Universal Television. UK tx 1991 ITV.

CR Christopher Crowe. **EXEC PR** Tom Selleck. **PR** Alan Barnette. **DR** William A Fraker, Tony Wharmby, Jerry Jameson, Burt Reynolds, Hal Needham, Alan J Levi, Stuart Margolin, Jack B Sowards. **WR** Leon Piedmont, Walter Klenhard, Chris Abbott, Hal Powell & Jay Huguely, Joe Gores, Tim Burns, Joan H Parker & Robert Parker, Tommy Thompson, Neil Cohen.
CAST B L Stryker (Burt Reynolds) Oz Jackson (Ossie Davis) Kimberly Baskin (Rita Moreno) Lyynda Lennox (Dana Kaminsky) Chief McGee (Michael O Smith) Oliver (Alfie Wise).

Burt (*Deliverance*) Reynolds, who had begun his career on TV (*Gunsmoke*, 1955, *Riverboat*, 1959, >*Hawk*, 1966, >*Dan August*, 1970), returned a couple of decades and many movies later to play B L Stryker, private eye. BL (Buddy Lee), a burnt-out New Orleans cop who, exited from the force after a clash with a serial killer, went back home to Palm Beach to bum around in a beaten-up old Caddy and live aboard a rundown old houseboat. But curiosity and a high crime rate among the rich socialites of his chosen location got him involved with the local police and he was back taking cases as a low-rent PI – to pay the rent. Aiding and abetting him in his efforts were ex-boxer Oz, his pal and enforcer, aspiring actress Lyynda, his free-spirited secretary, Oliver, his wealthy but trouble-prone landlord, and Kimberly Baskin, played by Puerto Rico-born Rita Moreno (real name Rosita Dolores Alverio), Stryker's ex-wife who had remarried four times since their divorce, the last time to a millionaire, and who lived as a widow in Palm Beach.

Stryker was a one-time college footballer, a Vietnam war hero, and an amateur boxer. The all-action role suited hunk Burt Reynolds (who posed naked for a *Cosmopolitan* spread in 1972) – he had himself attended Florida State University on a football scholarship as a star running back. His college football career was ended after only two seasons by a knee injury and serious car accident.

B L Stryker was one of the rotating elements of the revived *ABC Mystery Movie* and was seen every three weeks or so. (The show first appeared a week after Peter Falk returned as *Columbo*.) Writers included crime novelist Robert B Parker and directors included Reynolds himself. A character called Mitch Slade, a Ferrari-driving private detective, was added as an in-joke for the series because one of the series executive producers was Tom Selleck. Reynolds' later TV work included *Evening Shade*, 1991, for which he won an Emmy. (Plus a TV ad for Kodak Max Film, 1998, and a TV ad for Elizabeth Taylor's 'White Diamond' perfume, 1997.) The star-studded guest list included Loni Anderson, Reynolds' second wife

(1988–93). His first wife (1963–65) was English actress Judy Carne, real name Joyce Botterill, a regular performer in *Rowan and Martin's Laugh-In*.

The episodes were: *The Dancer's Touch/ Carolann/Blind Chess/Auntie Sue/Blues for Buder/The King of Jazz/Die Laughing/Winner Takes All/Grand Theft Hotel/High Rise/Plates/ Night Train.*

GUEST CAST: Douglas Fairbanks Jr, Ned Beatty, Doug McClure, Dom DeLuise, James Best, Abe Vigoda, Harry Carey Jr, Eriq La Salle, Jo Ann Pflug, Morgan Brittany.

THE BLUE KNIGHT

USA 1975–6 13 x 60m col CBS. A CBS Production. UK tx 1985 ITV.
CR *Joseph Wambaugh.* **EXEC PR** *Lee Rich, Philip Capice.* **PR** *Joel Rogosin.* **DR** *Various, including Gordon Hessler, Richard Benedict, Robert Butler, Robert Scheerer.* **MUS** *Henry Mancini.*
CAST *Bumper Morgan (George Kennedy) Sgt Newman (Philip Pine) Wimpy (John Steadman) Sgt Cabe (Charles Siebert) Lt Hauser (Lin McCarthy).*

Based on the best-selling novel by one-time LAPD man Joseph Wambaugh, *The Blue Knight* first rode on to the flickering screen as a mini-series on NBC. This version, a straight adaptation of the book, starred William Holden and Lee Remick, and won Holden an Emmy. The later CBS full series was based around Wambaugh's character Bumper Morgan, an old-style foot-patrol cop who cared for every person he encountered on his beat and fell for a hard luck story in the interests of harmony. He cared about his job, too, with a dedication that erred towards obstinacy and ruffled the uniform of boss Sergeant Newman. Streetwise informant Wimpy fleshed out the inner-city patch cast of characters.

Lee Rich was executive producer, but even so cast and script did not match up in the second rendition, and this nostalgic take on LAPD cops, complete with its smooth Mancini soundtrack, fell prey to the grittier, glitzier series showing elsewhere.

BONEY

Australia 26 x 50m col. Norfolk International/Scottish TV. UK tx 1975–6 ITV.
EXEC PR Bob Austin, Lee Robinson. **PR** John McCallum.
CAST Det Insp Napoleon 'Boney' Bonaparte (James Laurenson).

Languid murder cases of the Australian outback, investigated by Aboriginal Detective Inspector Napoleon Bonaparte (played, incongruously, by blacked-up white New Zealand actor James Laurenson), who used bush tucker man skills to track his quarry.

Production wise, casting foolish.

Adapted from the novels of Arthur W Upfield. Laurenson later resurfaced on the screen – sans boot polish – in >Prime Suspect 4 and the Napoleonic-era adventure series Sharpe's – as Major-General Ross.

BRONK

USA 1975–6 24 x 60m col CBS. An MGM Television Production. UK tx 1977 ITV.
CR Carroll O'Connor. **EXEC PR** Bruce Geller, Carroll O'Connor. **PR** Leigh Vance. **DR** Various, including Russ Mayberry, Sutton Roley, Richard Donner, Reza Badiyi, Corey Allen, Paul Krasny, Allan Baron, John Peyser, Stuart Hagman.
WR Various. **MUS** Jack Urbont, Lalo Schifrin, George Romanis.
CAST Det Lt Alexander 'Bronk' Bronkov (Jack Palance) Mayor Pete Santori (Joseph Mascolo) Sgt John Webber (Tom King) Harry Mark (Henry Beckman) Off Jane Harley (Sally Kirkland) Elen Bronkov (Dina Ousley).

Short-run police series, casting screen legend Jack Palance against tough-psycho type to play pipe-smoking, pontificating Lieutenant Alex Bronkov. At the request of his old friend, Mayor Santori, Bronkov cleaned up crime'n'corruption in Ocean City, South California. Those aiding and abetting 'Bronk' were Sergeant Webber and buddy Harry Mark, a former cop turned auto junkyard proprietor. Also

34

appearing in the cast of characters was Bronkov's paraplegic daughter, who had been crippled in the same accident which had killed his wife. The show was created by Carroll O'Connor, better known as Archie Bunker in hit US sitcom *All in the Family* and later the star of the small-screen version of >*In the Heat of the Night*.

BROOKLYN SOUTH

USA 1997–8 1 x 90m, 21 x 60m col CBS.
Steven Bochco Productions.

CR *Steven Bochco, David Milch.* **EXEC PR** *Steven Bochco, William M Finkelstein, David Milch, Michael S Churnuchin.* **DR** *Various, including Mark Tinker, Paris Barclay, Michael W Watkins, James Whitmore Jr.* **MUS** *Mike Post.*
CAST *Patrol Sgt Francis X Donovan (Jon Tenney) IAB Lt Stan Jonas (James B Sikking) Off Jimmy Doyle (Dylan Walsh) Off Jack Lowery (Titus Welliver) Off Ann-Marie Kersey (Yancy Butler) Off Phil Roussakoff (Michael DeLuise) Off Terry Doyle (Patrick McGaw) Sgt Richard Santoro (Gary Basaraba) Off Nona Valentine (Klea Scott) Off Clement Johnson (Richard T Jones) Off Hector Villanueva (Adam Rodriguez).*

'*Brooklyn South will tell the stories, personal and professional, of the footsoldiers who patrol the borough which is never mistaken for Manhattan and is as tough to nail down as the accent that everyone imitates, but few get right.*'

So ran the press release from CBS for Steven Bochco's *Brooklyn South*, a downstairs version of his detective show >*NYPD Blue*. Developed as part of Bochco's exclusive deal with CBS, *Brooklyn South* opened with a bang – a cop having his head blown off – which immediately created controversy and good opening figures (twelve per cent of available audience share), plus an Emmy for Mark Tinker's direction. Reminiscent of Bochco's >*Hill Street Blues* for its large ensemble cast, it also shadowed that show in its troubled early history, with viewers finding the cast of street cop characters too large and, um, too uniform. Unlike NBC with *Hill Street*, however, CBS refused to back *Brooklyn South* through shrinking figures and terminated it, their minds also concentrated by financial matters; CBS, which did not own *Brooklyn South*, was noticeably filling its airwaves with programmes it produced itself. The end came just as critics and fans were beginning to detect improvement, due to a pared-down cast, improved storylines and more of the sticky ethical situations that are the hallmark of the school of Bochco. The main characters were nice-guy Patrol Sergeant Francis Donovan (who was also a field associate of *Internal Affairs*), Officer Terry Doyle, IAB Lieutenant Stan Jonas (James B Sikking, in his fourth Bochco series), Officer Ann-Marie Kersey, cocksure Phil Roussakoff and the marriage-troubled Officer Jack Lowery.

The episodes were: *Pilot/Life Under*

Castro/Why Can't Even a Couple of Us Get
Along?/Touched by a Checkered Cab/Clown
without Pity/A Reverend Runs Through It/Love
Hurts/Wild Irish Woes/McMurder One/Dublin
or Nothin'/Gay Avec/Exposing Johnson/Tears
on My Willow/Violet Inviolate/Fisticuffs/Don't
You Be My Valentine/Dead Man Sleeping/Fools
Russian/Doggonit/Cinnamon Buns/Skel in a
Cell/Queens for a Day.
GUEST CAST: Erika Eleniak (as Officer Christine
Bannon).

BURKE'S LAW

USA 1963–6 81 x 60m bw ABC. Four Star. UK
tx 1963–6 ITV.

CR Ivan Goff, Ben Roberts, Ernest Kinoy. **PR** Aaron
Spelling. **DR** Various, including Don Weis, Walter
Graumann, Stanley Z Cherry, Murray Golden,
Don Taylor, Jerry Hopper, Lewis Allen. **WR** Various,
including Harlan Ellison. **MUS** Herschel Burke
Gilbert.

CAST Capt Amos Burke (Gene Barry) Det Tim
Tillson (Gary Conway) Det Sgt Lester Hart (Regim
Toomey) Henry (the chauffeur) (Leon Lontoc) Sgt
Ames (Eileen O'Neill) 'The Man' (spymaster,
1965–6) (Carl Benton Reed).

The crime cases of an urbane Los Angeles
police chief.

Originally intended as a TV vehicle for
Hollywood's Dick Powell – who played the title
character in a presentation ('Who Killed Julia
Greer?') of his own *Dick Powell Theater* – it
eventually fell to Gene Barry to fill the elegant
shoes of Captain Amos Burke in series form.
(Barry was already versed in small-screen
dandyism, having played dapper cowpoke-
lawman *Bat Masterson* for NBC, 1959–61.)
Episodes of *Burke's Law*, in which the millionaire
Burke slipped along to the scene of crime in his
chauffeur-driven Rolls Royce, were trade-
markedly titled 'Who Killed – ?' and filled to the
frames with guest stars – 63 in the first eight
episodes alone. Few were used to dramatic
purpose, but like the rest of the show they looked
glossily good. Assisting Burke in his detective
endeavours – which rarely involved anything as
infra dig as a murder among the downtown hoi
polloi – were a number of sidekicks over the
seasons, beginning with preppy Tim Tillson,
proceeding to seasoned oldster Les Hart, and
ending with shapely Sergeant Ames. The equally
shapely PI, Honey West, meanwhile appeared in
the 1965 episode 'Who Killed the Jackpot?'
which acted as a pilot for her own sleuth show
>*Honey West*.

After two years of law enforcement in LA, Burke
quit for the spy business (glamorous end of,
naturally), a change of occupation largely
prompted by the producers' desire to ride the
success of the Bond films. Accordingly, the show
was retitled *Amos Burke – Secret Agent* for its last

season. It was altered back to *Burke's Law* thirty years later, when the series was revived (having already spawned a clone, >*McMillan and Wife*) with Barry once again playing the debonair Burke, albeit in wrinklier form. He was joined by Bever-Leigh Banfield as Libby, Peter Barton as Peter Burke and Dom DeLuises Vinnie. Aaron Spelling, who had produced the original show, was co executive producer.

GUEST CAST (1963–6): Zsa Zsa Gabor, Sammy Davis Jr, Dorothy Lamour, Ida Lupino, Agnes Morehead, William Shatner, Hoagy Carmichael, Elizabeth Montgomery, Don Ameche, John Cassavetes, Gloria Swanson, Carl Reiner, Gloria Graheme, Buster Keaton, Nancy Kovack.

CADE'S COUNTY

USA 1971–2 24 x 60m col CBS. David Gerber Productions/20th Century Fox TV/CBS TV. UK tx 1972 ITV.
CR Rick Husky, Tony Wilson. **EXEC PR** David Gerber. **PR** Charles Lawson. **DR** Various, including Marvin Chomsky, Robert Day, George Marshall, Reza Badiyi, Richard Donner, Leo Penn, Paul Stanley, Joseph Pevney, David Lowell Rich, Alf Kjellin. **WR** Various. **MUS** Henry Mancini.
CAST Sheriff Sam Cade (Glenn Ford) Deputy J J Jackson (Edgar Buchanan) Joannie Little Bird

◈ Burke's Law – *former Bat Masterson starred as dapper detective Amos Burke.*

(Sandra Ego) Pete (Peter Ford) Deputy Arlo Pritchard (Taylor Lacher) Kitty Ann Sundown (Betty Ann Carr) Deputy Rudy Davillo (Victor Campos).

Police show cum contemporary western set in Madrid County, California, with Sheriff Sam Cade policing everything from professional killers to Apache Indians, now riding pick-up trucks rather than painted ponies. Aside from stunning desertscapes, the series was notable for its positive, unstereotypical attitude to Native Americans, and the role of police dispatcher was played in turn by American Indian actors Sandra Ego and Betty Ann Carr. The part of Cade himself was taken by Hollywood's Glenn Ford. His son, Peter, also featured in the cast. The part of aged Deputy J J Jackson went to Edgar Buchanan from *Hopalong Cassidy*. Three TV movies emerged from the show: *Marshal Madrid*, *Sam Cade* and *Slay Ride*. Executive producer David Gerber was one of the top independent producers of the 1970s. He was executive producer of, among others, >*Police Story*, >*Police Woman* and *Joe Forrester* (1975–6, NBC, featuring Lloyd Bridges as the eponymous kindly NY street cop). Later he was head of television at MGM-UA and MGM Pathé.

GUEST CAST: Loretta Swit, Martin Sheen, James Sikking, Jay 'Tonto' Silverheels, Cameron Mitchell, William Shatner, Darren McGavin, Dennis Fimple, Sharon Acker, L Q Jones, Jack Starrett.

CADFAEL

UK 1994– 13+ x 90m col ITV. Central/Carlton Television. US tx 1995– PBS.

EXEC PR Ted Childs, Rob Pursey. **PR** Stephen Smallwood. **DR** Various, including Ken Grieves, Herbert Wise, Graham Theakston, Mary McMurray. **WR** Various, including Christopher Russell, Simon Burke, Ben Rostul. **MUS** Colin Towns.

CAST Cadfael (Derek Jacobi) Hugh Beringar (Sean Pertwee/Eion McCarthy/Anthony Green) Prior

⊗ Hollywood legend Glenn Ford (second left) in Western cop show Cade's County.

Robert (Michael Culver) Abbot Herribert (Peter Copley) Brother Jerome (Julian Firth) Brother Oswin (Mark Charnock). **VIDEO** Acorn Media.

👁 Medieval monkish murder mysteries, adapted from the novels of Ellis Peters (aka Edith Pargeter) in 90-minute pieces neatly pitched for the Sunday evening couch-out in that they were stimulating enough to hold viewer attention without being so demanding that they actually required effort. Sir Derek Jacobi starred as Cadfael (pronounced 'Cadvile', for those who care to know), a former Crusader turned holyman, herbalist and amateur sleuth. The actor's performance trailed disconcerting echoes (hesitancy of manner, intellectual sharpness) for those who remembered him in the classic *I, Claudius*, and there were further cavils in the hastily raised styrofoam sets and the sometimes anachronistic writing. Since few parts of England were undeveloped enough to pass for twelfth-century Shrewsbury, the series was filmed in Hungary.

The episodes to date: *One Corpse Too Many/The Sanctuary Sparrow/Monk's Hood/The Leper of St Giles/The Devil's Novice/The Virgin in the Ice/St Peter's Fair/The Rose Rent/A Morbid Taste for Bones/The Raven in the Foregate/The Holy Thief/The Potter's Field/The Pilgrim of Hate.*
GUEST CAST: Anna Friel ('Monk's Hood'), Crispin Bonham Carter.

⌂ *The sleuthing habit Derek Jacobi as monk detective Cadfael.*

CAGNEY AND LACEY
USA 1982–8 125 x 60m col CBS. A Mace Neufeld/Barney Rosenzweig Production/Orion. UK tx 1982–8 BBC1.
CR *Barney Rosenzweig, Barbara Corday, Barbara Avedon.* **EXEC PR** *Barney Rosenzweig.* **PR** *Steve Brown, Terry Louise Fisher, Peter Lefcourt, Liz Coe,* *Ralph S Singleton, Patricia Green, P K Knelman, Georgia Jeffries, Jonathan Estrin, Shelley List.*
DR *Various, including Arthur Karen, Georg Stanford Brown, Bill Dukes, Jackie Cooper, Michael Vijar.* **WR** *Various, including Patricia M Green, Terry Louise Fisher, Alison Hock, Larry Kenner, Ronie Wenker-Konner.* **MUS** *Bill Conti (theme), Ron Ramin.*

40

CAST *Det Mary Beth Lacey (Tyne Daly) Det Sgt Christine Cagney (Meg Foster (season one)/Sharon Gless) Harvey Lacey (John Karlen) Lt Bert Samuels (Al Waxman) Det Mark Petrie (Carl Lumbly) Det Victor Isbecki (Martin Kove) Det LaGuardia (Sidney Clute) Det Esposito (Robert Hegyes) Sgt Dory McKenna (Barry Primus) Harvey Lacey Jr (Tony La Torre) Michael Lacey (Troy Slaten) Desk Sgt Ronald Coleman (Harvey Atkin) Charlie Cagney (Dick O'Neill) Dep Insp Marquette (Jason Bernard) David Keeler (Stephen Macht) Det John Newman (Dan Shor) Alice Lacey (Dana and Paige Bardolph/Michele Sepe).*

The long-awaited female buddy show. US TV had fielded a (sexy) lone female (>*Police Woman*) and a team of three pin-up detectives working for a male boss (>*Charlie's Angels*), but here were two women characters with a strong bond, flat shoes and sensible hairdos, pulling their weight as detectives. *Cagney and Lacey* ran for six Emmy-studded years, winning audiences and plaudits around the world – but it took nearly a decade to make it happen.

The series was conceived way back in 1974 by producer Barney Rosenzweig, his then wife Barbara Corday and co-creator Barbara Avedon. Corday, a writer for American daytime soaps such as *The Days of our Lives* (and later to rise to the presidency of Columbia Pictures Television),

wanted to score a first with a series starring two equal women in partnership. The fact that Cagney and Lacey were police officers was just a way to get the concept on TV.

All three networks turned *Cagney and Lacey* down as a series, and it was not until October 1981 that CBS aired it as a made-for-TV movie starring Tyne Daly and Loretta Swit. Huge audience response led to a short-run series which, because Swit was still playing Major 'Hotlips' Houlihan in >*M*A*S*H*, starred Meg Foster in her part. Subsequent poor ratings for the mini-series, a CBS executive explained, were because the American public 'perceived them [Cagney and Lacey] as dykes'. Enter beautiful blonde Sharon Gless to set the record straight and get gay groups outraged (the protests didn't last; *Lesbian Times* decided Gless looked 'kick-ass' in jeans running along the street, and she became a major sapphic icon). Still the ratings were low, and the series was cancelled after the 1982–3 season. But not for long – loyal viewers inundated CBS with letters, and that September the series won its first Emmy. In 1984 Cagney and Lacey were back to stay, and TV Guide proclaimed: 'You Want Them! You've Got Them!'

What they got was a tough, human series that dealt head-on with difficult issues. At its centre was a real relationship – hard times, arguments and all – between two believable women. They

 *Sharon Gless (left) and Tyne Daly in the award-winning* Cagney & Lacey.

were different – Christine Cagney was ambitious, single and hard-headed at work, Mary Beth Lacey wore her heart on her sleeve and had a husband and kids to go home to – but they were united by the .38s they carried on duty, an ability to drive like saloon-car racers and a total commitment to putting villains behind bars by any means just within the law.

Not all of their cases worked out. Like >*Hill Street Blues* and other 'reality' shows, *Cagney and Lacey* reflected the rough world of the big-city cop. The two women made mistakes, made wrong judgements and let feelings get in the way. And the place they discussed all this was the ladies' room.

Storylines could be overtly political. Mary Beth was arrested off-duty for demonstrating against nuclear waste transportation in 'Special Treatment', and the episode 'The Clinic', in which the female cop odd couple escorted a Latino woman to an abortion centre, later firebombed, was judged sufficiently controversial for some affiliates to ditch it. And sometimes stories could be straight cops and robbers, such as 'Happiness is a Warm Gun', which saw Mary Beth gunned down on a dirty tenement roof by a teenage robbery suspect. As the series went on, however, the women's personal lives became more prominent. Chris's life as a single woman became a means of exploring difficult issues – in the 'Do I Know You?' segment she was the victim of date rape, and she long struggled with alcoholism (a prime-time case of TV imitating life, since Gless herself was dried out in the Hazleden Foundation in Minnesota).

Series regulars at work included tough but caring boss Lieutenant Samuels, earnest Detective Mark Petrie and womanising Detective Victor Isbecki. At home Mary Beth's supportive husband Harvey, sons Harvey Jr and Michael, and later daughter Alice, were mainstays.

Both Gless and Daly had done service in a number of TV series before winning lead roles in *Cagney and Lacey*. Gless played secretary to the PI in the ex-cop-and-ex-con series *Switch* (1975–8, CBS) starring Robert Wagner, and had roles in *Clinic on 18th Street, Faraday and Company, House Calls, Marcus Welby MD, >McCloud, Palms Precinct* and *Turnabout*. Daly's past work included the role of Jenny Lochner, wife of hero Dr Paul Lochner in CBS's long-running series *Medical Center* (1969–76).

Producer Barney Rosenzweig went on to produce *The Trials of Rosie O'Neill* (1990–) for CBS, also starring Sharon Gless, whom he later married.

Cagney and Lacey won the following Emmy awards: Outstanding Drama Series: 1985, 1986; Outstanding Leading Actress: Tyne Daly 1983, 1984, 1985, 1988; Sharon Gless 1986, 1987; Outstanding Directing in a Drama Series (single episode): Arthur Karen, 'Heat' 1985; Georg Stanford Brown, 'Parting Shots' 1986; Outstanding Writing for a Drama Series (single episode): Patricia M Green, 'Who Said It's Fair? – Part II' 1986; Outstanding Supporting Actor: John Karlen 1986.

Although the series was ended in 1988, *Cagney and Lacey* trod the small-screen beat again in the inevitable Nineties reunion TVMs. They were: *Cagney and Lacey: The Return* (1994)/*Cagney and Lacey: True Conviction*

(1995)/*Cagney and Lacey: The View Through the Glass Ceiling* (1995)/*Cagney and Lacey: Together Again* (1995).

GUEST CAST: Shannen Doherty, Lance Henriksen.

CAMPION

UK 1989–90 16 x 55m col BBC1. BBC TV/WGBH Boston, Consolidated Productions. USA tx 1989–91 syndicated.

PR *Ken Riddington, Jonathan Alwyn.* **DR** *Robin Chetwyn.*

CAST *Albert Campion (Peter Davison) Magersfontein Lugg (Brian Glover) Chief Inspector Stanislaus Oates (Andrew Burt).*

When the going gets tough, the toff gets going. A quintessential gentleman amateur sleuth from the Thirties 'Golden Age' of the English whodunnit, Margery Allingham's Albert Campion first appeared on screen in two BBC serials, *Dancers in Mourning* (1959) and *Death of a Ghost* (1960), starring Bernard Horsfall. For his 1980 resurrection Peter Davison was cast as Campion, playing the part in the daffy-diffident manner he had perfected on *All Creatures Great and Small* (and would later employ on *Dr Who*). A vintage Lagonda was Campion's means of tootling to the scene of the dastardly deed; his sidekick was faithful Cockney manservant-cum-sidekick, Magersfontein Lugg, a reformed burglar played by ex-professional wrestler Brian Glover.

Chief Inspector Oates was the obligatory oikish contact at the Yard.

There were eight two-parters: *Look to the Lady/Police at the Funeral/The Case of the Late Pig/Death of a Ghost/Sweet Danger/Dancers in Mourning/Flowers for the Judge/Mystery Mile.*

Toodlepip!

GUEST CAST: Timothy West, Peter Tuddenham.

CANNON

USA 1971–6 120 x 60m col CBS. A Quinn Martin Production. UK tx 1972–8 BBC1.

CR *Quinn Martin.* **EXEC PR** *Quinn Martin.* **PR** *Alan A Armer, Harold Gast, Anthony Spinner, Winston Miller.* **DR** *Various, including Corey Allen, John Badham, Michael Caffey, Hershel Daugherty, Richard Donner, Alf Kjellin, George McCowan, Don Medford, Michael O'Herlihy, Virgil Vogel, Edward M Abroms, Marvin J Chomsky, Marc Daniels, Charles S Dubin, Harry Falk, William Hale, Jerry Jameson, Leslie H Martinson, Leo Penn, William Wiard, Seymour Robbie, Paul Stanley, Gene Nelson.* **WR** *Various, including George Bellak, Harold Gast, Edward Hume, Stephen Kandel, Robert W Lenski, Worley Thorne, Rick Husky, Carey Wilber, Robert Hamner, David Moessinger, Paul Playdon, Robert Lewin, Shirl Hendryx.* **MUS** *John Carl Parker (theme), George Romanis, Duane Tatro, John Cannon.*

CAST *Frank Cannon (William Conrad).*

An archetypal early Seventies private eye drama, down to the one-word title and the disadvantaged hero. (In shameless exploitation of the social liberation movements of the day the US small screen came up with a wave of minority PIs with tough names, viz the Polish-American >*Banacek*, the black >*Shaft*, and the paraplegic >*Ironside*.) Frank Cannon's handicap was that he was plain obese, weighing in at nineteen stones. In *Cannon* episodes the villain would inevitably run, leaving the balding, moustachioed Los Angeles PI wheezing far behind. Hindered by his considerable morphology, Cannon relied on smarts to solve his cases. His fees were at the top

'Too fat and unattractive' for most screen roles William Conrad found fame as corpulent P.I. Cannon.

producer on such shows as *Gunsmoke*, >*Naked City*, >*77 Sunset Strip*. After *Cannon*, most of his TV work was acting as … a fat detective. In 1981 he played Rex Stout's >*Nero Wolfe*. More recently he was the co-star of >*Jake and the Fatman*.

The series *Cannon* was first developed as a 100-minute CBS TVM . The show had a close relationship with another Quinn Martin detective caper, >*Barnaby Jones*, with Cannon occasionally appearing in *BJ* episodes. A 1980 TVM saw the fatman cometh again to the small screen in *The Return of Frank Cannon*.

GUEST CAST: Roy Scheider ('No Pocket in the Shroud'), Tab Hunter, Martin Sheen, Larry Linville, Joan Fontaine, Clu Gulager, Robert Pine, David Soul, Leslie Nielsen (police lieutenant in 'The Man Who Died Twice'), Jay Silverheels, David Janssen.

CASSIE & CO

USA 1982 13 x 60m col NBC. A Carson Production for Columbia Pictures Television.
CAST Cassie Holland (Angie Dickinson) Meryl Foxx (Dori Brenner) Benny Silva (A Martinez Lyman) 'Shack' Shackleford (John Ireland) DA Mike Holland (Alex Cord).

⊗ *After* Police Woman *Angie Dickinson continued sexy detection in* Cassie & Company.

end of the scale, his interest in justice tempered by his need for money to pay for gourmet cooking and the upkeep on his luxury Lincoln Continental. The mysteries themselves were often a slow plod, but *Cannon* was a genuine television PI creation.

The part was specifically created for William Conrad by Quinn Martin (*The Fugitive*). Conrad had first come to prominence as the voice of Matt Dillon in the radio version of *Gunsmoke* in the mid 1950s, but had not been chosen to play the role on screen; in his own words he had been 'too fat and unattractive'. Before *Cannon* most of Conrad's TV work had been as a director and

◉ Or >*Police Woman* turns Private Eye. After starring as spice girl cop Pepper Anderson in *Police Woman*, Angie Dickinson carried on sexing it up in *Cassie & Company*, the polka dot

46

of difference being that the character she played here was a private detective agent. This was Cassie Holland, who took over the business of retired gumshoe 'Shack' Shackelford (John Ireland); like Pepper, Cassie relied heavily on her feminine wiles to bring the guilty to justice. When even these were not enough, old Shack himself and secretary Meryl helped out. Gym trainer Benny Silva did da rough stuff while Cassie's ex-husband Mike Holland, the City District Attorney, could be relied on to drop useful inside info snippets her way.

C.A.T.S. EYES

UK 1985–7 1 x 90m, 30 x 60m col ITV. A TVS Network Production.

CR Terence Feely. **EXEC PR** Rex Firkin. **PR** Dickie Bamber, Frank Cox (season one), Raymond Menmuir (seasons two and three). **DR** William Brayne, James Hill (I), Ian Toynton, Robert Fuest, Tom Clegg, Dennis Abbey, Ian Sharp, Raymond Menmuir, Carol Wiseman, Anthony Simmons, Terry Marcel, Edward Bennett (I), Gerry Mill, J B Wood, Alan Bell, Claude Whatham, Francis Megahy. **WR** Terence Feely, Ray Jenkins, Martin Worth, Don Houghton, Ben Steed, Anthony Skene, Ray Jenkins, Jeremy Burnham, Paul Wheeler, Gerry O'Hara, Barry Appleton, Reg Ford, Jenny McDade, Andy De La Tour, Francis Megahy. **MUS** John Kongos (season one), Barbara Thompson (seasons two and three).

CAST Pru Standfast (Rosalyn Landor) Maggie Forbes (Jill Gascoine) Frederika 'Fred' Smith (Leslie Ash) Nigel Beaumont (Don Warrington) Tessa Robinson (Tracy-Louise Ward).

>Charlie's Angels' all-American, all-women action team was a runaway success on British small screens from 1977 to 1982, but it was not until 1985 that ITV chiefs realised a similar formula was missing from home-grown product. Enter the stiff-upper-lipped British version, C.A.T.S. Eyes: three gun-toting action women with a suitable history and sufficiently sensible hairstyles for native taste.

The trio worked for the Eyes Enquiry Agency – on the surface a run-of-the-mill investigation outfit, but actually a cover for the top-secret Home Office security squad known as C.A.T.S. (Covert Activities Thames Section). Leader of the three was Pru Standfast, a tall Oxford University graduate (and former student union president) with a War Office background. Also on board was Maggie Forbes, played by Jill Gascoine. Widowed ex-detective Forbes – with eighteen years' police experience under her belt, five of them in CID – had been Britain's first policewoman star in her own ITV series >The Gentle Touch (1980–4). As well as her all-action job, as loyal viewers knew, Forbes had plenty of problems at home bringing up a teenage son single-handed. The third member of the team, and the youngest, was Frederika 'Fred' Smith, played by Leslie Ash, later to become a household name in *Men Behaving Badly*. Smith's dual talents were driving at breakneck speed and a precocious flair for computers which had attracted attention in the Civil Service. Helping the women with their investigations was 'man from the ministry' Nigel Beaumont, their link to those in command.

The series was set up by a 90-minute pilot, 'Goodbye Jenny Wren', written by creator Terence Feely, in which Maggie Forbes joins the team on the day Jenny Cartwright, another team member, is killed. From then on jewels, foreign scoundrels, the Mafia and Triads routinely supplied the cases, with specifically female interest supplied by a marriage racket using Asian girls, a woman terrorist, and (in season two) the need for Tessa Robinson to go undercover as a club barmaid while Maggie took the spotlight and sang the blues.

C.A.T.S. Eyes' ratings never compared with those of glitzy precursor *Charlie's Angels*, although season one was quality fare with high-calibre writers, directors and theme music (composed by John Kongos). From season two on, however, there were major changes both in front of the camera (Maggie Forbes was promoted to leader and Pru Standfast was replaced by Tessa Robinson) and behind. Producers relied on an inferior creative team (and even a different theme tune), and the compromise was all too apparent on screen.

GUEST CAST: Isla Blair, Ed Devereaux, Alan Downer, Sneh Gupta, Phyllida Law, George Sewell, Peter Vaughan, Penelope Wilton, Ray Winstone.

CHARLIE'S ANGELS

USA 1976–81 109 x 60m col ABC. A Ben Roberts/20th Century Fox Production. UK tx 1977–82 ITV.

CR *Ben Roberts, Ivan Goff.* **EXEC PR** *Aaron Spelling, Leonard Goldberg.* **PR** *Rick Husky, David Levinson, Edward J Lasko, Barney Rosenzweig, Elaine Rich, Robert Janes.* **DR** *Various, including Richard Benedict, Don Chaffey, Phil Bondelli, John Moxey, Bernard McEveety, Bill Bixby, Cliff Bole, David Doyle, Bob Kelljan, Georg Stanford Brown, Allen Baron, Don Chaffey, Dennis Donnelly, Charles S Dubin, Ronald Austin, John D F Black, George W Brooks, Leon Carrere, Lawrence Dobkin, Daniel Haller, Curtis Harrington, Ron Satlof, Don Weis, George McCowan, Richard Lang, Kim Manners, Paul Stanley, Larry Stewart, Allen Barron.* **WR** *Various, including John D F Black, David Levinson, Rick Husky, Lee Sheldon, Kathryn Michaelian Powers, Michael Michaelian, Robert Earll, Jack V Fogarty, Stephen Kandel, B W Sandefur, Robert Biheller, Ray Brenner, Richard Carr, Les Carter, Rick Edelstein, Rift Fournier, Ron Friedman, William Froug, Jeff Myrow, Larry Mitchell, Esther Mitchell, Sue Milburn, Edward J Lasko, Skip Webster,*

Lee Sheldon, Lee Travis, John Whepley.
MUS *Henry Mancini (theme), Jack Elliott, Allyn Ferguson, Edward J Lasko (lyrics), Lynne Marta.*
CAST *Sabrina Duncan (Kate Jackson) Jill Munroe (Farrah Fawcett) (aka Farrah Fawcett-Majors) Kelly Garrett (Jaclyn Smith) Kris Munroe (Cheryl Ladd) Tiffany Welles (Shelley Hack) Julie Rogers (Tanya Roberts) John Bosley (David Doyle) Charlie Townsend (voice only) (John Forsythe).*

'Once upon time there were three girls who went to the police academy and were each assigned very hazardous duties, but I took them away from all that and now they work for me. My name is Charlie.'

 Girlie private eye show, derided – even by its own cast – for its blatant sexism. Sabrina Duncan, Kelly Garrett and Jill Munroe were three LAPD officers rescued from humdrum meter-maiding by Charlie Townsend, wealthy head of Townsend Investigations, and dispatched to do some serious crime-busting. Alas for the TV crime aficionado, the show's plots were less concerned with sleuthing than, in executive producer Aaron Spelling's admirably candid admission, 'hairdos and gowns'. Women tuned in for fashion tips, men turned on to the Angels who, each week, were placed in a contrived undercover situation where they were required to pose around in scanty clothing (as strippers,

cheerleaders, health spa attendants and the like).

The assignments, notably, were always delivered telephonically by Charlie (voiced by John Forsythe, aka John Freund, the star of the *John Forsythe Show* and later *Dynasty*). Aside from the Angels, also jumping to the master's voice was John Bosley, who provided the Angels' logistical back-up. (In the pilot David Ogden Stiers, later *M*A*S*H*, also apppeared alongside Bosley as a middleman but was dropped for the series.) After a single season lion-maned Farrah Fawcett left the show to be replaced by Cheryl Ladd (aka Cheryl Stoppelmoor), daughter-in-law of the diminutive Hollywood star, Alan Ladd, as Kris Munroe, Jill's sister. Thereafter, the introduction of a new Angel became an almost annual occurrence. In 1979 actress Kate Jackson left, to be replaced by former Charlie perfume girl Shelley Hack as Tiffany Welles, daughter of a Connecticut police chief. Hack lasted a single year, to be replaced by Tanya Roberts (later *Sheena Queen of the Jungle* and a Bond girl in *A View to a Kill*) as streetwise Julie Roberts. When the show ended in 1981, Jaclyn Smith (wife of British film director Tony Richardson) was the only survivor of the original Angel trio. An attempt to revive the show as *Angels 88* fell to earth with a thud. Yet the influence of *Charlie's Angels* is hard

» *More concerned with 'hairdos and gowns' than plotting – Charlie's Angels (played by, left to right, Kate Jackson, Farrah Fawcett, Jaclyn Smith).*

to underestimate. As Fawcett-Majors noted at the time, 'When the show was number three, I figured it was our acting. When it got to be number one, I decided it could only be because none of us wears a bra.' A poster of Farrah Fawcett – she became Farrah Fawcett-Majors briefly on her ill-fated marriage to *Six Million Dollar Man* star Lee Majors – as athletic angel Munroe sold millions.

The pioneer of 'jiggle' broadcasting, *Charlie's Angels* developed the trend towards titillating TV seen in series as diverse as *Dukes of Hazzard* and *Baywatch*. Appropriately enough, the show earned a soft-porn movie hommage in the shape of *Bobbie's Boobies*. Aaron Spelling, meanwhile, continued his preoccupation with hi-tack gloss in *Dynasty* and *Beverly Hills 90210*.

GUEST CAST: Tommy Lee Jones, Diana Muldaur, David Ogden Stiers, Kim Basinger (1976), Richard Mulligan, Tom Selleck, Rene Auberjonois, Ida Lupino, Michael Fox, Sammy Davis Jr, Taurean Blacque, L Q Jones, Dirk Benedict, Scatman Crothers, Dick Sargent, Dean Martin.

THE CHINESE DETECTIVE

UK 1981–2 14 x 50m col BBC1. BBC TV.
CR *Ian Kennedy Martin.* **PR** *Terence Williams.*
WR *Various, including Ian Kennedy Martin.*
CAST *Det Sgt Johnny Ho (David Yip) Det Chief Insp Berwick (Derek Martin) Det Sgt Donald Chegwyn (Arthur Kelly).*

Starred British-Chinese actor David Yip in the UK TV's first police show to feature a non-Caucasian hero. This was dishevelled Detective Sergeant John Ho of East London's Limehouse manor, attracted to carrying a warrant card in a bid to clear his father's name. Already a loner by nature, Ho found himself ostracised by his own community for his vocation and by the Met for the colour of his skin. Stories hovered uneasily between 'Yer nicked!' actioners (it came from the pen of >*Sweeney* creator Ian Kennedy Martin) and meaningful drama. Two short seasons proved its allotted lifespan.

CHIPS

USA 1977–83 139 x 60m col NBC. Rosner TV/An MGM Television Production. UK tx 1979–87 ITV.
CR *Rick Rosner.* **EXEC PR** *Cy Chermak.* **PR** *Rick Rosner, Ric Rondell.* **DR** *Various, including Michael Caffey, Don Weis, Gordon Hessler, Nicholas Colasanto, Barry Crane, Paul Krasny, Christian I. Nyby II, Don Chaffey, Larry Wilcox, John Florea, John Astin, Ric Rondell, Winrich Kolbe, Edward M Abroms, Leslie H Martinson, Ivan Nagy, Nicholas Sgarro, Earl Bellamy, John D Patterson, Harvey S Laidman, Don Mc Dougall, John Peyser, Lee H Katzin.* **WR** *Various, including Jim Carlson, Marshall Herskowitz, Stephen Kandel, Ivan Nagy, Mort Thaw, James Schmerer, Jerry Thomas.* **MUS** *Mike Post, Pete Carpenter, John Parker (theme).*

CAST *Off Jon Baker (Larry Wilcox) Off Frank 'Ponch' Poncherello (Erik Estrada) Sgt Joe Getraer (Robert Pine) Off Sindy Cahill (Brianne Leary) Harlan Arliss (Lou Wagner) Off Bonnie Clark (Randi Oakes) Off Bobby 'Hot Dog' Nelson (Tom Reilly) Off Jebediah Turner (Michael Dorn) Off Grossman (Paul Linke) Cadet/Off Bruce Nelson (Bruce Penhall) Off Barry Baricza (Brodie Greer).*

The freeways and byways of Los Angeles provided the beat for Officers Jon Baker and Frank 'Ponch' Poncherello, a pair of clean-cut, good-looking cops who rode motorcycles for the California Highway Patrol (CHiPS). Jon Baker was pure country, 'Ponch' a barrio kid whom good old Jon boy had persuaded to join the force. The body-count was low (indeed, zero, since Ponch and Jon never once fired their guns) for a cop series, but there were plenty of high-speed chases of hot-rodders, hijackers and Hell's Angels, with an enormous death rate among automobiles. Off duty and on, the guys kept their teeth white and their eyes peeled for 'foxy ladies'. And these had a curious habit of turning up in abundance, although the episode in which Jon and Ponch stopped a speeding transit, to find it full of nude women volleyball players, was enough to stretch the credulity even of a 15-year-old adolescent couch male.

Complex *CHiPS* was not. The stars were Erik Estrada (born Henry Enrique Estrada), a Spanish-

✪ *Jon and Ponch – eyes peeled for 'foxy ladies' – in motor cycle cop caper CHiPS.*

American actor who came to prominence in the film *The Cross and the Switchblade* (1970), and blond Vietnam veteran and professional cowboy Larry Wilcox (also *The Adventures of Lassie*). In 1981 Bruce Jenner, ex-Olympic decathlete, rode with Wilcox (as Officer McCleish) while Estrada was involved with the production company in a salary dispute. During the last season Wilcox left the show after refusing to work with Estrada any longer, and was replaced by Tom Reilly (who, somewhat ignominiously, was soon busted for possession of marijuana by the real-life cops). Other actors who came and went were Randi Oakes, as glamorous 'Chippie' Bonnie Clark, Robert Pine, who played the cop duo's long-suffering superior, Sergeant Getraer, and former sportsman Bruce Penhall. Michael Dorn, later Worf in *Star Trek: The Next Generation,* played Officer Jebediah Turner.

The series was a hit in both the USA (breaking into the Nielsen top twenty) and the UK, and Estrada and Wilcox became pin-ups on countless teen bedroom walls. At the show's peak, Estrada alone received three thousand fan letters a week.

In 1992 Estrada and Wilcox revealed an unexpected sense of irony when they obliged with a *CHiPS* guest spot in the spoof police film, *National Lampoon's Loaded Weapon 1.* Although the original show ended in 1983, it was not to be the end of the road for the actors of *CHiPS.* There was the inevitable Nineties reunion TVM. This aired on TNT in 1988 as *CHiPS '99.*
GUEST CAST: Broderick Crawford, L Q Jones, Larry Linville, Lee Meriwether, Ed McMahon, Robert Mandan, Sonny Bono, Milton Berle, Phil Silvers, Ellen Travolta, Michael Ansara, Edward James Olmos, Troy Donahue, Jared Martin, Larry Storch.

COLONEL MARCH OF SCOTLAND YARD
UK 1955 26 x 30m bw ITV. Panda Productions. US tx 1957 syndicated.
PR *Hannah Weinstein.* **DR** *Various, including Cyril Raker Endfield*
CAST *Colonel March (Boris Karloff) Inspector Ames (Ewan Williams).*

Classic half-hour series based on the Carter Dickson collection of short stories, *The Department of Queer Complaints.* For the TV incarnation, veteran horror star Boris Karloff (alas, truly called William Henry Pratt) took the role of the sophisticated eye-patch-wearing Colonel in a spree of crime cases which embraced common-or-garden murder but were sometimes supernaturally tinged (his adversaries included the Abominable Snowman). A feature film, edited from three Colonel March episodes, was released as *Colonel March Investigates* in 1953.

The episodes were: *Passage of Arms/The Sorcerer/The Abominable Snowman/Present Tense/All Night Cats Are Grey/The Invisible Knife/The Case of the Kidnapped Poodle/The Headless Hat/The Missing Link/The Second Mona Lisa/The Case of the Misguided Missal/ Death in Inner Space/The Talking Head/The Deadly Gift/The Case of the Lively Ghost/The Devil Sells His Soul/Murder in Permanent/The Silent Vow/Death and the Other Monkey/*

Strange Events at Roman Fall/The Stolen Crime/ The Silver Curtain/Error at Daybreak/Hot Money/The New Invisible Man/Death in the Dressing Room.

COLUMBO

USA 1971–7, 1989–, 27 x 90m, 41 x 120m col NBC. Universal Television. UK tx 1972–9, 1989– ITV.

CR *Richard Levinson, William Link.*
EXEC PR *Richard Levinson, William Link, Roland Kibbee, Dean Hargrove, Richard Alan Simmons, Peter Falk.* **PR** *Douglas Benton, Everett Chambers, Dean Hargrove, Richard Alan Simmons, Edward K Dodds, Roland Kibbee, Robert F O'Neill.* **DR** *Various, including Hy Averback, Robert Butler, John Cassavetes, Jonathan Demme, Dennis Dugan, Daryl Duke, Peter Falk, Bernard L Kowalski, Patrick McGoohan, Leo Penn, Steven Spielberg, Jeannot Szwarc, E W Swackhamer, James Frawley, Ted Post, Vincent J McEveety, Sam Wanamaker, Edward M Abroms, Robert Douglas, Alf Kjellin, Alan J Levi, Ben Gazzara, Walter Grauman.*
WR *Various, including Myrna Bercovici, Robert Bless, Steven Bochco, Steven J Cannell, Larry Cohen, Peter S Fischer, Dean Hargrove, Roland Kibbee, Richard Levinson, William Link, José Luis Navarro, Barney Slater, Robert Malcolm Young, Robert Van Scoyk.*
CAST *Lieutenant Columbo (Peter Falk).*

 The shambolic Lieutenant Columbo, everybody's folk hero, drove a beaten-up old Peugeot, wore a shabby, rumpled raincoat (he was once told he looked like an unmade bed) and went about his work with an air of naive puzzlement which threw the upper-class killers against whom he pitted his wits off guard. One of the many pleasures of this series was watching the idiosyncratic commoner detective getting the better of members of society's élite. 'Look, I don't mean any offence,' he would explain. 'I'm just trying to tie up loose ends' – and wealthy art collectors, powerful politicians and talented poets would fall prey to his indefatigable desire to find out the truth.

Unusually for a detective show, *Columbo* was not a whodunnit, but a howdunnit: the viewer knew the identity of the killer, and was witness at the beginning of each episode to the planning and execution of what would have been the 'perfect' murder. Thereafter the satisfaction lay in watching the Lieutenant meticulously put each piece of the puzzle into place. 'Just one more thing,' he would say, then snare his quarry. Even the villains had to applaud his methods.

Starring the charismatic Peter Falk (who had one eye surgically removed at the age of three because of cancer, hence the trademark glassy right eye), *Columbo* was the most popular segment of NBC's Mystery Movie package which also featured >*McMillan and Wife* and

>*McCloud*. Created by Richard Levinson and William Link (>*Mannix*, >*Ellery Queen*, >*Tenafly* and >*Murder, She Wrote*), the character was modelled on Petrovitch, the detective in Dostoyevski's *Crime and Punishment*. It was only Falk's reluctance that prevented this multiple award-winning show (the series won eight Emmys, four for Falk as lead actor) running as a series in its own right; the original NBC run ended in late 1977, and thereafter only the occasional new episode was filmed. In 1989, more than a decade later, Falk returned with some new films for ABC's *Mystery Wheel,* after which Columbo came back periodically in the form of TV movies.

Loath to lose the ratings of the series when its original run ended, NBC decided to invoke the oft-mentioned but never seen wife of the detective for a spin-off. They first cashed in on the well-loved name with *Mrs Columbo,* running from February to June 1979 and dealing with the life of pretty Kate Columbo (Kate Mulgrew, later >*Star Trek: Voyager*), journalist for the Weekly Advertiser in San Fernando, California. Next they tried to sever the links and ran *Kate Loves a Mystery,* which took up the story after Kate's divorce from the Lieutenant, when Kate resumed her maiden name Callahan and moved on to a job as reporter for *San Fernando's Valley Advocate*. This series lasted from October to December 1979, after which Columbo's missus was laid to rest.

Born in New York City, half-Italian, half-Hungarian, Peter Falk (actually the producers' second choice for Columbo – the first actor approached was Bing Crosby), began as a stage actor, making his first TV appearances in programmes such as *Studio One* (1957) and *The Dick Powell Show* (1962) and playing gangster roles in >*The Untouchables* and >*Naked City*. The charm, wisdom and naivety of his screen persona in *Columbo* later led to a major part as an angel-made-mortal in Wim Wenders' 1987 feature film *Wings of Desire*.

Columbo's reputation pulled in guest stars of variety and calibre. Patrick McGoohan won two Emmys for his guest appearances as well as directing episodes of the series: 'Agenda for Murder', 1990, 'Murder with Too Many Notes', 1995, 'Ashes to Ashes' (co-director with Peter Falk), 1998. William Shatner materialised in a few episodes, Billy Connolly appeared in 1995 and Donald Pleasance cropped up as guest star in both *Columbo* and ill-fated spin-off *Mrs Columbo*. The series also boasted a star-studded list of directors which included Peter Falk himself, Steven Spielberg, Sam Wanamaker, John Cassavetes and Jonathan Demme, while writers included Larry Cohen, creator of >*The Invaders* and >*Branded*, and *Steven Bochco*.

» *'Just one more thing' – Peter Falk as* Columbo, *a character derived from a Dostoyevski novel.*

GUEST CAST: William Shatner, Patrick McGoohan, Jamie Lee Curtis, Samantha Eggar, Janet Leigh, Martin Landau, Honor Blackman, Wilfrid Hyde-White, Martin Sheen, Vincent Price, John Cassavetes, Myrna Loy, Rod Steiger, George Wendt, Tyne Daly, George Hamilton, Lesley Ann Warren.

COP ROCK

USA 1990 11 x 60m ABC. A Steven Bochco Production for Twentieth Century Fox Television. UK tx 1991 BBC1.

CR *Steven Bochco, William M Finkelstein.*
PR *Steven Bochco, John Romano, Gregory Hoblit.*
MUS *Randy Newman (theme).*
CAST *Off Andy Campo (David Gianopoulos) Off Vicki Quinn (Anne Bobby) Chief Roger Kendrick (Ronny Cox (I)) Capt John Hollander (Larry Joshua) Det Lt Ralph Ruskin (Ron McLarty) Det Joseph Gaines (Mick Murray) Mayor Louise Plank (Barbara Bosson) Trish Vaughn (Teri Austin) Ray Rodbart (Jeffrey Alan Chandler) Cdr Warren Osborne (Vondie Curtis-Hall) Sidney Weitz (Dennis Lipscomb) Det Bob McIntire (Paul McCrane) Off Franklin Rose (James McDaniel) Det Vincent La Russo (Peter Onorati) Det William Donald Potts (William Thomas Jr).*

A tango too far for Steven Bochco (>*Hill Street Blues*, >*LA Law*). After a flawless run of gritty, ground-breaking detective dramas the cop creator par excellence took a step in the wrong direction and got his cast dancing. One of the shortest-lived series on US network television, *Cop Rock* was part 'Real Stories of the Highway Patrol' and part 'Sound of Music'. After chasing down a criminal, the force would take to the street for an organised dance number, then haul their quarry back to HQ for questioning. Here we had a familiar Los Angeles backdrop, mean urban cops and a musical score that ranged from rock to rap, gospel to ballads. The men of this law enforcement team may have been hard, but they had feelings too and they expressed them frequently – in song, five tunes per episode.

The Cop Rockers themselves were a pretty standard assortment of characters: Chief of Police Roger Kendrick was a solid leader with a love of the Old West, Captain John Hollander was the curt but caring CO, Detective Joseph Gaines was green but keen, and portly Ralph Ruskin was the team forensics expert and husband of Officer Vicki Quinn, 25 years his junior. Handsome Officer Andy Campo supplied Quinn with a little distraction, and the cast also included Bochco's wife Barbara Bosson as Mayor Louise Plank.

It must have seemed like a great idea on paper. Luckily Bochco soon regained his balance and went on to whiplash camerawork in >*NYPD Blue*. Meanwhile those who caught Cop Rock's tragically brief run are left with a smile on their lips and the knowledge that Bochco had a sense of humour, too.

THE CORRIDOR PEOPLE

UK 1966 4 x 60m bw ITV. Granada TV.
CR Edward Boyd. **PR** Richard Everitt. **DR** David Boisseau. **WR** Edward Boyd.
CAST Phil Scrotty (Gary Cockrell) Kronk (John Sharp) Inspector Blood (Alan Curtis) Sergeant Hound (William Maxwell) Syrie Van Epp (Elizabeth Shepherd) Nonesuch (William Trigger).

Self-consciously surreal detective series, much influenced by *The Avengers,* in which international vamp and villainess Syrie Van Epp perpetrated outlandish schemes (eg controlling a scientist who could raise the dead). The men on her case were private eye Scrotty, and Kronk, Blood and Hound of the Yard.

Short-lived but stylish, the show came from the pen of Edward Boyd, who had earlier devised the offbeat thriller *The Odd Man* (1962–3).

The episodes were: *Victim as Birdwatcher/ Victim as Whitebait/Victim as Red/Victim as Black.*

GUEST CAST: Nina Baden-Semper.

CRACKER

UK 1993–6 25 x 60m col ITV. Granada TV. US tx 1994–6 PBS.
CR Jimmy McGovern. **PR** Gub Neal, Paul Abbott, Hilary Bevan Jones. **DR** Various, including Tim Fywell, Charles McDougal, Roy Battersby, Julian Jarrold, Michael Winterbottom, Andy Wilson, Simon Cellan Jones, Jean Stewart, Richard Standeven. **WR** Jimmy McGovern, Paul Abbott, Ted Whitehead. **MUS** Roger Jackson.
CAST Eddie 'Fitz' Fitzgerald (Robbie Coltrane) Judith Fitzgerald (Barbara Flynn) DS Jane Penhaligon (Geraldine Somerville) DCI Bilborough (Christopher Eccleston) DS Jimmy Beck (Lorcan Cranitch) Chief Insp Wise (Ricky Tomlinson) Mark Fitzgerald (Kieran O'Brien) Katie Fitzgerald (Tess Thomson).

Brooding British crime show featuring a forensic psychologist who helped the Greater Manchester Police Force with their murder enquiries. He was corpulent Dr Eddie 'Fitz' Fitzgerald, whose brilliant deductive methods included criminal profiles and mind-reading. Outside the office, however, his life was a mess (alcohol, cigarettes, gambling, loose women), and his wife Judith walked, leaving him to pursue a tempestuous affair with Detective Sergeant Jane 'Panhandle' Penhaligon, the woman usually assigned to accompany him on cases. Even when creator Jimmy McGovern dispensed with any proper semblance of police work and masochistically began killing off the main characters of the show, the taut plots, the Dostoyevskian central hero, the mesmerising lead performance by Robbie Coltrane (previously best known for light brigade work, such as *The Comic*

57

Strip Presents and *Tutti Frutti*) and the grim but contemporary subject-matter (rape, serial killing) kept millions of viewers handcuffed to the screen. Real-life psychologist Ian Stephen, the man who had tracked down the notorious serial killer Bible John, acted as series advisor.

Cracker sold around the world, and prompted a US version (*Fitz*, 1997) starring Robert Pastorelli as Gerry Fitzgerald, Angela Featherstone as Detective Hannah Tyler and Carolyn McCormick

⊗ *Robbie Coltrane as forensic psychologist Eddie Fitzgerald in* Cracker.

as Judith Fitzgerald. It came from Kushner-Locke and Granada Entertainment USA.

The cases of the original Cracker comprised: *The Mad Woman in the Attic/To Say I Love You/ One Day a Lemming Will Fly/To Be a Somebody/ The Big Crunch/Men Should Weep/Brotherly Love/Best Boys/True Romance/White Ghost.*
GUEST CAST: David Calder, Robert Carlyle ('To Be a Somebody'), Clive Russell (as Danny Fitzgerald).

CRIME STORY

USA 1986–8 48 x 60m col NBC. New World TV. UK tx 1989 ITV.
CR *Chuck Adamson, Gustave Reininger.*
PR *Michael Mann.* **DR** *Various, including Michael Mann, Colin Bucksey.* **WR** *Various.* **MUS** *Del Shannon (theme).*
CAST *Lt Michael Torello (Dennis Farina) Pauli Taglia (John Santucci) Ray Luca (Anthony Denison) Atty David Abrams (Stephen Lang) Det Danny Krychek (Bill Smitrovich) Det Joey Indelli (William Campbell) Det Walter Clemmons (Paul Butler) Det Nate Grossman (Steve Ryan) Frank Holman (Ted Levine) Manny Weisbord (Joseph Wiseman) Cori Luca (Johann Carlo) Max Goldman (Andrew Dice Clay) Julie Torello (Darlanne Fluegel) Inga Thorson (Patricia Charbonneau) Ted Kehoe (Mark Hutter) Chief Kramer (Ron Dean) Phil Bartoli (Jon Polito) Steven Kordo (Jay O Sanders).*

⊗ *Lt Mike Torello on the case in period cop show* Crime Story.

👁 Tough-looking period cop show, set in Sixties Chicago, from Michael Mann, and preceded by a TVM of the same moniker directed by Abel Ferrara.

A hit among crime aficionados, though not a big ratings success, *Crime Story* told the story of Lieutenant Michael Torello, chief of the city's MCU (Major Crime Unit), and his fight against gangster Ray Luca and his mob. Joining Torello in his struggle were Danny, Joey, Walter and Nate, his team of hardbitten but honest detectives. Julie was his estranged wife. Initially mobster's son attorney David Abrams was also on the side of law and order, but by season two Abrams had returned to his roots and joined Luca's camp. The action moved cities when Luca transferred his base to Los Angeles and Torello followed, but the squad was no match for the young gangster, and Luca's empire continued to prosper with the help of old-time mobsters Manny Weisbord and Phil Bartoli.

A kind of latter-day >Untouchables, the series was guaranteed authenticity by the fact that co-creator Chuck Adamson had served seventeen years with the Chicago PD, and Dennis Farina, also an ex-cop, had actually been a member of the unit on which the squad was based. The villains' pock-marked look, meanwhile, was enhanced by the choice of unknown actors from the right stuff background – Anthony Denison (Luca) was a one-time professional gambler and John Santucci (Taglia) was a former jewel thief.

With a budget of around $1.5 million per episode, the series was one of the most expensive ever made for network TV. Like Mann's marshmallow >Miami Vice, CS mixed speed, visuals (the stark night-time scenes were of particular note) and music (Del Shannon's 'Runaway' provided the theme), all of which pulsed forcefully through the action and got the emotions going.

After CS, Mann himself largely decamped to the movies, though his 1995 thriller flic, Heat (with Al Pacino and Robert De Niro), proved something of a retread – with its premise of two men on opposite sides of the law in titanic battle – of Crime Story itself.

GUEST CAST: Ving Rhames, Julia Roberts, Christian Slater, Kevin Spacey.

DAN AUGUST

USA 1970–1 26 x 60m col ABC. Quinn Martin Productions. UK tx 1976–8 ITV.

EXEC PR Adrian Samish, Anthony Spinner.
DR Various, including Virgil W Vogel, Ralph Senensky, Robert Douglas. **WR** Various, including Rick Husky. **MUS** Dave Grusin.
CAST Det Lt Dan August (Burt Reynolds) Sgt Wilentz (Normal Fell) Sgt Joe Rivera (Ned Romero) Chief George Untermeyer (Richard Anderson) Katy Grant (Ena Hartman).

In which Burt Reynolds played Detective Lieutenant Dan August, a cop whose crime beat was his own home town, Santa Luisa, California, which meant that he knew most of those mixed up in the cases assigned to him. His partner was Sergeant Wilentz.

Fast-moving, well-produced Quinn Martin police actioner, which was preceded by two 1970 TVMs, The House on Greenapple Road (with Christopher George as August) and Double Jeopardy. Poor ratings led to the series being axed in April 1971. However, a year later Burt Reynolds became a major star following his role as Lewis Medlock in the movie Deliverance, and subsequent reshowings of Dan August pulled in large audiences.

The episodes were: *In the Eyes of God/Murder by Proxy/The Murder of a Small Town/ Quadrangle for Death/The Soldier/Love is a Nickel Bag/The Law/The Colour of Fury/The King is Dead/Epitaph for a Swinger/When the Shouting Dies/Passing Fair/Invitation to Murder/ The Union Forever/Death Chain/Trackdown/ Days of Rage/The Titan Dead/Witness to a Killing/Bullet for a Hero/Circle of Lies/Prognosis Homicide/The Assassin/The Worst Crime/The Meal Ticket/The Manufactured Man.*

GUEST CAST: Martin Sheen, Mickey Rooney, Robert Fuller.

DAVID CASSIDY — MAN UNDERCOVER

USA 1978–9 4 x 60m col NBC. A Columbia Pictures Television Production.

CR Richard Fielder. **EXEC PR** David Gerber. **PR** Mark Rodgers, Mel Swope.

CAST Off Dan Shay (David Cassidy) Joanne Shay (Wendy Rastatter) Cindy Shay (Elizabeth Reddin) Lt Abrams (Simon Oakland) Off Paul Sanchez (Michael A Salcido) Off T J Epps (Ray Vitte).

Anyone with a long memory or a junk-lot of Seventies records will recall David Cassidy as a fast-rocket teen sensation and star of the sitcom *The Partridge Family.* Less well known is this, alas rarely seen, piece of TV kitsch. Conceived as a means of cashing in on the star's popularity, *David Cassidy – Man Undercover* cast the unfeasibly boyish Cassidy as a twentysomething undercover agent with the LAPD. Cases had Cassidy's Dan Shay character investigating teenage bank robbers, illegal drug use – indeed anything which might tempt the curiosity of Cassidy's child/pubescent fans. It wasn't cool, and Cassidy – brother of Shaun (>*American Gothic, The Hardy Boys*) – wasn't hot any longer anyway. Joanne was Shay's loving wife, Cindy his young daughter, while Lieutenant Abrams was the man in charge at work. It was developed for TV by David Gerber and came via an episode of Joseph Wambaugh's >*Police Story.*

DELLAVENTURA

USA 1997–8 13 x 60m CBS. Rysher Entertainment.

EXEC PR Richard Di Lello, Danny Aiello. **DR** Rick Rosenthal. **MUS** Joe Delia.

CAST Andy Dellaventura (Danny Aiello) Geri Zarias (Anne Ramsay) Teddy Naples (Ricky Aiello).

Starred Danny Aiello (*The Last Don*) as Andy Dellaventura, a veteran police detective turned shamus. Like >*The Equalizer* before him, he took the cases the police wouldn't

61

62

or couldn't handle, and so was there to 'help the people who had nowhere else to turn' (as the CBS press release had it). But Dellaventura was no mere tough guy, as was shown by the profundity of his personal philosophy: 'You see, everything we are is everything we were, and everything we were is everything we will be.' He was aided in his detective work by a team of renegade ex-cops and criminals.

The episodes were: *Pilot/Above Reproach/ Music of the Night/Joe Fallon's Daughter/Clean Slate/Fathers/Hell's Kitchen/The Deadly Fashion/With a Vengeance/Dreamers/The Biggest Miracle/David and Goliath/Made in America.*

GUEST CAST: Howard Spiegel.

DELVECCHIO

USA 1976–7 20 x 60m col NBC. A Universal Television Production.
CR *Sam Rolfe, Joseph Polizzi, Steven Bochco.*
EXEC PR *William Sackheim, Lane Slate.*
PR *Michael Rhodes.* **DR** *Various, including Arnold Laven, Ivan Nagy, Walter Doniger, Lou Antonio, Jerry London.* **WR** *Various, including Steven Bochco.* **MUS** *Billy Goldenberg, Richard Clements.*
CAST *Sgt Dominick Delvecchio (Judd Hirsch) Lt Macavan (Michael Conrad) Sgt Paul Shonski (Charles Haid) Sgt Rivera (Jay Varela) Asst DA Dorfman (George Wyner).*

Delvecchio was the story of a hard-nosed independent cop (badge 425) who worked the Washington Heights area of LA, with his partner Paul Shonski. Assigning the cases – which ranged from grand theft auto to homicide – was Lieutenant Macavan. Tomaso was Delvecchio's elderly immigrant father, a barbershop proprietor continually bemused as to why his son had given up a career as an attorney to become a policeman. Shot on location, the show interested in its own right; it also played a pivotal role in the development of the cop TV genre. A certain youthful Steven Bochco was a co-creator (along with *Man from UNCLE*'s Sam Rolfe), and when Bochco later devised >*Hill Street Blues* he took no fewer than three of Delvecchio's lead players (Charles Haid, Michael Conrad, George Wyner) with him. Judd Hirsch, meanwhile, went on to star in the New York sitcom *Taxi.*

DEMPSEY AND MAKEPEACE

UK 1985–6 1 x 105, 30 x 60m col ITV. A Golden Eagle Films Production for London Weekend TV. US tx 1985 syndicated.
CR *Tony Wharmby.* **PR** *Tony Wharmby, Nick Elliott, Ranald Graham.* **DR** *Tony Wharmby, William Brayne, Christian Marnham, Robert Tronson, Gerry Mill, Michael Brandon, Roger Tucker, Viktors Ritelis, Baz Taylor, Graham*

Theakston, Christopher King.
WR Various, including Ranald
Graham, Jesse Carr-Martindale,
Murray Smith, Dave Humphries,
Jonathan Hales. **MUS** Alan
Parker.
CAST Lt James Dempsey
(Michael Brandon) Det Sgt
Harriet Alexandra Charlotte
'Harry' Makepeace (Glynis
Barber) Chief Supt Gordon
Spikings (Ray Smith) Det Sgt
Charles 'Chas' Jarvis (Tony
Osoba).

Mid-Atlantic cop TV
product in which brash,
trigger-happy New York
Lieutenant James Dempsey
(played by Michael Brandon,
born Feldman, sometime
husband of Lindsay 'Bionic
Woman' Wagner) was
sent over to Britain after
uncovering corruption among
his Ninth Precinct colleagues.
In Blighty, he was partnered by
Lady Harriet Makepeace
(pneumatic Glynis Barber of
Blake's 7 and Jane, born
Glynis Van der Reit in South

Africa), an upper-class English
blonde with a Cambridge
degree in science and distant
claims to the throne. This
uneasy pairing worked in
and around London for
Scotland Yard's élite covert
division S1–10 and while
'Lootenant' Dempsey never left
home without his .357
Magnum, 'Harry'
Makepeace preferred to
use her friends in high
places. Overseeing the
pair's antics was loudmouth
Liverpudlian Gordon Spikings,
while Detective Sergeant Chas
Jarvis (Tony Osoba, from jail
sitcom Porridge) also lent his
skills on occasion.

Preposterous but enduringly
popular action series which
covered up its criminally past-sell-
by-date plots with a heavy dose of
schmaltz in the form of a will-they-
won't-they? between the cop
leads. This, fortunately for the

63

« Michael Brandon and Glynis
Barber as Dempsey and
Makepeace. The actors later
married in real life.

64

producers, gained considerable spice from the much publicised off-screen romance between its stars, who later married.

GUEST CAST: Terence Alexander, Ralph Arliss, Kate O'Mara, Patty Boulaye.

DEPARTMENT S

UK 1969–70 28 x 60m col ITV. ITC. USA tx 1971 syndicated.

CR Monty Berman, Dennis Spooner. **PR** Monty Berman. **DR** Ray Austin, John Gilling, Cyril Frankel, Paul Dickson, Gill Taylor, Roy Ward Baker, Leslie Norman. **WR** Gerald Kelsey, Philip Broadley, Terry Nation, Tony Williamson, Harry H Junkin, Leslie Darbon, Donald James. **MUS** Edwin Astley.

CAST Jason King (Peter Wyngarde) Stewart Sullivan (Joel Fabiani) Annabelle Hurst (Rosemary Nichols) Sir Curtis Seretse (Dennis Alaba Peters). **VIDEO** ITC.

Moustachioed actor Peter Wyngarde played the flamboyant Jason King ('Whenever I feel the need for exercise I lie down until it passes'), head investigator of Department S, an Interpol branch which specialised in 'unsolvable' crimes. A detective novelist in his spare time, King chose to approach each Department S case as though he himself were Mark Caine, his own ace sleuth creation – a somewhat fanciful modus operandi which

continually irked his co-workers, the prosaic Stewart Sullivan and computer expert Annabelle Hurst. The trio's boss was Sir Curtis Seretse (played by black actor Dennis Alaba Peters), and it was he who gave them their international assignments. These were usually murder or kidnapping mysteries which had a strong element of the fantastic: 'The Pied Piper of Hambledown' concerned the mass abduction of an English village, 'One of Our Aircraft is Empty' a pilotless plane, and 'The Man in the Elegant Room' a killing in a palatial chamber in an otherwise abandoned factory. The scripts were highly polished, and no matter how seemingly implausible the plots, they were usually convincingly resolved. The guest cast included Kate O'Mara – a trooper in a range of Sixties action series – and Alexandra Bastedo (>The Champions).

Less successful, though, was the spin-off >Jason King in which Wyngarde (aka Cyril Louis Goldbert) reprised his King character as a solo, non-Department S, crime-busting operative.

The episodes were: Six Days/The Trojan Tanker/A Cellar Full of Silence/The Pied Piper of Hambledown/One of Our Aircraft is Empty/The Man in the Elegant Room/Handicap Dead/Black Out/Who Plays the Dummy?/The Treasure of the Costa del Sol/The Man Who Got a New

» Mike Maguire on the wrong end of a pistol-whipping in 50s classic Dial 999.

Face/Les Fleurs du Mal/The Shift That Never Was/The Man from 'X'/Dead Men Die Twice/The Perfect Operation/The Duplicated Man/The Mysterious Man in the Flying Machine/Death on Reflection/The Last Train to Redbridge/The Bones of Byrom Blaine/Spenser Bailey is Sixty Years Old/The Ghost of Mary Burnham/A Fish Out of Water/Soup of the Day/A Ticket to Nowhere/The Double Death of Charlie Crippen.

GUEST CAST: Peter Bowles, Alexandra Bastedo, Kate O'Mara, Anthony Hopkins, John Louis Mansi, Anthony Valentine, Ronald Lacey, David Prowse, Duncan Lamont.

DIAL 999

UK 1958–9 39 x 30m bw ITV. A Towers of London Production in association with Ziv TV Programmes. US tx 1959 syndicated.

PR Harry Alan Towers. **DR** Various, including Alvin Rakoff. **MUS** Sidney Torch.

CAST Mike Maguire (Robert Beatty) Det Insp Winter (Duncan Lamont) Det Sgt West (John Witty).

Vintage cop series from the black-and-white age, featuring a tough-named Mountie, Mike Maguire, seconded to London's Scotland Yard. Naturally, he always got his man. Filmed almost entirely on location, the series was a co-production with American quickie factory Ziv TV, and contained a generous weekly slug of car chase and fisticuffs, these ingredients thought necessary for the action-minded American viewer. Canadian film star Robert Beatty – who was almost 50 when the show began – played Mountie Mike with vigorous professionalism, while Duncan Lamont (previously in Quatermass) was perfectly cast as his bemusedly refined London counterpart, Detective Inspector Winter.

DICK BARTON – SPECIAL AGENT

UK 1979 26 x 15m col ITV. A Southern Network Production.

EXEC PR Terence Baker, Lewis Rudd. **PR** Jon Scoffield. **DR** Jon Scoffield. **WR** Clive Exton, Julian Bond.

CAST Dick Barton (Tony Vogel) Snowey White (Anthony Heaton) Jock Anderson (James Cosmo).

Small-screen make-over of a 1940s radio favourite. The snappy twice-weekly serial followed Barton's investigation – with help from old army chums Snowey and Jock – into the disappearance of the offspring of Sir Richard Marley. To no great surprise, it turned out to be Barton's arch-enemy Megalnik who dunnit.

If the TV version sensibly kept the old wireless DB theme, it less astutely gave the ex-commando hero seamy, thoroughly modern looks. Which never quite square-jawed with an audience used to Dick Barton as an archetype of lion-hearted British do-goodery.

DICK TRACY

US 1950–1 23 x 30m bw ABC. An ABC Production.

PR Dick Moore, Keith Kalmer.

CAST Dick Tracy (Ralph Byrd) Police Chief Murphy (Dick Elliott) Sam Catchem (Joe Devlin) Tess Trueheart (Angela Greene) Police Officer Mary Faelb (Margia Dean).

TV version of Chester Gould's famous comic strip hero. Ralph Byrd played the title NYPD plainclothes tough guy, as he had in a slew of film serials and radio shows since 1937 – with him violently slugging it out on the small screen in exactly the same manner as the other media. All the supporting characters came too: sidekick Sam Catchem, Chief Murphy, villains The Joker and The Mole, and girlfriend Tess Trueheart. After a brief run on the ABC network, Byrd continued to make Tracy TV films for the syndicated market until his premature death in 1952 (from a heart attack, at the age of 43). Nearly a decade later an animated *Dick Tracy Show* was syndicated, with Everett Sloane voicing Tracy (also in the voice cast were Mel Blanc, Benny Rubin and Paul Frees). In 1990 a big-budget movie version cast Warren Beatty as the jut-jawed Dick and Madonna as breathless temptress Mahoney, the success of which prompted a trio of TVMs edited down from Byrd's serials: *Dick Tracy's G-Men*, *Dick Tracy vs Crime Inc* and *Dick Tracy*.

DIXON OF DOCK GREEN

UK 1955–76 365 x 30/45m bw/col BBC1. A BBC TV Production.

CR Ted Willis. **PR** Various, including Douglas Moodie, Ronald Marsh, Philip Barker, Joe Waters, G B Lupino, Robin Nash. **DR** Various, including A A Englander, David Askey, Robin Nash, Vere Lorrimer, Michael Goodwin, Douglas Argent, Mary Ridge, Michael E Briant. **WR** Various, including Ted Willis, Arthur Swinson, Eric Paice, Gerald Kelsey, N J Crisp, Jack Trevor Story, P J Hammond, Robert Holmes, Tony Williamson, David Ellis, Peter Ling, Richard Waring, Derek Benfield, Rex Edwards, Ivor Jay, John Wiles, Cyril Abraham, Dick Sharples.

CAST PC George Dixon (Jack Warner) Det Sgt Crawford (Peter Byrne) Mary Crawford (Billie Whitelaw [1955]/Jeannette Hutchinson (from 1955]/Anna Dawson) PC 'Laudy' Lauderdale (Geoffrey Adams) Desk Sgt Flint (Arthur Rigby) PC Willis (Nicholas Donnelly) PC Tubb Barrell (Neil Wilson) Sgt Grace Millard (Moira Mannion) Cadet Jamie MacPherson (David Webster) PC Bob Penney (Anthony Parker) WPC Kay Shaw/Lauderdale (Jocelyne Rhodes) Bob Cooper (Duncan Lamont) PC Swain (Robert Arnold) WPC Liz Harris (Zeph Gladstone) PC Newton (Michael Osborne) Insp Cherry (Stanley Beard/Robert Crawdon) PC Bob Penney (Anthony Parker) PC/Sgt Johnny Wills (Nicholas Donnelly).

'Evenin' all.' Former war hero Jack Warner played *the eponymous* Dixon of Dock Green.

'Evenin' all.' Avuncular PC George Dixon was the first British copper to tread the TV beat and, with 21 years on screen, the longest-lasting. The character was first seen in the Rank movie *The Blue Lamp* (1950), where he was famously killed by young Dirk Bogarde's villain in the climax. But so popular was the kindly, tea-drinking copper that the BBC unashamedly brought him back to life, with co-creator Ted Willis penning most of his early small-screen appearances. The character of PC Dixon (played by Jack Warner, aka Horace John Waters, who in the First World War had won a Meritorious Service Medal) was based by Willis on a real policeman from Leman Street in the East End, and on an archetype of the English bobby. Keen to have an air of reality about the series, Willis kept on his payroll 250 real-life policemen who would pass on anecdotes about their job.

The emphasis in the series, which was reassuringly cosy and quaint even in the Fifties, was on small, everyday experiences, not major-league crime and sensationalism, with Dixon a benevolent father figure to the local community. 'Murder cases are not as frequent as some crime writers would lead us to imagine' was how the *Radio Times* primly introduced the first episode, 'PC Crawford's First Pinch'. But no matter what the crime, justice was always done, usually with Dixon persuading the villain – who had apparently stepped out of Lombroso's catalogue of criminal stereotypes – to 'give it up, son', and the episode finishing with a heart-warming homily from Dixon standing under the station's blue lamp.

Other characters at Dock Green who made the move from the movie along with Dixon included Andy Crawford, later to become a Detective Sergeant and to marry Dixon's daughter Mary, PC 'Taudy' Lauderdale, and Desk Sergeant Flint (Arthur Rigby), who lodged with Dixon's mother.

In 1964 Dixon was promoted to sergeant and became more desk-bound, too old to pound the beat any more. He finally retired in 1976, as the show was beginning to pale in comparison with such energetic vehicles as >*The Sweeney*. Still, for a TV generation or more, the image of Dixon looming out of a foggy London night whistling 'Maybe It's Because I'm a Londoner' – the show's opening sequence – remains a classic image.

When Jack Warner died in 1981, aged 85, his coffin was borne by police officers from Paddington Green and the show's theme tune, 'An Ordinary Copper', was played over the PA. It was the end of an era and a British institution. Never again would the British police be served so well on the small screen.

Ted Willis, who created Dixon, was something of a British monument himself. His output included 34 stage plays, 39 films and 40 television series, and he earned a place in the *Guinness Book of Records* as TV's most prolific writer. He made a controversial start to his career as a radio writer for *Mrs Dale's Diary*, writing an episode in which Mrs Dale and friends plunged to their deaths after reversing a car over Beachy Head. He was promptly fired. Credited as the pioneer of the 'kitchen sink' dramas of the Fifties, he was made a Labour peer by Harold Wilson in 1963. Lord Willis died in 1992.

GUEST CAST: Sean Connery, David Hemmings, Kenneth Cope, Harold Scott (as recurring character 'Duffy'), Paul Eddington, Richard O'Sullivan, Patrick Mower, Malcolm McDowall.

DOG AND CAT

USA 1977 10 x 60m col ABC. A Paramount Television Production.
CR Walter Hill. **EXEC PR** Lawrence Gordon. **PR** Robert Singer. **DR** Various, including Arnold Laven, Steven Hilliard Stern, Michael Preece, Paul

Stanley. **WR** Various. **MUS** Barry De Vorzon.
CAST Det Sgt Jack Ramsey (Dog) (Lou Antonio) Off
J Z Kane (Cat) (Kim Basinger) Lt Arthur Kipling
(Matt Clark).

To test the feasibility of male and female
detective teams, the 42nd Division of the
LAPD assigns the beautiful rookie J Z Kane to
partner tough Detective Sergeant Jack Ramsey.

Dog and Cat *was a him'n'her crime show devised
by Hollywood director Walter Hill.*

Cheesy hour-long police drama, which
introduced actress Kim Basinger to the waiting
world of male viewerdom. It also set the mark for
mixed-sex detective partnerships, with >Dempsey
and Makepeace *and* >Moonlighting *following in
its gumshoes. The show was preceded by a TVM*

of the same title which, like the series, was devised by writer-director Walter Hill (*The Getaway, Red Heat, Geronimo, Alien 3*) and filmed on location in LA.

DRAGNET

USA 1952–8 263 x 30m bw, 1967-70 98 x 30m col NBC. MCA TV/Mark VII/Universal TV. UK tx 1955-9 ITV.

CR *Jack Webb, Richard L Breen.* **EXEC PR** *Jack Webb.* **PR** *Robert A Cinader, William Stark, Jack Webb.* **DR** *Jack Webb.* **WR** *Various, including James Moser, Richard L Breen, Henry Irving, Sidney Morse, Jerry D Lewis, Robert Soderburg, Preston Wood, Robert C Dennis, David Vowell, Burt Prelutsky, James Doherty.* **MUS** *Walter Schumann.*

CAST *Sgt Joe Friday (Jack Webb) Sgt Ben Romero (Barton Yarborough) Sgt Ed Jacobs (Barney Philips) Off Frank Smith (Herb Ellis/Ben Alexander) Off Bill Gannon (Harry Morgan) Introducer (voice) (George Fenneman/Hal Gibney).* **VIDEO** *Columbia House/Shokus.*

'The story you are about to see is true. Only the names have been changed to protect the innocent.'

Thus thundered the introduction to every episode of Jack Webb's hyper-realistic *Dragnet*, one of the most popular and influential

⌃ *Arguably the most influential cop show in TV history, the hyper-realistic* Dragnet *used cases from the files of the real LAPD. Jack Webb (left) created and starred.*

police series in TV history. While other cop shows traded in super-heroic detectives who carried a blonde in one hand and a stuttering machine-gun in the other, Webb – as director, producer and star – played it low-key, with documentary-style photography and laconic voice-over narration. Authenticity was assured by using cases actually pulled from files of the Los Angeles Police Department, with many of the walk-on parts played by those involved in the real crime. Webb spent two years riding in LAPD patrol cars to learn police jargon and behaviour. Sergeant Joe Friday, too, was suitably downbeat, not given to loquaciousness, emotion, shoot-outs (Webb only allowed one bullet to be fired every four episodes) or fights, only hard plodding policework. 'Just the facts, Ma'm', 'That's my job' and 'I carry a badge' were Friday's standard lines for every eventuality.

The hero may have been uncharismatic, and the style *vérité*, but *Dragnet* was far from boring. Webb's direction was taut, with lots of close-ups, while Walter Schumann's music provided dramatic changes of pace and mood. (Schumann's famous 'dum-de-dum-dum' theme became a hit record in 1953.) The programme's fault was the occasional lapse into sententious moralising on behalf of the fine, decent, upstanding nature of American law enforcement. And, indeed, sententious moralising generally; the show's best remembered episode, 'The LSD Story', written by Webb under the pseudonym John Rudolph, featured drug use by the young, but was so risibly hysterical that it was reminiscent of the infamous Hollywood anti-cannabis film, *Reefer Madness*.

Like several other small-screen hit dramas of the Fifties, *Dragnet* began life as a radio series. It was first transmitted as a segment in *Chesterfield Sound Off Time* in 1951, before going independent in the following year. In 1955 it became the first US police show to be screened in Britain (and one of ITV's first hits), where it ran against the infinitely tamer native >*Dixon of Dock Green*. *Dragnet*'s prime-time run in the USA came to an end in 1959, by which time Friday had been promoted to lieutenant and had had three sidekicks (Romero, Jacobs and Smith). But you cannot keep a good TV series down, and Webb resurrected *Dragnet* as a colour 60-minute show in 1967. Friday was back to a sergeant again and his new partner was Officer Bill Gannon, a married hypochondriac played by Harry Morgan (later to be promoted to Colonel Sherman Potter in *M*A*S*H*). Around the same time, the original *Dragnet* was syndicated under the title *Badge 714* (Friday's warrant number).

Since the death of Jack Webb (a sometime head of Warner TV, and the producer of such later detective shows as >*O'Hara, US Treasury* and *Hec Ramsey*) in 1982, yet another *Dragnet* (an Arthur Company Production for WWOR-TV, 1989–90, 52 episodes) has appeared, with the leads played by Jeffrey Osterhage and Bernard White. There was also a 1987 film feature *Dragnet*, directed by Tom Mankiewicz, with Dan Ackroyd playing Friday as an amusingly starched, cleaner-than-clean parody of the original. Harry Morgan guested in affectionate homage to his years on the show.

GUEST CAST: Anthony Eisley, Vic Perrin, Virginia Gregg, Scatman Crothers.

DUE SOUTH

Canada 1994–8 1 x 120m, 61 x 60 x 60m
col. Alliance Communications/BBC TV. UK tx
1995–8 Sky I, US tx 1995–8 CBS/Polygram
Syndication.

CR Paul Haggis. **EXEC PR** Paul Haggis, Jeff King,
Kathy Slevin, Paul Gross. **PR** Robert Wertheimer.
DR Various, including George Bloomfield, Paul
Lynch, Paul Haggis, Steve DiMarco, David Warry-
Smith, Joseph L Scanlon, Malcolm Cross, Francis
Damberger. **WR** Various, including Paul Lynch.
MUS Various, including Jack Lenz, John McCarthy.

CAST Constable Benton Fraser (Paul Gross)
Raymond Vecchio (David Marciano) Stanley
(Raymond Kowalski) Callum (Keith Rennie) Louis
Gardeno (Daniel Kash) Lt Harding Welsh (Beau
Starr) Insp Margaret 'Meg' Thatcher (Camilla
Scott) Thomas E Dewey (Tom Melissis) Robert
Fraser (Gordon Pinsent) Francesca Vecchio
(Ramona Milano) Det Jack Huey (Tony Craig).
VIDEO Clearvision.

⊗ 'Thank you kindly.' Fraser and Vecchio in quirky
Canadian cop show Due South.

74

Quirky Canadian series about a charming straight-arrow Mountie, Constable Benton Fraser (Paul Gross, *Tales of the City*), assigned to duty in Chicago, where he buddied up with cynical detective Ray Vecchio (David Marciano, *Lethal Weapon II*). Naturally, Fraser always got his man, though unusual powers (heightened sense of smell and sight, the ability to see the ghost of his dead father) and a deaf but lip-reading wolf-husky named Diefenbaker helped some.

Aimed somewhere between *Northern Exposure* and >*McCloud,* the series boasted wise-cracking scripts (some by Gross himself) and dialogue. It was filmed in Toronto – where streets had to be dirtied to pass for 'the windy city' – and guest players included Leslie Nielsen, who taught Gross how to lace his boots in correct RCMP manner; Nielsen's father had been a real Mountie. A hit in Canada and the UK, the show was unable to defeat bad US ratings, causing its cancellation after two series. A funding deal by Canada's Alliance Communications and the BBC, however, produced one more season, in which David Marciano made only limited appearances, leaving Callum Keith Rennie's Kowalski character to step into the role of sidekick.

As Fraser would have said, 'Thank you kindly.'
GUEST CAST: Leslie Nielsen, Michele Scarabelli, Bruce Weitz, Lee Purcell, Sherry Miller, Alison Sealy-Smith.

EISCHIED

USA 1979–83 13 x 60m col NBC. Gerber Productions/Columbia Pictures TV.
EXEC PR *David Gerber.* **PR** *Matthew Rapf, Jay Daniel.* **MUS** *Roger Webb.*
CAST *Chief Earl Eischied (Joe Don Baker) Dep Commissioner Kimbrough (Alan Fudge) Capt Finnerty (Alan Oppenheimer) Chief Insp Ed Parks (Eddie Egan) Rick Alessi (Vincent Bufano) Carol Wright (Suzanne Leder) Det Malfitano (Joe Cirillo).*

It was pronounced 'eye-shy-ed'. Violent police series featuring the burly, hardbitten NYPD Chief of Detectives, Earl Eischied (Joe Don Baker, later >*In the Heat of the Night*), a cop who knew the rule-book but generally preferred to ignore it – much to the worry of his politically ambitious boss, Deputy Commissioner Kimbrough. Rick Alessi, Carol Wright and Captain Finnerty were the main – and highly devoted – members of Eischied's special squad. Like fellow Seventies screen cops >*Kojak* and Steve McGarrett in >*Hawaii Five-O,* the Southern-born Eischied was a consummate professional, and thus had no time for a wife, girlfriend or family. His sole home companion was cat PC.

In the UK the show aired as *Chief of Detectives;* it was spun off from the 1978 TVM *To Kill a Cop* (**DR** Gary Nelson, **WR** Ernest Tidyman, *Shaft*), itself based on the novel by Robert Daley.
'You done good.'

ELLERY QUEEN

USA 1975–6 1 x 120m, 22 x 60m col NBC. A Fairmont-Foxcroft Production/Universal TV. UK tx 1976 BBC1.

EXEC PR Richard Levinson, William Link. **PR** Peter S Fischer, Michael Rhodes. **DR** David Greene, Charles S Dubin, Peter H Hunt, Jack Arnold, James Sheldon, Seymour Robbie, Edward Abroms. **MUS** Elmer Bernstein, Hal Mooney. **CAST** Ellery Queen (Jim Hutton) Insp Richard Queen (David Wayne) Sgt Velie (Tom Reese) Frank Flannigan (Ken Swofford) Simon Brimmer (John Hillerman).

Invented in a 1929 novel, *The Roman Hat Mystery*, by Frederic Dannay and Manfred Bennington Lee, *Ellery Queen* was first brought to the small screen by Richard Hart in the 1950 series, *The Adventures of Ellery Queen*. When Hart died of a heart attack, the title role of the New York author turned supersleuth then passed in turn to Lee Bowman, George Nader and Lee Phillips. After fifteen years the character was revived by American network NBC in this 1940s period piece, overseen by Richard Levinson and William Link. They added a pleasant leavening of self-conscious humour, epitomised by Queen's turning to the audience just before the denouement to ask: 'Have you figured it out?' Here the part of Queen was taken by Jim Hutton, later cast in the abortive US version of *Butterflies*.

David Wayne, who played Queen's policeman father, was previously on the other side of the law as the Batman villain, 'Mad Hatter'. Two years after handing in his badge as Queen senior he resurfaced as Willard 'Digger' Barnes in *Dallas*.

GUEST CAST: Rene Auberjonois, Nancy Kovack, Bobby Sherman, Joan Collins, George Burns, June Lockhart, Ed McMahon.

'Have you figured it out?' Jim Hutton as NY's finest amateur sleuth, Ellery Queen.

THE EQUALIZER

USA 1985–9 88 x 60m col CBS. Universal TV.
UK tx 1986–9 ITV.

CR *Michael Sloan, Richard Lindheim.*
EXEC PR *James McAdams.* **PR** *Various, including
Alan Barnette, Colman Luck, Scott Shepherd,
Daniel Lieberstein, Peter A Runfolo, Alan Metzger.*
DR *Various, including Russ Mayberry, Richard
Compton, Alan Metzger, Bradford May, Rod
Holcomb, Richard Colla, Tobe Hooper, Paul
Krasny, Michael O'Herlihy, Mark Sobel, James
Sheldon, Aaron Lipstadt, Marc Laub.*
WR *Various, including Joel Surnow, Maurice
Hurley, Victor Hsu, Howard Chesle, Mark Frost,
Robert Crais, Carleton Eastlake, Robert Eisele,
Coleman Luck, Scott Shepherd, Michael Sloan.*
MUS *Various, including Stewart Copeland
(theme), Cameron Allan, Bob Christianson, Joseph
Conlan.*
CAST *Robert McCall ('The Equalizer') (Edward
Woodward) Control (Robert Lansing) Mickey
Kostmayer (Keith Szarabajka) Lt Isadore Smalls
(Ron O'Neal) Lt Burnett (Steven Williams) Scott
McCall (William Zabka) Sgt Alice Shepherd
(Chad Redding) Lt Brannigan (Eddie Jones).*

*'Got a problem? Odds against you? Call the
Equalizer.'*

Take >*Callan*, add a dash of American
dressing, a soupçon of Bronson's *Death*

⊗ *'Got a problem?' Edward Woodward as* The
Equalizer.

Wish, a dollop of venerable oater *Have Gun –
Will Travel* and, hey presto, you have *The
Equalizer*. Edward Woodward (formerly *Callan*)
played a muttering Manhattan former secret

service agent for 'The Company' (ie the CIA) turned PI/bodyguard who drove a Jaguar car, dressed immaculately and righted wrongs, usually by dint of his gun. Careful to avoid anything too strenuous, 'The Equalizer' passed over the legwork to assistant Mickey Kostmayer. A violent vigilante fantasy (most of those to die were NY muggers and rapists) the show was lapped up in the USA – after CBS threw some scheduling

Bruce Seton as Fabian of the Yard, *which dramatised the cases of the real life DI Fabian.*

weight behind it – and then all around the world. The theme music was composed by Stewart Copeland from post-punk band, The Police, who also guested in the episode 'Re-entry' (as did Hollywood legend Robert Mitchum, no less). Although CBS positively loved *The Equalizer* – dubbing it affectionately 'Call Daddy', in homage both to Woodward's character and also its novelty as an actioner with a hero over 50 – they cancelled it in a tit-for-tat retaliation against Universal when the latter hiked up the price of >*Murder, She Wrote* episodes. Woodward adroitly continued his 'Equalizer' ice-killer persona to present the true-crime show, *In Suspicious Circumstances*, before throwing typecasting to the wind to star in the garbage-men comedy *Common as Muck*.

GUEST CAST: Robert Mitchum, Brad Dourif, Jenny Agutter, John Goodman, Anthony Zerbe, Michael Moriarty, Kevin Spacey.

FABIAN OF THE YARD

UK 1954–6 39 x 30m bw BBC. Anthony Beauchamp Productions/Trinity Productions. US tx 1955 syndicated.

PR John Larkin, Anthony Beauchamp. **DR** *Various, including Anthony Beauchamp, John Lemont, Bernard Knowles, Alex Bryce.* **WR** *Various, including Arthur La Bern, Rex Rienits, Arnold Goldsworthy, Donald Bull.*
CAST Det Insp Robert Fabian (Bruce Seton).

Classic British police series from the Fifties, fictionalising the cases of the Yard's real-life Detective Inspector Fabian. Shot on film, with Bruce Seton, stiff upper lip clamped on pipe, as the consummately dedicated Fabian, it cast a giant TV shadow; for the post-war generation Fabian was not just the first British police hero of the small screen, but the best. *Fabian of the Yard* sold to America, where it screened as *Inspector Fabian of Scotland Yard* or – in reference to the hero's Humber Hawk – *Patrol Car*. The real Fabian, incidentally, retired from the force for a sinecure as 'Guardian of the Questions' on the *$64,000 Question* quiz show, the cheapskate British version of the USA's *$64,000 Question*.

THE FALL GUY

USA 1981–6 113 x 60m col ABC. Twentieth Century Fox. UK tx 1982–6 ITV.

CR *Glen A Larson.* **EXEC PR** *Glen A Larson.* **PR** *Various, including Robert Jones, Harry Thompson, Lee Majors.* **DR** *Various, including Tom Connors, Daniel Haller, Ray Austin, Vincent Edwards.* **WR** *Various, including Larry Brand, Rebecca Reynolds.* **MUS** *Glen A Larson, David Somerville, Gail Jensen (theme), Stu Phillips.* **CAST** *Colt Seavers (Lee Majors) Howie Munson (Douglas Barr) Jody Banks (Heather Thomas) Samantha 'Big' Jack (JoAnn Pflug) Terri Shannon/Michaels (Markie Post) Edmund Trench (Robert Donner).*

Lee Majors in his fourth prime-time hit (after *The Big Valley, Men from Shiloh* and *The Six Million Dollar Man*) played Colt Seavers, a Hollywood stuntman who earned extra bucks tracking down bail jumpers. Naturally, this latter-day bounty hunting required stuntwork even more spectacular than that Seavers performed for the movies. He was assisted in his sleuthing work by eager-beaver cousin Howie and beautiful stuntwoman Jody Banks. To distract from the often routine plotlines, the producers plied such age-old TV tricks as packing episodes with beautiful women (one episode alone, 'Always Say Always', included former Bond girls Britt Ekland and Lana Wood), slapstick and glamorous locales. Episodes also had a tendency to include showbiz in-jokes; thus the instalment 'Happy Trails', named after the theme song of *The Roy Rogers Show*, not only featured the old singing cowpoke himself, but also his sidekick Pat Buttram, plus *Virginian* stars James Drury and Doug McClure. The 'Unknown Stuntman' theme, meanwhile, was croaked by Majors himself.

GUEST CAST: Britt Ekland, Lana Wood, Farrah Fawcett, James Coburn, Richard Kiel, Lou Ferrigno, Tom Selleck, Monte Markham, Heather Locklear, Peter Breck, L Q Jones, Clu Gulager, Roy Rogers, Pat Buttram, James Drury, Doug McClure, William Conrad, Tab Hunter, Morgan Brittany, Stuart Margolin, Archie Moore, Sugar Ray Robinson, Priscilla Presley, David Carradine,

Jonathan Frakes, Buz Aldrin, Scott Carpenter, Barry Newman, Cameron Mitchell.

FATHER BROWN

UK 1974 11 x 60m col ITV. An ATV Network Production. US tx 1982 WGBH Boston.

PR Ian Fordyce. **DR** Robert Tronson, Peter Jeffries. **WR** Hugh Leonard, Peter Wildeblood, Michael Voysey, John Portman. **MUS** Jack Parnell.
CAST Father Brown (Kenneth More) Detective Flambeau (Dennis Burgess).

Affable period detective series featuring Kenneth More as G K Chesterton's clumsy but cerebral clerical sleuth (motto: 'Have Bible – Will Travel'). One of the last sighs of the gentle school of TV detection before the screen was overrun by actioners such as >*Starsky and Hutch*, the series was a personal project of British TV supremo Sir Lew Grade, who astutely badgered More into the lead role to ensure perfect casting.

The episodes were: *The Hammer of God/The Oracle of the Dog/The Curse of the Golden Cross/The Quick One/The Man with Two Beards/The Head of Caesar/The Eye of Apollo/ The Dagger with Wings/The Actor and the Alibi/The Arrow of Heaven/The Secret Garden.*

FATHER DOWLING MYSTERIES

USA 1989–91 45 x 60m col NBC/ABC. Viacom. UK tx 1990–4 ITV.

CR Donald E Westlake. **EXEC PR** Fred Silverman, Dean Hargrove. **PR** Barry Steinberg, Joyce Burditt. **DR** Various, including Harry Harris, Sharron Miller, Charles S Dubin, James Frawley, Ron Satloff, Christopher Hibler, Alan Cooke. **WR** Various, including Gerry Conway, James H Brown, Doc Barrett, Robert Schlitt, Joyce Burditt, Jeri Taylor, Dean Hargrove, Dave Hoffman. **MUS** Artie Kane, Dick De Benedictis, Bruce Babcock, Joel Rosenbaum, Arthur Kempel.
CAST Father Frank Dowling (Tom Bosley) Sister Stephanie Laskowsky ('Sister Steve') (Tracy Nelson) Father Philip Prestwick (James Stephens) Marie Murkin (Mary Wickes) Sgt Clancy (Regina Krueger).

Tom Bosley, in his first starring role since sitcom *Happy Days*, played a Chicago Catholic priest whose hobby was amateur 'tec work. He was aided in his investigation by a credulity-breaking streetwise nun, Sister Steve, and in his screen charm by a clapped-out station-wagon.

Not good enough for TV Heaven, but not quite offensive enough for TV Hell either. Purgatory, perhaps. Based on Ralph McInerny's novels, which the suspicious might say were an updated make-over of Chesterton's >*Father Brown* cycle. It was developed for television by Donald E Westlake, better known as the hardboiled author Richard 'Point Blank' Stark. In the UK it was transmitted as *Father Dowling Investigates*.

GUEST CAST: Leslie Nielsen, Anthony LaPaglia, Yaphet Kotto, Michele Scarabelli.

THE FBI

USA 1965-74 239 x 60m col ABC. Quinn Martin Productions/Warner Bros. UK tx 1965-74 ITV.

EXEC PR *Quinn Martin.* **PR** *Charles Larson, Anthony Spinner, Philip Saltzman.* **DR** *Various, including Earl Bellamy, Richard Donner, Walter Grauman, Jesse Hibbs, Allen Reisner, William Wiard, Philip Abbott, Robert Douglas, William Hale, Christian Nyby, William A Graham, Don Edford.* **WR** *John D F Black, Richard Landau, Morman Lessing, Andy Lewis.* **MUS** *Bronislau Kaper ('FBI theme'), Richard Markowitz, John Elizade.*

CAST *Insp Lew Erskine (Efrem Zimbalist Jr) Asst Dir Arthur Ward (Philip Abbott) Barbara Erskine (Lynn Loring) Special Agent Tom Colby (William Reynolds) Special Agent Jim Rhodes (Stephen Brooks) Chris Daniels (Shelly Novack) Chet Randolph (Anthony Eisley) Narrator (Marvin Miller).*

'The FBI. A Quinn Martin Production ...'

Tough-guy tales of the Federal Bureau of Investigation. Efrem Zimbalist Jr (late of >*77 Sunset Strip* and future voice of Alfred Pennyworth in innumerable Bat products of the Nineties) played incorruptible G-man Inspector Lewis Erskine, a zombie-like pursuer of commies and crooks, whose devotion to duty suffered no personal life. (A daughter, Barbara, seen in early episodes, was killed off by the producers because she was 'a distraction'.) Erskine, always to be found impeccably dressed in regulation FBI dark suit, reported to Assistant Director Arthur Ward, and was aided in his mission by a succession of sidekicks, of whom Tom Colby lasted the longest. Although pedestrianly made, the show's favourable depiction of the FBI earned enthusiastic encomiums from J Edgar Hoover, the real-life FBI head honcho, who even allowed location shooting at Bureau headquarters in Washington (episode narratives were also supposedly pulled from authentic FBI files). In a quid pro quo, executive producer Quinn Martin (>*The Fugitive*, >*Cannon*) ensured that FBI episodes signed off with a plea to viewers for help in catching America's real-life most wanted, complete with the offender's mugshot. The official sponsors of the show were the Ford Motor Company, whose gleaming – and oft-seen – sedans were the agents' main form of transportation. As one of the USA's longest-running crime shows it cast a giant shadow, and there

have been periodic attempts to imitate it, including *Today's FBI* (1981, starring Mike Connors) and *FBI: The Untold Stories* (1991–3, hosted by Pernell Roberts).

GUEST CAST: Jeffrey Hunter, Julie Parrish, Warren Oates, Jack Klugman, Robert Blake, Noam Pitlik, Dabney Coleman, Pete Duel, Robert Duvall, Beau Bridges, Jack Lord, Martin Sheen, Burt Reynolds, Ron Howard, Daniel J Travanti (as Dan Travanty), Ivan Dixon, Larry Linville, Bruce Dern, Gene Hackman.

⊗ The FBI – *a show sponsored by Ford, who placed their product in nearly every scene.*

FREEBIE AND THE BEAN

USA 1980–1 6 x 60m col CBS. A Warner Bros Production. UK tx 1981 BBC1.

CR Dick Nelson. **PR** *Philip Saltzman.*

CAST Det Sgt Tim Walker ('Freebie') (Tom Mason) Det Sgt Dan Delgado ('Bean') (Hector Elizondo) DA Walter W Cruikshank (William Daniels) Rodney Blake ('Axle') (Mel Stewart).

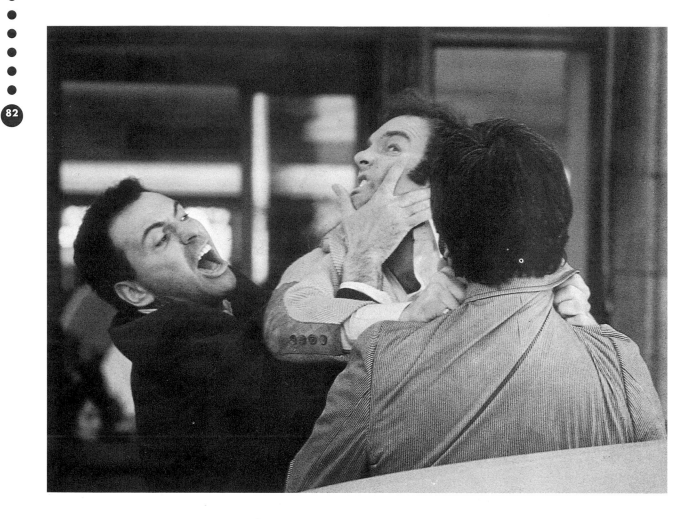

Freebie was a swinging single plainclothes detective working special assignments for San Francisco District Attorney Walter Cruikshank. Bean was Freebie's straight-arrow partner.

A study-in-contrasts cop show, it was a spin-off from the hit 1974 movie of the same name (Dr Richard Rush), starring Alan Arkin and James Caan. There was plenty of action – usually wild car chases which left police mechanic Axle busy

Things start to get heavy on Freebie and the Bean, *a cop show from 1980 starring Tom Mason as Freebie and Hector Elizondo as Bean.*

in the garage afterwards – together with hefty truncheonings of slapstick humour. It confused as to whether it was a police drama or something with lighter intentions, and when *The Love Boat* was the attraction on rival channel ABC, too few viewers bothered to watch.

THE GENTLE TOUCH

UK 1980–4 56 x 60m col ITV. An LWT Network Production.

CR Brian Finch. **EXEC PR** Tony Wharmby, Nick Elliott. **PR** Kim Mills, Jack Williams, Michael Verney-Elliott. **DR** Various, including Tony Wharmby, John Reardon, Christopher Hodson. **WR** Various, including Brian Finch, Roger Marshall, Terence Feely. **MUS** Roger Webb.

The Gentle Touch *was British TV's first cop show with a female lead.*

CAST DI Maggie Forbes (Jill Gascoine) DCI Russell (William Marlowe) DI Bob Croft (Brian Gwaspari) DS Jake Barratt (Paul Moriarty) DS Peter Philips (Kevin O'Shea) Steve Forbes (Nigel Rathbone) DS Jimmy Fenton (Derek Thompson).

Introduced Britain's first starring female cop, Detective Inspector Maggie Forbes (beating >*Juliet Bravo* by a mere five months), who worked out of the Seven Dials station in London's Soho. As the widowed mother of a

teenage son – her police constable spouse, Ray, was shot dead by some armed blaggers in the opener – initially much of her attention (and thus the viewers') was given over to her downer home life. As seasons passed, however, the show moved into actioner mode (although the non-driving actress Gascoine, wife of Alfred Molina, had always to be filmed behind the wheel of a stationary car), with Forbes blown up by a grenade at the conclusion of season four. This failed to end her life, however, or apparently even ruffle her perm, and Gascoine came back for another thirteen episodes.

A knock-on series, >C.A.T.S. Eyes, saw the tough-gal cop promoted to an élite Home Office security squad.

GUEST CAST: George Baker, Leslie Ash, Joss Ackland, George Sewell, Joanne Whalley-Kilmer, Art Malik.

GET CHRISTIE LOVE

USA 1974–5 22 x 60m col ABC. A Universal Television Production.

EXEC PR David L Wolper. **PR** Paul Mason. **DR** Various, including Edward Abrams, Gene Nelson. **WR** Det Olga Ford, NYPD.

CAST Det Christie Love (Teresa Graves) Lt Matt Reardon (1974) (Charles Cioffi) Capt Arthur P Ryan (1975) (Jack Kelly) Sgt Pete Gallagher (1975) (Michael Pataki) Det Valencia (Scott Peters) Det Joe Caruso (Andy Romano).

Mid-Seventies action series cashing in on the big-screen vogue for badass hero blacks. *Shaft* (1971) begat blaxploitation, which spawned karate-kicking-tough-black-mama movie queens Tamara Dobson and Pam Grier (*Foxy Brown*, 1974, recently paid homage by Quentin Tarantino). Enter, small-screen left, television's first black female cop, in the form of Christie Love, undercover policewoman for the LAPD Special Investigations Division. She was slick, hip and broke the rules. And, unrestrained by the sober influence of uniform, she had a chance to show off a sassy wardrobe and physique. The *New York Times* declared her 'stunningly sexy', but this didn't make her gritty enough for an urban action show. Neither did the black woman gimmick set the series enough apart to make it last beyond one season. Christie Love was played by one-time *Laugh-In* regular Teresa Graves after a series of TV comedy roles brought her notice (*Turn On*, 1969, *Rowan and Martin's Laugh-In*, 1968–73, *Funny Side*, 1971, *Keeping Up with the Jones's*, 1972). The part brought her a Golden Globe nomination in 1975 for Best TV Actress, Drama. Love's hard-nosed boss was Lieutenant Matt Reardon, played by Charles Cioffi, a face well known from *Shaft*, *Klute*, *Lucky Luciano*, >*Kojak*, >*Dog and Cat* and >*Peter Gunn*. Reardon was later replaced by Captain Ryan, played by Jack Kelly, ex-*Hardy Boys* and star of *Maverick* (he played Bart, brother to James Garner's Bret). The female LAPD officer's sidekick was Sergeant Pete Gallagher.

After *Get Christie Love* Charles Cioffi went on to roles in a series of small-screen cop shows, as well as a part in *The X-Files* (as Section Chief Scott Blevins). Teresa Graves, despite putting in good service breaking moulds, unfortunately faded from sight. Executive producer David Wolper, whose company, Wolper Productions, mostly specialised in documentaries, later hit the

 Ghost Squad *was based on the memoirs of Scotland Yard's John Gosling.*

jackpot when he bought the rights to Alex Haley's *Roots*, reportedly for $250,000, and produced the twelve-hour mini-series that became, in January 1977, the highest-rated programme in TV history. He also produced the sequel, *Roots: The Next Generations*, a big hit in 1979.

GHOST SQUAD

UK 1961–4 52 x 60m bw. Rank Organisation/ATV. US tx 1960 syndicated.
PR *Connery Chapell, Anthony Kearey, Dennis Vance.* **PR** *Various, including Don Sharp, Norman Harrison, Phil Brown, James Ferman, William G Stewart, Peter Sasdy, Eric Price.* **WR** *Various, including Lindsay Galloway, Robert Stewart, Patrick Campbell, Brian Clemens.* **MUS** *Philip Green.*
CAST *Nick Craig (Michael Quinn) Sir Andrew Wilson (Donald Wolfit) Tony Miller (Neil Hallett) Helen Winters (Angela Browne) Geoffrey Stock (Anthony Marlowe) Jean Carter (Claire Nielson) Peter Clarke (Ray Barrett) Billy Clay (Ray Austin).*

An élite Scotland Yard unit infiltrates the British underworld.

Classic police series from the early Sixties, based on the memoirs of real-life undercover Scotland Yard detective John Gosling. Shakespearean actor Sir Donald Wolfit played the squad's head honcho, with busy Australian Ray Barrett (*Emergency Ward 10*, *Stingray*,

Thunderbirds) as the quietly lethal op Peter Clarke. The other main agents were: American master of disguise Nick Craig, strong-armed Tony Miller and typist-turned-tec Jean Carter. For the later part of its run, the series was broadcast as *GS5*. Among the producers was James Ferman, who later became chief of the British Board of Film Censors.

GUEST CAST: Honor Blackman, John Woodvine, Warren Mitchell, William Gaunt, Roger Delgado, Lois Maxwell, Willoughby Goddard, William Hartnell.

GIDEON'S WAY

UK 1965–6 26 x 50m bw ITV. New World/ITC/ATV.US tx 1966 syndicated.

CR *John Creasey.* **PR** *Monty Berman, Robert S Baker.* **DR** *Various, including John Llewellyn Moxey, Roy Ward Baker, Cyril Frankel, Robert Tronson, James Hill, Leslie Norman, Roy Ward Baker.* **WR** *Various, including Harry W Junkin.* **MUS** *Edwin Astley.*
CAST *Cdr George Gideon (John Gregson) Det Chief Insp David Keen (Alexander Davion) Det Chief Supt Bell (Ian Rossiter) Kate Gideon (Daphne Anderson).*

Hour-long British police procedural featuring the cases of a CID chief inspector, set against a gritty London cityscape. Made visually arresting by documentary-style photography (courtesy of the influence of US show >*Dragnet* and such rising talents as John Llewellyn Moxey at the helm), but even in the mid Sixties the 'chalk-and-cheese cop' routine (the intuitive Gideon conflicting with scientifically minded assistant DCI Keen) grated on viewer sensibilities. Based on the novels of John Creasey, under the pen name J J Marric, and coming to TV on the heels of the successful 1958 feature, *Gideon's Way*, starring Jack Hawkins. The TV series was syndicated in the US under the title *Gideon CID*.

GUEST CAST: Donald Sutherland, George Cole, Nicola Pagett, John Hurt, Alfie Bass, George Baker.

THE GREEN HORNET

USA 1966–7 26 x 30m col ABC. Greenway Productions/20th Century Fox Television. UK tx 1996 Bravo.

CR *George W Trendle.* **EXEC PR** *William Dozier.* **PR** *Richard Blue.* **DR** *Various, including Leslie Martinson, Allen Reisner, Darrel Hallenbeck, Norman Foster, William Beaudine.* **WR** *Various, including Art Weingarten, William L Stuart, Lorenzo Semple, Ken Pettus, Charles Hoffman.* **MUS** *Rimsky-Korsakov's 'The Flight of the Bumble Bee', updated by Al Hirt (theme), Billy May.*
CAST *The Green Hornet/Britt Reid (Van Williams) Kato (Bruce Lee) Leonore 'Casey' Case (Wende Wagner) Mike Axford (Lloyd Gough) District Attorney F P Scanlon (Walter Brooke).*

Flying high on the success of >*Batman*, producer William Dozier decided to introduce another daring masked crime-buster to the small screen – the Green Hornet. Accompanied by faithful Oriental chauffeur Kato, the Hornet sped to the scene of crime ('Faster, Kato!') in the 'rolling arsenal' known as the Black Beauty (a customised 1966 Chrysler Imperial), and then set about sleuthing the villain of the piece. When identified, the baddie would be immobilised by the Green Hornet's non-lethal Sting Gun, which used high-pitched soundwaves, or dealt with by Kato's dashing martial arts. Unmasked, Hornet was really Britt Reid, crusading editor-publisher of the *Daily Sentinel* and TV-station owner but only Kato, Reid's secretary Casey and the DA knew his identity. Considered criminal by the police, the Green Hornet and Kato always disappeared from the scene of their arresting success before the authorities arrived to take over.

The series was a flop. It was too similar to *Batman*, while having none of that show's knowing camp. Probably Hornet's sole

« *Chop, chop! Bruce Lee (right) as Kato in* The Green Hornet.

88

interest was the extraordinary kung fu fighting character of Kato, played by Bruce Lee in his first appearance on American screens. Born in 1940 in San Francisco to Chinese parents there on a theatrical tour, Lee Jun Fan – as Lee was named in Mandarin – was brought up in the British colony of Hong Kong, where he became an expert in the wing chun ('Beautiful Springtime') style of kung fu as well as a child actor. Returning to America in 1959, aged nineteen, Lee made a sensational appearance at the International Karate Championship at Long Beach, California, in 1964, where his stylish, dynamic kicking and punching was witnessed by Hollywood hair stylist Jay Sebring. Some time later, when Sebring (who would eventually be murdered by the Manson gang when they invaded the home of Sharon Tate) was cutting the hair of TV producer Dozier, he mentioned Lee. Dozier, who at that stage was looking for someone to play Charlie Chan's Number-One Son in a TV series, sent for a film of Lee's demonstration at Long Beach. Dozier liked what he saw and optioned Lee for $180. Scratching the Charlie Chan series, Dozier installed Lee as the black-suited, black-masked Kato in *The Green Hornet* – Lee joking that he got the part because he was 'the only Chinaman in all California who could pronounce Britt Reid'. So quick were Lee's martial arts movements that he was forced to slow them down for the show's cameras. Audiences were appreciative of their

first taste of kung fu, and Lee went on to spice up episodes of >*Ironside*, *Blondie*, >*Longstreet* and *Here Come the Brides*. Lee also helped develop the idea of a wandering Shaolin monk which became *Kung Fu*, and was bitterly disappointed when Warner Bros and ABC-TV gave the lead role to the more experienced – and Caucasian – David Carradine. However, unknown to Lee, *The Green Hornet* had become a television phenomenon in the Far East – where it was retitled *The Kato Show* – and he had ascended to celestial celebrity. In 1971 the Golden Harvest studios of Hong Kong sent a senior producer to the USA to sign up Lee for a movie deal; Lee then returned East to make a cycle of kung fu films which would include *The Big Boss*, *Fists of Fury* and *Enter the Dragon*. The rest is legend.

By way of footnote, the *Green Hornet* was created as a radio character in 1936 by George W Trendle, who also invented the *Lone Ranger*, to whom the masked, clean-cut Hornet has obvious similarities. Britt Reid first appeared on the wireless waves as the son of Dan Reid, the Lone Ranger's nephew.

GRIFF

USA 1973–4 12 x 60m col ABC. Universal. UK tx 1974–6 ITV.
CR Larry Cohen. **EXEC PR** David Victor. **PR** Steven Bochco. **DR** Various, including Edward Abrams. **MUS** Elliott Kaplan, Mike Post, Pete Carpenter.

CAST *Wade Griffin (Lorne Greene) Mike Murdoch (Ben Murphy) Gracie Newcombe (Patricia Stich) Capt Barney Marcus (Vic Tayback).*

👁 Starred Lorne Greene as a retired police captain who went into business on his own, as Wade Griffin Investigations, in the hip Westwood area of Los Angeles. Ben Murphy (*Alias Smith and Jones*) played his young sidekick, Mike Murdoch. The show came from the pen of Larry Cohen (creator of *Branded* and *The Invaders*) but the initial unavailability of Greene – the studio's choice – delayed filming for six months. By then CBS had pushed through their own show with a near identical format – >*Barnaby Jones* – and *Griff* lost out in the ratings. And, in truth, Buddy Ebsen proved a more convincing veteran cop on screen than Greene, who for most viewers indelibly remained Pa Cartwright from *Bonanza*. The original pilot for *Griff* aired as a 120-minute TVM, *Man on the Outside*, in 1975 (dr Boris Sagal).

HALF NELSON

USA 1985 1 x 120m col, 6 x 60m col NBC. A Glen Larson Production.

CR *Glen Larson, Lou Shaw.* **EXEC PR** *Glen Larson.* **PR** *Harker Wade.*
CAST *Rocky Nelson (Joe Pesci) Chester Long (Fred Williamson) Annie O'Hara (Victoria Jackson) Detective Hammill (Gary Grubbs) Beau (Bubba Smith) Kurt (Dick Butkus).*

👁 Rocky Nelson was a diminutive detective who tired of the NYPD beat and moved to Beverly Hills, where he joined a fashionable PI firm which provided security for the very, very rich. All this, and Nelson wanted to break into the movies, too; unfortunately, few were interested in casting a person of his stature (or lack of), though Nelson did find that his short-issue size came in useful when gumshoeing – people either failed to notice him or refused to take such a 'little guy' seriously, enabling him to sneak in and find the clues.

Half-cocked detective show with comic edges. Joe Pesci (Joey La Motta in *Raging Bull,* and later *GoodFellas*) in mid-career did all that could be done with heavy-handed scripts, but it wasn't enough and the show was unplugged before it could finish its début season. Black actor Fred Williamson, previously better known for such badass movies as *The Legend of Nigger Charley* (1972) and *Black Caesar* (1973), played Nelson's bemused boss at the PI company.

'He is standing up...'
GUEST CAST: Dean Martin.

HAMISH MACBETH

UK 1995-7 20 x 50m col BBC1. Zenith/Skyline. US tx 1996-7 ABC.

CR *M C Beaton.* **EXEC PR** *Andrea Calderwood, Scott Meek, Trevor Davies.* **PR** *Deidre Keir, Charles Salmon.* **DR** *Various, including Patrick Lau, Nicholas Renton, Sid Roberson, Ian Knox,*

90

Mandie Fletcher. **WR** *Daniel Boyle, Dominic Minghella, Bryan Elsley, Julian Spilsbury, Stuart Hepburn.* **MUS** *John Lunn.*
CAST *Hamish Macbeth (Robert Carlyle) TV John (Ralph Riach) Isobel Sutherland (Shirley Henderson) Rory Campbell (Brian Pettifer) Miss Meikeljohn (Anne Kirsten) Major Roddy Maclean (David Ashton) Dolores Balfour (Morag Hood) Harry Balfour (Campbell Morrison) Alex (Valerie Grogan) Esme Murray (Anne Lacey) Agnes (Barbara Rafferty) Barney (Stuart McGugan) Jubel (Brian Alexander) Lachie Sr (Jimmy Yuill) Lachie Jr (Stuart Davids) Edie (Mona Bruce).* **VIDEO** *BBC.*

'*It's baffling, Jock, pure baffling!*' PC Hamish Macbeth

Rural police drama featuring Robert Carlyle (later *Trainspotting* and *The Full Monty*) as the eponymous easy-going PC of the remote (and fictional) Scottish village of Lochdubh. Accompanied by West Highland terrier Wee Jock, Hamish Macbeth pursued bucolic villains and offbeat cases, with 'The Great Lochdubh Salt Robbery' (what connection between the theft of a large quantity of table salt from the local shop and the disappearance of local bully Geordie Robb?) setting the tone. Macbeth also had a notably troublesome love life, torn between the blonde (Alex) and the brunette (Lochdubh journalist Isobel). Evidently influenced by such US non-mainstream shows as *Northern Exposure* and >*Twin Peaks*, HM mixed light whimsy with dark tragedy, and backgrounded a stock of quaint characters, among them grocer Rory (Brian Pettifer from military sitcom *Get Some In*) and TV John ('I think I'll have a nip of something about twelve years old'). The series was filmed on location at Plockton in the Scottish Highlands.

The episodes were: *The Great Lochdubh Salt Robbery/A Pillar of the Community/The Big Freeze/West Coast Story/Wee Jack's Lament/A Bit of an Epic/A Perfectly Simple Explanation/In Search of a Rose/Isobel Pulls It Off/Radio Lochdubh/No Man is an Island/The Lochdubh Deluxe/The Honourable Policeman/Deferred Sentence/The Lochdubh Assassin/The Good Thief/The Trouble with Rory/More than a Game/Destiny I/Destiny II.*

HARRY O
USA 1974–6 1 x 1 20m, 1 x 90m, 43 x 60m col ABC. A Warner Bros Television Production. UK tx 1974–7 BBC1.
CR *Howard Rodman.* **EXEC PR** *Jerry Thorpe.* **PR** *Robert E Thompson, Robert Dozier, Buck Houghton, Alex Beaton, Rita Dillon.* **DR** *Barry Crane, Richard Bennett, Daryl Duke, Harry Falk, Richard Lang, Robert Michael Lewis, Jerry London, Joe Manduke, Russ Mayberry, John Newland, Jerry Thorpe, Don Weiss, Paul Wendkos.* **WR** *Various, including John Meredyth Lucas,*

Michael Adams, Dorothy Blees, Larry Forrester, Robert Dozier, Susan Glasgow, Ron Jacoby, Stephen Kandel, Robert C Dennis, Herman Groves, Michael Sloan. **MUS** Jerry Goldsmith, John Rubinstein.

CAST Harry Orwell (David Janssen) Det Lt Manny Quinlan (Henry Darrow) Lt K C Trench (Anthony Zerbe) Lester Hodges (Les Lannom) Dr Creighton Fong (Keye Luke) Sgt Frank Cole (Tom Atkins) Sue Ingham (Farrah Fawcett-Majors) Sgt Don Roberts (Paul Tulley) Betsy (Kathrine Baumann).

👁 While responding to a burglary in progress, Los Angeles police officer Harry O (for Orwell) is shot in the back and disabled when the bullet lodges in his spine. He retires from the force and becomes one of TV's more bohemian private eyes, living in a beachfront cottage near San Diego. Here the dour ex-marine takes on only those cases that interest him. These usually involve luscious girls – Harry's next-door neighbour, flight attendant Sue Ingham, was played by *Charlie's Angels'* Farrah Fawcett-Majors – but Harry O shows little desire to pursue them.

Harry's sometime nemesis, sometime ally was his contact Lieutenant Manny Quinlan of the San Diego Police Department (played by TV veteran Henry Darrow from *Zorro*). But Manny was killed off in a February 1975 telecast, after which Harry moved his base of operations to Santa Monica and inherited a new official nemesis, Lieutenant Trench, plus occasional unsolicited help with his cases from amateur criminologists Lester Hodges and Dr Fong. The series needed two pilots – *Harry O* (aka *Such Dust as Dreams Are Made On*) and *Smile Jenny You're Dead* (featuring a twelve-year-old Jodie Foster) – before it got off the ground, and when it did it lost out to NBC's rival Californian PI, James Rockford. Starting out at the same time, >*The Rockford Files* far outran the disabled Orwell, lasting until 1980.

In fact *Harry O* had little to recommend it apart from the gimmick that Orwell's MG sports car was in an almost permanent state of disrepair, leaving him to bus it to the scene of the crime, and the charisma of its star, David Janssen, well known to viewers as *The Fugitive* and with a track record in TV crime which included producer Jack Webb's >*O'Hara, United States Treasury* and >*Richard Diamond, Private Detective*.

GUEST CAST: Margot Kidder, Linda Evans, Kurt Russell, Larry Hagman, Loni Anderson, Louis Gossett Jr, Cheryl Ladd, Martin Sheen, Jodie Foster, Broderick Crawford, Rene Auberjonois, Roddy McDowall.

HART TO HART

USA 1979–84 110 x 60m col ABC. Spelling-Goldberg. UK tx 1980–5.

CR Sidney Sheldon. **EXEC PR** Aaron Spelling, Leonard Goldberg. **PR** David Levinson, Matt Crowley. **DR** Various, including Bruce Kessler, Earl

Bellamy, Tom Mankiewicz, Stuart Margolin, Leo Penn, Peter Medak, Reza S Badiyi, Seymour Robbie, Ralph Senensky, Sam Wanamaker, Dennis Donnelly, Harry Winer, George W Brooks. **WR** *Various, including Catherine Bacos, Earl Bellamy, Allan Folsom, Stephen Kandel, David Levinson, Anthony Yerkovich, Edward Martino, Martin Roth, Lana Sands, Rick Husky,*

⊗ *Their hobby was 'moider'. The stars of the irresistibly schlocky Hart to Hart.*

Tom Mankiewicz, Sidney Sheldon. **MUS** *Various, including Mark Snow, John Davis, Richard Lewis Warren, Ron Ramin, Robert Folk.*
CAST *Jonathan Hart (Robert Wagner) Jennifer Hart (Stefanie Powers) Max (Lionel Stander).*

'This is my boss, Jonathan Hart, a self-made millionaire. Quite a guy. This is Mrs H. She's gorgeous. She's one lady who knows how to take care of herself ... By the way, my name is Max. I take care of them both, which ain't easy – 'cause when they met it was moider.'

Thus spake the Hart's rasp-voiced retainer over the opening credits of Aaron Spelling's *Hart to Hart,* a glossy romantic caper about a husband and wife amateur sleuthing duo, Jonathan and Jennifer Hart, who discovered corpses galore as they jet-setted around the world. A particular peril for the Harts was that Jennifer Hart was peculiarly prone to being kidnapped. Stalwart good-looking lead Robert ('RJ') Wagner *(It Takes a Thief, Colditz, >Switch)* and former *Girl from UNCLE* Stefanie Powers starred; the other cast regulars were Lionel Stander as Max, the Harts' cigar-smoking Mr Mopp, and a dog, Freeway, usually to be found on the couch at their lavish mansion at 3100 Willow Pond Drive, Bel Air, California.

In the credits best-selling novelist Sidney Sheldon was listed as the programme's creator; but the series was merely an update of the popular *Thin Man* movies of the Thirties, which in turn were derived from the novels of Dashiell Hammett. (A previous TV series using Hammett's characters, >*The Thin Man,* had been made by MGM in the Fifties.) *Hart to Hart* lacked the urbane, sophisticated wit of the films – which starred William Powell and Myrna Loy – not to mention their passable plots. The Harts were also indecently gooey, always ending the day with pyjamas, milk and cookies, before turning off the light for another honeymoon. Unfortunately, their sheer good spirits and a certain self-mockingness made them compulsively watchable.

And thus it was that the Harts were reunited in the mid Nineties for a sequence of reunion TVMs, beginning with *Hart to Hart Returns* (1993), and continuing through *Hart to Hart: Home is Where the Hart Is* (1994)/*Hart to Hart: Old Friends Never Die* (1994)/*Hart to Hart: Crimes of the Hart* (1994)/*Hart to Hart: Two Harts in Three-Quarters Time* (1995)/*Hart to Hart: Till Death Us Do Hart* (1996)/*Hart to Hart: Harts in High Season* (1996).

GUEST CAST: Gordon Jackson, Robert Englund, David Hedison, Edward Mulhare.

HAWAII FIVE-O

USA 1968–80 274 x 50m col CBS. Leonard Freeman Productions. UK tx 1970–82 ITV.
CR *Leonard Freeman, Jack Lord.* **EXEC PR** *Leonard Freeman, Philip Leacock, Douglas Greene.* **PR** *Bill Finnegan, Bob Sweeney, Richard Newton, Gene Levitt, B W Sandefur, Stanley Kallis, Leonard Katzman, Leonard B Kaufman, Jack Lord.*
DR *Various, including Michael O'Herlihy, Gordon Hessler, Sutton Roley, Alvin Ganzer, Corey Allen,*

93

Herschel Daugherty, Alf Kjellin, Marvin Chomsky, Reza S Badiyi, Nicholas Colasanto, Paul Krasny, Philip Leacock, Jerry Thorpe, Irving J Moore, Jerry Jameson, Jack Lord, John Moxey, Robert Butler, Harvey S Laidman, Barry Crane, William Hale, Ernest Pintoff, Sutton Roley, Brad Van Ecker.
WR Various, including Robert Lewin, Leonard Freeman, Arthur Bernard Lewis, Robert C Dennis, Stephen Kandel, Norman Lessing, John D F Black, Shirl Hendryx, Edward J Lask, Glen Olson, Martin Roth, Robert Hamner, Dean Tait, William Robert Yates. **MUS** Morton Stevens (theme), Peter Rugolo, Jerrold Immel, Richard Shores.
CAST Steve McGarrett (Jack Lord) Det Danny 'Danno' Williams (James MacArthur) Det Chin Ho Kelly (Kam Fong) Det Kono Kalakaua (Zulu) Doc Bergman (Al Eben) Jenny Sherman (Peggy Ryan) Wo Fat (Khigh Dhiegh) Lt Lori Wilson (Sharon Farrell) Det Ben Kokua (Al Harrington) Che Fong (Harry Endo) Det Duke Lukela (Herman Wedemeyer) Che Fong (Harry Endo) Gov Paul Jameson (Richard Denning) Jenny Sherman (Peggy Ryan) Atty Gen John Manicote (Glenn Cannon).
VIDEO Columbia House.

'Gentlemen, I want you to turn this place inside out …'

Originally to be entitled *The Man*, *Hawaii Five-O* was the longest-running cop series in the history of American TV. Ex-Stoney Burke star Jack Lord played Steve McGarrett of the Hawaii State Police, head of a special detective squad working out of the Iolani Palace which reported directly to the governor. Too important for everyday crime-busting, the team – principally the be-quiffed McGarrett himself, boyish Danny 'Danno' Williams and native islanders Chin Ho Kelly and Kono Kalakaua – concentrated on psychopathic killers and Triad-like forces from the Hawaiian underworld. A particularly cunning and elusive Mr Big was Wo Fat (Khigh Dhiegh), 'a Red Chinese agent in charge of the entire Pacific Asiatic theatre'. Fighting Wo Fat and his ilk was a full-time mission for McGarrett; he had no apparent life outside the office, save for an occasional sail in his dinghy, and his home (first at 404 Piikoi Street, then 2085 Ala Wai Boulevard) was rarely glimpsed.

The kindest thing to say about the acting of the principals in *Hawaii Five-O* is that it was consistent: Lord never registered an emotion, MacArthur never looked anything other than surprised. The rank-and-file police, played by off-duty cops, were often more accomplished. And the stories were frequently flimsy. However, few shows have looked more stunning than *Hawaii Five-O*, which was shot entirely on location in Hawaii. Even when plot and character dragged,

❯ *Jack Lord in* Hawaii Five-O, *US TV's longest-running cop show.*

viewer attention was taken by the exotic setting, enhanced by exquisite photography.

For a series of such longevity (it began in flower-power September 1968, with a pilot, 'Cocoon', but was philosophically indebted to the morally straight-arrow Fifties cop shows of the >*Dragnet* type), cast changes were few. Presumably the working conditions were too good to give up. Zulu departed in 1972, but Kam Fong and MacArthur played McGarrett's assistants until the end of the Seventies. With the departure of MacArthur (the adoptive son of Helen Hayes, 'the first lady of American theatre'), the show's famous catchphrase, 'Book 'em, Danno', had to go too, and somehow things were never the same. The ratings were falling anyway, and the introduction of a new woman detective in 1979, Lori Wilson, played by Sharon Farrell, did nothing to halt them. No doubt, however, it was some satisfaction to Lord/McGarrett that in the last episode before the series was unplugged he finally caught Wo Fat ('Woe to Wo Fat').

The memorable theme music, played over the stylish front and end credits (the latter showing Polynesians powering an outrigger canoe) was composed by Morton Stevens, who duly received an Emmy. Despite the murder rate of the series it did much to promote Hawaiian tourism. Hawaii now has a 'Jack Lord Day' on its calendar. After the close of the show, Lord himself, made a millionaire by H5-O (which, at its peak, was seen in 80 countries, with an audience of 300 million), retired to a beach-front condo in Kahala, Hawaii, and returned to his original career – a painter. (He had sold his first art work to The Metropolitan Museum of Art in New York when he was only eighteen, and plain John Joseph Ryan.) Lord died in Honolulu in January 1998.

GUEST CAST: William Shatner, George Takei, Loretta Swit, Donald Pleasence, Martin Sheen, Vic Morrow, Buddy Ebsen, Abe Vigoda, Andy Griffith, Ricardo Montalban, Cyd Charisse.

HAWAIIAN EYE

USA 1959–63 133 x 60m bw ABC. Warner Bros Television Production. UK tx 1960–3 ITV.
EXEC PR *William T Orr.* **PR** *Charles Hoffman, Stanley Niss, Ed Jurist.* **DR** *Various, including Robert Altman, Leslie H Martinson, Richard Sarafian.* **MUS** *Mack David, Jerry Livingston.* **CAST** *Thomas Jefferson Lopaka (Robert Conrad) Tracy Steele (Anthony Eisley) Cricket Blake (Connie Stevens) Phil Barton (Troy Donahue) Greg Mackenzie (Grant Williams) Kazuo Kim (Poncie Ponce) Quon (Mel Prestidge).*

PI show from the same slick'n'glamorous but ultimately vacuous Warner Bros drawer as >*77 Sunset Strip*. Set in Honolulu, *HE* featured handsome gumshoes Tracy Steele and Thomas Jefferson Lopaka, who worked out of the swish Hawaiian Village Hotel, where the resident

 *Photogenic but vacuous, Warner Bros'* Hawaiian Eye – *a makeover of 77* Sunset Strip *with palm trees.*

chanteuse was one Cricket Blake (played by Connie Stevens, who used her time on the show to build up a successful singing career). Cricket and the equally IQ-challenged taxi driver Kim –

he of the 'crazy' straw hat – played the detectives' idiot sidekicks. At the end of the 1960 season another peeper, Greg MacKenzie, joined the team, while Stu Bailey from *77 Sunset Strip* developed the habit of dropping down to Honolulu to help out the boys – and get an Hawaiian Eye full of the local girls, girls, girls paraded through every instalment. Originally to be entitled *Diamond Head,* the series gave Jack Nicolson one of his earliest screen appearances in the 1961 episode, 'The Stanhope Brand'. The show also set a trend for using Hawaii as a beautiful backdrop for crime shows, with >*Hawaii Five-O* and *Hawaiian Heat,* among others, following on its heels.

GUEST CAST: Jack Nicolson, Mary Tyler Moore, Lee Van Cleef.

HAWK

USA 1966 17 x 60m col ABC. A Columbia Pictures Television Production. UK tx 1973 ITV (Granada).

CR *Allan Sloane.* **EXEC PR** *Hubbell Robinson.* **PR** *Paul Bogart.* **DR** *Richard Benedict (II), Tom Donovan, Paul Henreid, Leonard Horn, Burt Reynolds, Sam Wanamaker, Charles Dubin, Paul Bogart, Alexander Singer.* **MUS** *Kenyon Hopkins, Nelson Riddle.*

CAST *Lt John Hawk (Burt Reynolds) Det Dan Carter (Wayne Grice) Asst DA Murray Slaken (Bruce Glover) Asst DA Ed Gorton (Leon Janney).*

Detective Lieutenant John Hawk was an Iroquois Indian working the night beat for the New York District Attorney's Office. Quirky, original, this show was ahead of its time both in its ethnic gimmick and for the fact that it was filmed on location in and around New York City at night. Cases scratched the veneer of metropolitan life from penthouse Park Avenue to tenement West Side. And Hawk, as befitted his name and background, left no track unfollowed. Partner Detective Carter accompanied him in his quests. A young Burt Reynolds, himself part Indian, played John Hawk in his third series for TV after *Gunsmoke* (1955) and *Riverboat* (1959). He went on to star in >*Dan August* (1970), taking a break for movie stardom before > *B L Stryker* (1989). NBC repeated *Hawk* a decade after it was aired by ABC to capitalise on Reynolds' celebrity status. Directors for the quality series were accomplished veterans and included Sam Wanamaker, Richard Benedict and Paul Henreid, one-time star of *Casablanca* and director of, among other series, *Bonanza* and *Maverick.* Reynolds himself also took a spell behind the camera.

HAWKINS

USA 1973 8 x 90m col CBS. Arena Productions in association with MGM-TV.

EXEC PR *Norman Felton.* **PR** *Jud Taylor.*

CAST *Billy Jim Hawkins (James Stewart) R J Hawkins (Strother Martin).*

James Stewart played homespun country lawyer Billy Jim Hawkins, renowned expert in criminal cases, alongside Strother Martin as his cousin and assistant, R J Hawkins. Slow-talking, nice-guy Billy Jim had quit his job as Deputy District Attorney to go into private legal practice in rural West Virginia. Murder was his speciality, and his reputation for steely determination drew clients from all over America. He and RJ were prepared to travel as far as it took to clear a client and nail a guilty party. The casting of two such high-calibre movie stars in a small-screen series fitted the importance CBS ascribed to its 9.30–11 p.m. slot, filled by *Hawkins* as one of three rotating elements, along with >*Shaft* and *The New CBS Tuesday Night Movies*.

James Maitland Stewart (1908–1997), movie icon and war hero (the first star to join up for service in the Second World War, ending it with the rank of Air Force brigadier), had worked with all the great directors: Cukor, Capra, Wilder, Mann, Lubitsch, Ford. Starting in the 1930s, he had played in down-and-dirty westerns (*Destry Rides Again*, 1939, *Bend of the River*, 1952, *The Man from Laramie*, 1955, *The Man Who Shot Liberty Valance*, 1962), wrung our hearts in all's-right-with-the-world weepie *It's a Wonderful Life* (1946), and acted out Hitchcock's sexual obsessions in *Rope* (1948), *Rear Window* (1954) and *Vertigo* (1958). His awards spanned five decades, from an Oscar for Best Actor in 1940 to a Golden Berlin Bear in 1982.

Strother Martin (1919–1980) starred in *Cool Hand Luke* (1967), *The Wild Bunch* (1969) and *Butch Cassidy and the Sundance Kid* (1969). He was the man of whom Sam Peckinpah said, 'He just happens to be one of the finest actors in the world.' The pair were well matched, and *Hawkins* won both its stars prizes: Strother Martin won Best Supporting Actor, Television, in 1973 and was nominated for a Golden Globe in 1974, James Stewart won Best TV Actor, Drama, in 1973 and won a Golden Globe in 1974. Executive producer Norman Felton (*Dr Kildare*, *Mr Novak*) oversaw the quality series.

GUEST CAST: Bonnie Bedelia, Tyne Daly, Diana Ewing, Julie Harris.

HAZELL

UK 1978–80 22 x 60m col ITV. A Thames Television Network Production.
CR *Gordon Williams, Terry Venables.* **PR** *June Roberts (season one), Tim Aspinall (season two).*
DR *Don Leaver, Alistair Reid, Jim Goddard, Moira Armstrong, Peter Duguid, Colin Bucksey, Brian Farnham.* **WR** *Richard Harris, Gordon Williams, Tony Hoare, Peter Ransley, Trevor Preston, Terry Venables.* **MUS** *Andy McKay.*
CAST *James Hazell (Nicholas Ball) 'Choc' Minty (Roddy McMillan) Cousin Tell (Desmond McNamara).*

'Hazell is divorced, ex-police, big, good-looking, slightly battered … He has mass tastes – Daily Mirror, slightly old-fashioned pop

99

music, films, paperbacks ... His accent is variable, basically cockney.' These were novelist Gordon Williams' notes for the TV production team translating his private eye creation, James Hazell, to the small screen. Aged 33, cockney Jack-the-lad Hazell (played by Nicholas Ball, *The*

⊗ *'Kin'ell! Nicholas Ball as Hazell, a South London version of Philip Marlowe.*

Crezz, Colin's Sandwich, and first husband of Pamela Stephenson) worked seedy suburban London much as Chandler's Marlowe worked downtown Los Angeles. Down at heel, invalided out of the police with a dodgy ankle, with a penchant for saying ''kin'ell!', he had a drink problem that put an end to his marriage and a streak of disillusion beneath his East End humour. Always on the look-out for reasons to withdraw Hazell's PI licence was dour Scottish CID man 'Choc' Minty.

Hazell was the product of Thames Television's policy of producing contemporary drama with a London flavour. Under the guidance of Verity Lambert – brought in as head of drama by Programme Controller Jeremy Isaacs in 1974 – the series was developed from the *Hazell* novels of P B Yuill, aka journalist Gordon Williams (who wrote *The Siege of Trencher's Farm*, which formed the basis of the film *Straw Dogs*), and Terry Venables, ex-star football player for Chelsea, Spurs, Queen's Park Rangers and England, then manager of Crystal Palace, Spurs and England. In particular, Lambert approved of the books' 'cockney sense of humour' and potential to show 'the underbelly of London'. Thames hoped that *Hazell* would help ITV regain the ground it had been losing in its ratings battle against the BBC.

At £80,000 per episode, the series was comparatively cheap. Unlike its predecessor in the same slot, >*The Sweeney, Hazell* was shot in studio on tape with only ten or fifteen minutes per episode shot on film. Like the novels, the TV *Hazell* harked back to Chandler, but

interpretations of this differed. For June Roberts, the script executive, Chandler's Los Angeles was a state of mind, and she showed series writers the film noir classics *The Big Sleep* and *Double Indemnity* as a guide. For script editor Kenneth Ware (>*Z Cars*, >*Softly Softly*) and co-creator Gordon Williams, the 'real' London was to be a star of the series. The resulting mix had a Marlowe-style voice-over, stylish location filming in Soho and scenes of seedy reality shot in Acton, the East End, or Clapton dog stadium. Time pressures led to an absence of the film noir-style strong women characters June Roberts had hoped for; even Hazell's ex-Rodean debt-collector girlfriend (or rather, the East London Romeo's main girlfriend) turned out to be a passive onlooker. Another compromise was made on the theme tune. In keeping with the cockney feel of the series the producers had asked Ray Davies of The Kinks to write a theme tune along the lines of 'Dead End Street', but Davies pulled out at the last minute and Roxy Music's Andy McKay, who wrote the music for earlier Thames success >*Rock Follies*, stepped in.

Too violent for some tastes, *Hazell* was a top-grade series, but it never achieved Jeremy Isaacs' stated goal of 39 episodes. The BBC dealt the series a fatal blow by scheduling a season of Robert Redford films in the same time slot. After 22 memorable, idiosyncratic episodes, *Hazell* was a goner.

102

The episodes were: *Hazell Plays Solomon/
Hazell Pays a Debt/Hazell and the Walking
Blur/Hazell Settles the Accounts/Hazell Meets
the First Eleven/Hazell and the Rubber-heel
Brigade/Hazell Goes to the Dogs/Hazell and
the Weekend Man/Hazell Works for Nothing/
Hazell and the Maltese Vulture/Hazell and the
Baker Street Sleuth/Hazell and the Deptford
Virgin/Hazell Bangs the Drum/Hazell Gets the
Boot/Hazell Gets the Bird/Hazell and the Big
Sleep/Hazell and the Suffolk Ghost/Hazell and
Hyde/Hazell and the Happy Couple/Hazell
Gets the Part/Hazell and the Greasy Gunners/
Hazell and the Public Enemy.*

HIGH INCIDENT

USA 1996–7 32 x 60m col ABC. DreamWorks
SKG/ABC/Donwell.
EXEC PR Michael Pavone, Steven Spielberg, Dave
Alan Johnson, Ann Donahue, Charles Haid.
PR Jack Clement, W K Scott Meyer. **DR** Various,
including Steven Spielberg, Ralph Winter, Randall
Zisk. **MUS** Hans Zimmer (theme), Jeff Rona, John
Powell, Christopher Tyng.
CAST Off Terry Hagar (Matt Beck) Off Leslie Joyner
(Aunjanue Ellis) Off Lenny Gayer (Matt Craven)
Sgt Marge Sullivan (Lindsay Frost) Sgt Jim Marsh
(David Keith) Off Russell Topps (Louis Mustillo) Off
Randy Willitz (Cole Hauser) Off Jessica Helgado
(Lisa Vidal) Off Gayle Van Camp (Catherine
Kellner) Off Mike Rhoades (Blair Underwood).

Snappy look at life in the trenches for the
uniformed officers of the El Camino PD.
It came from Steven Spielberg's DreamWorks
company, with Spielberg himself taking on
uncredited directorial duties. However, slotted
against NBC's *Friends* it lost the ratings war, and
ABC declined a third season.

HIGHWAY PATROL

USA 1955-9 156 x 30m bw syndicated. A Ziv
Production. UK tx 1960–2 ITV.
EXEC PR Vernon E Clark. **MUS** Richard Lewellyn.
CAST Chief Dan Matthews (Broderick Crawford)
Sgt Ken Williams (William Boyett) Narrator (Art
Gilmore).

*'Whenever the laws of any state are broken, a
duly authorised organisation swings into action.
It may be called the State Police, State Troopers,
Militia, the Rangers or the Highway Patrol. These
are the stories of the men whose training, skill
and courage have enforced and preserved our
state laws...'*

Burly, gravel-voiced Broderick Crawford
(son of movie actress Helen Broderick) was
Dan Matthews, chief of the Highway Patrol in a
series that was one of the most popular

» *'Ten four – and out', Broderick Crawford in the
classic* Highway Patrol.

syndicated programmes in television history.

The action took place on the sprawling highway system of an unidentified western state, with plenty of hardware to help it along – patrol cars, motorbikes, helicopters. Storylines were straight crime dramas from a time when good was good and bad was bad, with the Chief and his uniformed officers nailing hijackers, smugglers and robbers. But it was the way fast-talking Dan Matthews leant against his patrol car to radio to headquarters that really captured the public imagination. 'Ten-four' (message received and understood) and 'Ten-twenty' (report your position) became catchphrases around the world. In one episode a young newlywed couple were hunted when they were sole witnesses to a café hold-up and murder; in another a bank messenger absconded with $50,000 and took it home – and his wife made off with the money. But whatever the narrative, a chase here, an all-points bulletin there, and Chief Matthews won every time in the name of the law. For the public good, he also gave viewers helpful tips on road safety.

Along with >Dragnet it was the founding father of the TV cop genre. Ten four – and out.

HILL STREET BLUES
USA 1980–7 145 x 60m col NBC. MTM Productions. UK tx 1981–4 ITV, 1984–9 C4.
CR Michael Kozoll, Steven Bochco.
EXEC PR Steven Bochco, Gregory Hoblit (seasons three and four). **DR** Robert Butler, Georg Stanford Brown, Arnold Laven, Jack Starrett, Robert C Thompson, Gregory Hoblit, Corey Allen, David Anspaugh, Rod Holcomb, Randa Haines, Jeff Bleckner, Thomas Carter, Lawrence Levy, Robert Kelljan, Christian I. Nyby II, Oz Scott, David Rosenbloom, Rick Wallace, Alexander Singer, Bill Duke, Arthur Seidelman, Gabrielle Beaumont, Richard Compton, Scott Brazil. **WR** Various, including Steven Bochco, Michael Kozoll, Anthony Yerkovich, Lee David Zlotoff, Geoffrey Fischer, Bill Taub, E Jack Kaplan, Gregory Hoblit, Alan Rachins, Robert Crais, Jeffrey Lewis, Michael Wagner, David Milch, Karen Hall, Robert Earll, Mark Frost, Peter Silverman, Dennis Cooper. **MUS** Mike Post (theme).
CAST Capt Frank Furillo (Daniel J Travanti) Sgt Phil Esterhaus (Michael Conrad) Off Bobby Hill (Michael Warren) Det Mick Belker (Bruce Weitz) Lt Howard Hunter (James B Sikking) Sgt Henry Goldblume (Joe Spano) Fay Furillo (Barbara Bosson) Det Neal Washington (Taurean Blacque) Det Johnny 'JD' La Rue (Kiel Martin) Lt Ray Calletano (Rene Enriquez) Off Lucy Bates (Betty Thomas) Off Andy Renko (Charles Haid) Joyce Davenport (Veronica Hamel) Det Harry Garibaldi (Ken Olin) Lt Norman Buntz (Dennis Franz) Sgt Stanislaus Jablonski (Robert Prosky) Off Joe Coffey (Ed Marinaro) Sidney Thursto ('Sid the Snitch') (Peter Jurasik) Det Tina Russo (Megan Gallagher) Det Patsy Mayo (Mimi Kuzyk).

⊗ *'Would you like internal bleeding?' Detective Mike Belker in the seminal* Hill Street Blues.

'And hey, let's be careful out there.'

From its familiar early morning roll-call episode-opener, *Hill Street Blues* looked different. Part soap opera, part cop-action melodrama, its first season left viewers quizzical and critics elated (it scooped eight Emmys in 1980). *Hill Street Blues* not only mixed its genres, it had an unwieldy regular cast number of around thirteen, ran up to half a dozen storylines and subplots in each episode and then left them dangling, and was shot *vérité*-style, with hand-held camera, choppy cuts and an eight-track sound previously only heard in *M*A*S*H*.

The officers who received their duties from Sgt Phil Esterhaus each morning worked out of Hill Street Station in the rundown area of a large unnamed eastern city (Maxwell House precinct in Chicago provided the station exterior). Quietly forceful Captain Frank Furillo was in charge of a bunch of officers of assorted ethnic mix (*Hill Street* gave a number of talented black actors and actresses a chance for challenging work) and personal habits. The vaguely off-beam Detective Mick Belker's forte was undercover work as a tramp, and he had a line in terrorising offenders: 'Would you like to sit down, hairball, or would you prefer internal bleeding?' Henry Goldblume was the station's liberal and anti-racist, while Howard Hunter was the team's redneck and trigger-happy leader of the SWAT team. Andy Renko and Bobby Hill were the black/white patrol team. Prominent later recruits included Sergeant Stan Jablonski – who replaced Esterhaus when the latter died of a coronary during sex with the widow Grace Gardener – the abrasive

Norman Buntz and detective Harry Garibaldi (Ken Olin, later *Thirtysomething*). Each episode ended late at night after a day that witnessed all the problems of the ghetto – drugs, prostitution, burglary, murder – entangled with the messy personal lives of the precinct's warts'n'all cops.

It was not long before each episode also ended with Furillo unwinding in Public Prosecutor Joyce Davenport's bed or bath. The object of many viewers' desires as well as Captain Frank Furillo's, Davenport ably fulfilled the demands of her profession as well as those of soap opera, first becoming Furillo's secret lover and later, in a lunchtime ceremony, his wife. But for a would-be soap opera *Hill Street* had few women in its regular cast, and two of these featured only as ongoing problems – Furillo's ex-wife and thorn-in-his-side Fay, who constantly badgered him for more alimony, and the maniacal Belker's mom at home, experienced only through irritating phonecalls. In other respects the series was unfashionably liberal, although unlike its MTM stablemate *Lou Grant* episodes were not 'about' social problems. Instead a storyline about a brutal policeman posted to the precinct became a personal story about a man under stress, and rather than making racism an issue, *Hill Street* wrote racists (Renko) and anti-racists (Goldblume) into its cast.

After the first ground-breaking season there were some changes, and in season two viewing figures went up and quality went down. At the start of *Hill Street* NBC had guaranteed no network interference in storylines, but for the second season NBC demanded that production company MTM tie up at least one storyline per episode. Co-creator Michael Kozoll distanced himself to the role of creative consultant and storyline composer, and by the end of the second series he was gone. In 1982 a Writers' Guild strike used up the backlog of scripts, which meant that episodes had to be churned out at one a week instead of one a fortnight. As a result *Hill Street* had more fights, shoot-outs, car wrecks and chases, and less creativity. The new formula, however, was a network's dream: it attracted those all-important young urban adults in the 18–49 age range (rated first among men, third among women), which meant NBC could charge advertisers more for slots in *Hill Street* than for higher-rated top ten hits. Mercedes Benz became a regular *Hill Street* advertiser in 1983, and Thorn EMI chose the slots for their first network ads for video software.

The second of the series' creators, Steven Bochco, left in 1985, supposedly fired by MTM for going over budget. Bochco had brought with him a wealth of experience (*Sarge*, 1971–2, *Six Million Dollar Man*, 1974, >*Griff*, >*Delvecchio*). Many of Hill Street's cast and technical personnel had worked together on Bochco's previous series >*Paris* (actors Michael Warren, Kiel Martin and

Joe Spano were all from the previous team). Bochco went on to create *LA Law*, *Doogie Howser MD* (1989–), >*Hooperman*, costly musical flop >*Cop Rock*, and the acclaimed >*NYPD Blue* and >*Murder One*. Meanwhile *Hill Street* continued until Travanti refused to do an eighth season in 1987, by which time it had become arguably the most influential TV policier of the Eighties and spun off a sideshow in >*Beverly Hills Buntz*.

GUEST CAST: Dennis Franz (originally as Detective Sal Benedetto), David Caruso, Edward James Olmos, Van Nessa Clarke, Fredye Chapman, Brent Spiner, Andy Garcia.

HOMICIDE

Australia 1964–77 376 x 60m bw, 133 x 60m col Channel 7. A Crawfords (Australia) Production. US tx 1967 syndicated.

EXEC PR *Ian Crawford, Henry Crawford, Hector Crawford, Dorothy Crawford.* **PR** *Don Battye, Igor Auzins, Ian Crawford, Simon Wincer.* **DR** *Various, including Igor Auzins, Graeme Arthur.*

CAST *Insp Connolly (Jack Fegan) Insp Fox (Alwyn Kurts) Insp Lawson (Charles Tingwell) Det Sgt Mackay (Leonard Teale) Detective Barnes (George Mallaby) Det Sgt Bronson (Terry McDermott) Det Harry White (Don Barker).*

 Long-running Australian series about the cases of the Melbourne Homicide Squad.

It featured Leonard Teale as Detective Sergeant Mackay, Jack Fegan as Inspector Connolly and Charles Tingwell (from soap *Emergency – Ward 10*) as Inspector Lawson. The show's realism made it difficult initially for Crawfords to sell, but after a successful début at home it travelled to the USA and was Australia's most successful TV export until the advent of supersoaps *Neighbours* and *Home and Away*. Later episodes of *Homicide* were shot on film.

HOMICIDE: LIFE ON THE STREET

USA 1993– 112+ x 60m col NBC. NBC/Fatima/MCEG/Baltimore Pictures. UK tx 1994– C4.

CR *Paul Attanasio.* **EXEC PR** *Tom Fontana, Barry Levinson.* **PR** *Anya Epstein, David Simon.* **DR** *Various, including Gwen Arner, Barbara Kipple, Peter Medak, Alan Taylor, Peter Weller, Barry Levinson, Kathy Bates, Kathryn Bigelow, Ken Fink, Steve Buscemi, John McNaughton, Christoper Menaul, Jean de Segonzac.* **WR** *Various, including Tom Fontana, James Yoshimura, Anya Epstein, Yaphet Kotto, David Simon, Jorge Zamacona, Julie Martin.* **MUS** *Tom Hajdu and Andy Milburn (theme).*

CAST *Lt Al 'Gee' Giardello (Yaphet Kotto) Det Steve Crosetti (Jon Polito) Det John Munch (Richard Belzer) Det Meldrick Lewis (Clark Johnson) Det Tim Bayliss (Kyle Secor) Det Francis Xavier 'Frank'*

Pembleton (Andre Braugher) Det Sgt Kay Howard (Melissa Leo) Det Beau Felton (Daniel Baldwin) Det Stanley Bolander (Ned Beatty) Det Paul Fasone (Jon Seda) Off/Det Stuart Gharty (Peter Gerety) Det Michael Scott 'Mike' Kellerman (Reed Diamond) Lt/Cap Det Megan Russert (Isabella Hoffmann) Det Terri Stivers (Toni Lewis) Chief Medical Examiner Julianna Cox (Michelle Forbes) Dr Laussanne (Herb Levinson).

'Ho-ho-Homicide!' Detective John Munch, answering the squadroom phone on Christmas Day.

Police drama from Barry Levinson (director of *Diner, Rainman, Tin Men*) featuring the detectives of a Baltimore Homicide Squad. Shot on Steadicam, entirely on location at Fells Point, with what Levinson termed a 'down and dirty sensibility', episodes followed an individual murder case from report to solution (sometimes). However, catching criminals took a narrative backseat to the interrelationships of the detectives in the squadroom, which was headed by black-Italian Lieutenant Al Giardello (Yaphet Kotto, from the 007 movie *Live and Let Die*, and born the Crown Prince of the Royal Bell family of Douala, Cameroon), which were pursued with a psychological accuracy rare in popular TV. The partnership bewteen detectives Pembleton and rookie Bayliss was especially nuanced, with a creeping homo-eroticism almost unnoticed by the characters themselves, but only given in unconscious dialogue (such as Pembleton's admission, to a gay character, that he and Bayliss were 'joined at the hip'). And when Pembleton's wife wanted to leave him, she instinctively knew that her departure would be eased if she could reconcile Pembleton with his erstwhile bunky Bayliss. To develop story and character, the production team (which was captained by Levinson and former *St Elsewhere* stalwart Tom Fontana) used such novel devices as 'long term stakes' (plot points which recurred over the life of the series), overlapping, even repeating dialogue, and the shooting of the same scene from different angles. There were no shoot-outs, car chases, only reality-based homicide investigations and truly human drama. *Homicide* was a cop show, but not as viewers knew it. Never a great ratings runner, the series was based on an account of a year spent shadowing the Baltimore homicide unit, *Homicide: A Year on the Killing Streets,* by the journalist David Simon, who co-produced the TV series.

GUEST CAST: Lily Tomlin ('The Hat'), Eric Stolz, Robin Williams, Rosanna Arquette, Barry Levinson, James Earl Jones, Melvin Van Peebles.

❯❯ *It was a cop show but not as viewers knew it – Barry Levinson's 'down and dirty'* Homicide: Life on the Street.

HONEY WEST

USA 1965–6 30 x 30m ABC. A Four Star Production. UK tx 1966 ABC Midlands.

EXEC PR *Aaron Spelling.* **PR** *Jules Levy, Arthur Gardiner, Arnold Laven.* **DR** *Various, including Paul Wendkos, Virgil W Vogel, Seymour Robbie, Ida Lupino, James Brown, Bill Colleran, Walter Grauman, James Goldstone, Thomas Carr, John Peyser, John Florea.* **WR** *Various, including Gen Bagni, Paul Dubov, Tony Barrett, William Link, Richard Levinson.* **MUS** *Joseph Mullendore.*
CAST *Honey West (Anne Francis) Sam Bolt (John Ericson) Aunt Meg (Irene Hervey).*

Purrr. Honey West was a blonde, judo-kicking, leather-clad private eye created by husband and wife writing team 'G G Fickling' (aka Skip and Gloria Fickling) in a series of late Fifties/early Sixties novels. She made her first television appearance in an episode of >Burke's Law, in which she succeeded in outwitting Captain Amos Burke himself (no small feat).

Honey turned to detective work after inheriting the family agency, complete with employee Sam Bolt, from her father. And she was spectacularly well equipped for the job. Not only a martial arts expert, she was also the owner of a positive arsenal of gadgetry which included such items as a radio transmitter concealed in a lipstick. Her undercover operations were undertaken from a specially equipped van labelled 'H W Bolt and Co, TV Service' and, like many PIs after her, her constant companion was a pet – Bruce the ocelot.

Inevitably compared to British series >The Avengers, Honey West did not match up. The concept was good and Honey deserves credit for working in a man's world in such prehistoric TV times, but the half-hour slots lacked much in their execution – the blonde was not sexy enough (despite being dubbed 'TV's pretty private eye-full') and the storylines were unimaginative. All this, plus poor production values and casting problems, meant the series only lasted one season in the States and made it to just one brief airing on ABC Midlands in Britain. Intended to be noteworthy for its gutsy heroine, it was in fact mostly memorable for the fight scenes in which a man with a blond wig was quite obviously wheeled in to do the stunts. Actress Anne Francis herself was one of Hollywood's 'never-quite-made-its'; despite being contracted several times to major studios she failed to achieve stellar celebrity and is best remembered by screen devotees for her role in the cult sci-fi flic *Forbidden Planet*.

GUEST CAST: Bobby Sherman, Edd Byrnes, Anthony Eisley, Marvin Kaplan, Byron Morrow, Wayne Rogers, Herschel Bernardi.

HOOPERMAN

USA 1987–9 42 x 30m col ABC. An Adam Production/20th Century Fox Television. UK tx 1988–9 ITV.

CR Steven Bochco, Terry Louise Fisher.
EXEC PR Robert Myman, Leon Tokatyan, Rick Kellard. **DR** Various, including Gregory Hoblit, Carl Gottlieb. **WR** Various, including R. W. Goodman. **MUS** Mike Post.
CAST Insp Harry Hooperman (John Ritter) Capt C 7 Stern (Barbara Bosson) Susan Smith (Debrah Farentino) Rick Silardi (Joseph Gian) Mo Dermott (Sydney Walsh) Bobo Pritzger (Clarence Celder) Clarence McNeil (Felton Perry).

'Dramedy' starring John Ritter (son of oater legend Tex) as Detective Harry Hooperman of the San Francisco PD. From the philosophical school of policing, Harry hated to use his gun, and his generally freewheeling methods caused the ire of his caustic boss, the appropriately named Captain Stern. Bobo was the office reactionary, and Mo the woman officer determined to persude her handsome-but-homosexual partner Rick to see the error of his gay ways.

The show also tracked Hooperman's chaotic home life. His landlady had been murdered, leaving him the rundown apartment building – not to mention her irritating terrier dog Bijoux. Unable to spare the time to landlord, Hooperman hired feisty handywoman and aspiring writer Susan as his superintendent. The two then assumed a somewhat up-down, on-off affair.

The show was created by Steven Bochco and

⊗ John (son of Tex) Ritter in Hooperman, an early show from Steven Bochco.

Terry Louise Fisher, and used something of the same mix of hard cop action and soft comedy that Bochco had pioneered on >Hill Street Blues. Bochco's wife, Barbara Bosson, played C Z Stern. **GUEST CAST:** Miguel Ferrer, Jane Leeves, Dan Laurie, Mitch Pileggi, Mark Hamill.

112

HUNTER

USA 1984–91 1 x 120m, 151 x 60m col NBC. A Stephen J Cannell Production. UK tx 1985–8 ITV/BSB/Sky 1.

CR Frank Lupo. **EXEC PR** Stephen J Cannell, Fred Dryer, George Geiger, Roy Huggins, Lawrence Kubik. **PR** Nick Anderson, Robert Hargrove, John Peter Kousakis, Terry D Nelson. **DR** Various, including James Whitmore Jr, David Soul, Michael Preece, Stephanie Kramer, Tony Mordente, Michael O'Herlihy, Corey Allen, Don Chaffey, James Darren, Fred Dryer, Dennis Dugan, Jeff Kibbee, Winrich Kolbe, John Peter Kousakis, Douglas Heyes, James L Conway, Don Chaffey, James Fargo, Charlie Picerni, Gus Trikonis, Ron Satlof, Kim Manners, Gary Winter. **WR** Various, including Sidney Ellis, Dallas L Barnes, Asher Brauner, Tom Chehak, Marianne Clarkson, Thomas Huggins, Frank Lupo, Joe Menosky, Dick Nelson, Robert Vincent O'Neil, Richard C Okie, Roy Huggins, Scott Rubenstein, Jo Montgomery, Charlotte Clay, Doug Heyes Jr, Tom Blonquist. **MUS** Various, including Nils Lofgren (theme), Peter Carpenter, Mike Post, Frank Denson.

CAST Det Sgt Rick Hunter (Fred Dryer) Det Sgt Dee Dee McCall (Stefanie Kramer) Sgt Chris Novak (Lauren Lane) Off Joanne Molenski (Darlanne Fluegel) Capt Charles Devane (Charles Hallahan) Capt Dolan (John Amos) Allison Novak (Courtney Barilla) Sgt Bernie Terwilliger (James Whitmore Jr) Arnold 'Sporty' James (Garrett Morris) Kirby (Don 'Bubba' Bexley) Capt Lester Cain (Michael Cavanaugh/Arthur Rosenberg) Off Beacon (Philip Sheppard) Carlos (Richard Beauchamp) Capt Wyler (Bruce Davison) Reuben Garcia (Rudy Ramos).

After the success of the Dirty Harry cycle at the movie house, it was inevitable that a version of the fascist cop would end up on the small screen. This was Detective Sergeant Rick Hunter of the LAPD. (A female version, 'Skirty Harry', appeared in >Lady Blue.) Both Harry Callahan and Hunter wielded .357 Magnums (Hunter's was called 'Simon'), both had by-the-book wimpy bosses who wanted their maverick butts kicked off the force. Whereas Harry said 'Make my day' to the slime he was about to blast apart, Hunter cooed 'Works for me'. Another small difference was that Hunter had a female sidekick, the beautiful but tough Dee Dee ('the brass cupcake'), and later, when Hunter was promoted to the LAPDS's élite Metro Division, Joanne Molenski. One big difference was that Don Siegel's initial and seminal Dirty Harry feature (1972), for all the critics' worries about its ultra-conservativism, was framed ambiguously; but Hunter was pure, unadultered redneckery.

In addition to his female cop partners, Hunter (played by former NFL star Fred Dryer) was assisted in his cleaning up of LA by Sporty James, street hustler and snitch, and Carlos, the assistant at the morgue. In later episodes, Hunter gained a girlfriend, Chris Novak, a fellow cop. Aside from 'Works for me', the show's other endearing catchphrase occurred every time Hunter told the episodes's psycho/pimp/pusher/rapist/arsonist to accompany him to the station. 'Who says?' the lowlife would sneer. 'Simon says,' replied Hunter, pulling out his .357.

GUEST CAST: Brent Spiner, Erik Estrada (as Sergeant Brad Navarro in 'City of Passion'), Robert Vaughn, James B Sikking, Tony Mordente.

INSPECTOR MORSE
UK 1987– 32 x 120m col ITV.
Central/Zenith/Carlton. US tx 1989– PBS.
EXEC PR Ted Childs, John Thaw. **PR** Kenny McBain, Chris Burt, David Lascelles, Deidre Keir.
DR Danny Boyle, Alastair Reid, Brian Parker, Adrian Shergold, Roy Battersby, Antonia Bird, Edward Bennett, Peter Duffell, Jim Goddard, Colin Gregg, Peter Hammond, Sandy Johnson, Herbert Wise, Stephen Whittaker, Anthony Simmons, James Scott, Stuart Orme, John Madden.
WR Various, including Julian Mitchell, Anthony Minghella, Thomas Ellice, Charles Wood, Peter Buckman, Alma Cullen, Peter Nichols, Malcolm Bradbury. **MUS** Barrington Pheloung (theme).
CAST Chief Insp Morse (John Thaw) Det Sgt Lewis (Kevin Whately) Chief Supt Strange (James Grout) Dr Grayling Russell (Amanda Hillwood) Dr Laura Hobson (Clare Holman) Det Sgt Maitland (Mary Jo Randle) Max (Peter Woodthorpe) Adrian Kershaw (Matthew Finney). **VIDEO** Central Video/Britannia Video Collection.

Exquisitely filmed police procedurals featuring Chief Inspector Morse of Thames Valley Police (Oxford beat), adapted from the novels of Colin Dexter. Accompanied by prosaic Geordie sidekick Lewis, the irascible Morse (hobbies: Mozart, crosswords, real ale) pursued plots of true middlebrowness, in that they bridged lowly whodunnit teleplays and cryptic, high-minded allegories. A case in point was Julian Mitchell's 'Masonic Mysteries', which was both a murder mystery and a parody of *The Magic Flute* and freemasonry within HM's Constabulary; another was Mitchell's 'Promised Land', which took a tilt at real-life policing by making Morse the subject of a wrongful conviction. With each episode developed over two hours – a cinematic length which, thanks to early producer Kenny McBain, was the real making of *Morse* – there was plenty of time for plot, character and atmosphere to develop. Languid, nostalgic,

113

redolent of dreaming spires, cobbled lanes and the ghost of Sebastian Flyte, *Morse* proved compulsive viewing for 750 million around the world. It was also a singular case of the box being better than the book. Although the programme officially ended in 1993, 'one offs' appeared thereafter at an almost annual rate. For the 1998 'The Wench is Dead', in which the cerebral Morse solved a murder mystery from the previous century, a new sidekick was introduced in the irreverent, fast-tracker shape of Adrian Kershaw.

SHOW TRIVIA: Novelist Colin Dexter appeared as an extra in every episode / Morse drove a red 1960 Mk II Jaguar, with registration plate 248 RPA / His first name, long hidden, was revealed, to much brouhaha, as the thoroughly contrived Endeavour / In the original books, Lewis was an elderly Welshman / Morse scriptwriter Anthony Minghella went on to write the films *Truly, Madly, Deeply* and *The English Patient* / Barrington Pheloung's theme music spelt out M-O-R-S-E in Morse code.

The episodes were: *The Dead of Jericho/The Silent World of Nicholas Quinn/Service of All the Dead/The Wolvercote Tongue/Last Seen Wearing/Settling of the Sun/Last Bus to Woodstock/Ghost in the Machine/The Last Enemy/Deceived by Flight/The Secret of Bay 5B/Infernal Serpent/The Sins of the Father/ Driven to Distraction/Masonic Mysteries/ Second Time Around/Fat Chance/Who Killed Harry Field?/Greeks Bearing Gifts/Promised Land/Dead on Time/Happy Families/Death of the Self/Absolute Conviction/Cherubim and Seraphim/Twilight of the Gods/The Day of the Devil/Deadly Slumber/The Way Through the Woods/The Daughters of Cain/Death is Now My Neighbour/The Wench is Dead.*

GUEST CAST: Keith Allen, John Gielgud, Patricia Hodge, Ronald Pickup, Julia Sawalha, Zoë Wanamaker, Patrick Malahide, Barry Foster, Holly Aird, Michael Hordern, Patrick Troughton.

IN THE HEAT OF THE NIGHT

USA 1988–95 140 x 60m col NBC. An MGM Production. UK tx 1988–90 ITV.

EXEC PR Fred Silverman, Juanita Bartlett, David Moessinger, Jeri Taylor, Carroll O'Connor. *PR* Joe Gannon. *DR* Various, including Carrol O'Connor, Larry Hagman, Paul Chavez, Winrich Kolbe. *WR* Various, including Matt Harris (aka Carroll O'Connor), Denise Nicholas. *MUS* Quincy Jones, Alan and Marilyn Bergman (theme), David Bell. *CAST* Chief William 'Bill' Gillespie (Carroll O'Connor) Det Virgil Tibbs (Howard Rollins) Sgt/Capt DL 'Bubba' Skinner (Alan Autry) Althea Tibbs (Anne-Marie Johnson) Ptlm/Det Lt Lonnie Jamison (Hugh O'Connor) Sgt Parker Williams

» *John Thaw (left) and Kevin Whately in* Inspector Morse, *one of the first UK policiers at cinematic length.*

(David Hart) Chief Hampton Forbes (Carl Weathers) Sgt Luann Corbin (Crystal Fox) Councilwoman Harriet DeLong (Denise Nicholas) Capt Tom Duggan (Joe Don Baker) Sgt Willson Sweet (Geoffrey Thorne) Joann St John (Lois Nettleton) Sgt Dee Shepherd (Dee Shaw) Ptlm Dennis Abernathy (Dennis Wofford) Etta Kirby (Tonea Stewart) Ptlm Randy Goode (Randall Franks) Ptlm Charlie Peake (CC Taylor).

'I want to like you people; and I want you people to like me. But there can be no liking without respect, and until there is that respect you will call me MISTER Tibbs!'

Any screen retread of John Ball's novel was bound to suffer in comparison with the multi-Oscared 1967 movie starring Rod Steiger and Sidney Poitier, but this atmospheric James Lee Barrett TV version held up pretty well. Cast in the role of (white) Police Chief Gillespie of Sparta, Mississippi, was Caroll O'Connor, from *All in the Family,* with Howard Rollins, from the film *Ragtime,* as returned-home black detective Virgil Tibbs. Obliged by the local mayor to work together on the murder case of a teenage white girl, the two policemen related abrasively but (unlike novel and film) this was less racial in nature than generational. In particular, Gillespie resented the new-fangled methods Tibbs advocated. As if to prove the TV version's difference from its predecessors, the small-screen Gillespie even

married a black woman, councillor Harriet DeLong; for his laid-back interpretation of Gillespie, O'Connor received a 1989 Emmy. Initially shot on location in Louisiana, the show switched filming to Covington, Georgia, the home of *The Dukes of Hazzard.* When Rollins quit the series in 1993 (Tibbs was said to be leaving Sparta for a law degree), ITHOTN continued through four reunion TVMs, *In the Heat of the Night: A Matter of Justice* (1994), *In the Heat of the Night: Who Was Geli Bendl?* (1994), *In the Heat of the Night: By Duty Bound* (1995), and *In the Heat of the Night: Grow Old Along with Me* (1995).

The Hugh O'Connor on the cast list was Carroll O'Connor's adopted son, whose character, Lonnie Jamison, began as a background patrolman but was eventually promoted to dramatic front rank as a detective lieutenant. Hugh O'Connor took his own life in 1995, after a long struggle against drug addiction.

GUEST CAST: Stacy Keach, Peter Fonda, Robert Goulet, Tippi Hedren, Steve Kanaly, O J Simpson, Burgess Meredith, George C Scott.

IRONSIDE
(British title: A Man Called Ironside)
USA 1967–75 197 x 60m, 3 x 120m col NBC. Harbour Productions/Universal TV/NBC. UK tx 1967–75 BBC.

» *Raymond Burr as Ironside. Playing the paraplegic detective's gofer was blaxploitation star Don Mitchell (rear).*

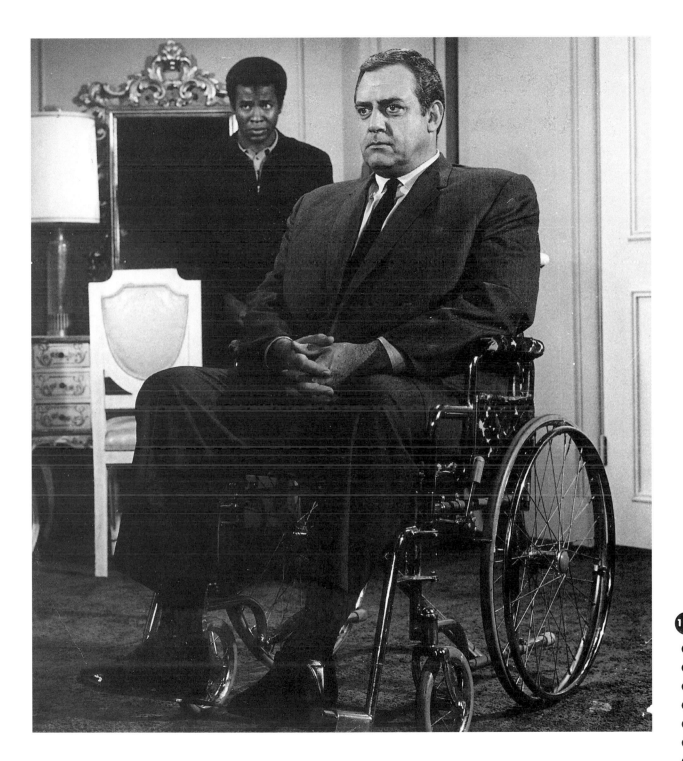

CR *Collier Young.* **EXEC PR** *Cy Chermak, Joel Rogosin, Frank Price, Collier Young.* **PR** *Albert Aley, Douglas Benton, Norman Jolley, Paul Mason, Jerry McAdams, Winston Miller, Lou Morheim, Collier Young.* **DR** *Abner Biberman, Michael Caffey, Richard Colla, Charles S Dubin, John Florea, David Friedkin, William Graham, Daniel Haller, Leonard Horn, Jerry Jameson, Bruce Kessler, Alf Kjellin, Russ Mayberry, Don McDougall, James Neilson, Christian I Nyby II, Leo Penn, Daniel Petrie, Allen Reisner, David Lowell Rich, Boris Sagal, Jimmy Sangster, Robert Scheerer, Ralph Senensky, Barry Shear, James Sheldon, Jeannot Szwarc, Don Weis.* **WR** *Don Mankiewicz, Collier Young, Albert Aley, Michael Philip Butler, Francine Carroll. Cy Chermak, James Doherty, William Gordon, Norman Jolley, Ken Kolb, William Douglas Langsford, Lou Morheim, Sy Salkowitz, Lane Slate, Christopher Trumbo.* **MUS** *Monty Paich, Oliver Nelson.* **CAST** *Chief Robert T Ironside (Raymond Burr) Det Sgt Ed Brown (Don Galloway) Eve Whitfield (Barbara Anderson) Mark Sanger (Don Mitchell) Fran Belding (Elizabeth Baur) Commissioner Dennis Randall (Gene Lyons) Lt Carl Reese (Johnny Seven) Diana Sanger (Joan Pringle).*

San Francisco Chief of Detectives Ironside, member of the force for 25 years, is paralysed from the waist down when a would-be assassin's bullet tears through his spinal column.

Such was the premise of *Ironside*, initially intended as a two-hour made-for-TV movie period. But this unusual hero proved so popular that an unplanned series took up where the movie left off. Here 215-pound, wheelchair-bound Ironside (played by former >*Perry Mason* star Raymond Burr) was duly given a permanent post as special consultant to the SFPD by Police Commissioner Randall, along with an operations base in the converted attic of Police Headquarters. Helping him wage his war against crime were top-flight police officers Sergeant Ed Brown, policewoman Eve Whitfield and Mark Sanger (Don Mitchell, also the blaxploitation flic *Scream, Blacula, Scream 2*), a black man with a history of run-ins with the law, who became Ironside's aide, bodyguard and driver of his customised van, specially equipped with telephone, tape-recorder and hydraulic lift.

Whitfield (played by Barbara Anderson of *Mission Impossible*) left the series at the end of the 1970–1 season over a contract dispute and was replaced by Elizabeth Baur as policewoman Fran Belding. Sergeant Brown and Mark Sanger were given expanded roles – Brown took on more undercover work, and Mark went to law school, graduating at the start of the 1974–5 season and getting married.

The appeal of this solid, old-fashioned police series, in which the robbers and murderers were always caught, lay in the commanding, magnetic

⌃ *Former* Cannon *star William Conrad stayed within typecasting in* Jake and the Fatman.

presence of Raymond Burr, who was so convincing in his role that viewers believed that Burr himself was paraplegic. Burr regarded the part as both a challenge and an eye-opener. 'There are many people incapacitated in many ways, not just paraplegics, who are being ignored,' he said. 'We kind of push them away into the dark.' Burr had some personal insight into Ironside's situation; he had been severely wounded during service with the US Navy in the Second World War.

The series, consistently rating in the top 25 for most of its eight-year run, was only terminated by

Burr's ill-health. In 1974 he suffered first a heart attack and then further illness requiring a spell in hospital. Burr retired to the Pacific Island of Naitauba, near Fiji, that wages from his previous role as Perry Mason had earned him, and laid the law book to rest. Until, that is, he came back in the new *Perry Mason* and a 1993 *Ironside* reunion movie, *The Return of Ironside* (120m col). Burr died in 1993.

GUEST CAST: Susan Saint James, Loretta Swit, Bruce Lee, DeForest Kelley, Walter Koenig, Myrna Loy, Desi Arnaz, Tyne Daly, Ron Masak, Scott Glenn, Tina Louise.

JAKE AND THE FATMAN

USA 1987–90 Approx 100 x 60m col CBS. A Viacom production. UK tx 1989–91 ITV.

CR *Dean Hargrove, Joel Steiger.* **EXEC PR** *Fred Silverman, Dean Hargrove, David Moessinger, Ed Waters.* **DR** *Various, including Jeri Taylor, Bernard Kowalski, Christian I Nyby, Russ Mayberry, Ron Satlof, Dale White, David Moessinger, Alexander Singer.* **MUS** *Richard DeBenedictis (theme).*

CAST *Jason Lochinvar 'JL' McCabe (William Conrad) Jake Styles (Joe Penny) Derek Mitchell (Alan Campbell) Katie Grant (Rebeccah Bush) Judge Smallwood (Jack Hogan) Gertrude (Lu Leonard) Sgt Rafferty (George O'Hanlon Jr) Lisbeth Berkeley-Smythe (Olga Russell).*

After playing corpulent detectives >*Cannon* and >*Nero Wolfe*, William Conrad stayed within typecasting to play the Fatman, a former Hawaiian cop turned Honolulu DA, in this serviceable vehicle from Viacom. The Fatman's constant companion was his pet bulldog Max, while the Jake of the title was the Fatman's pet PI, suave Jake Styles. A fair ratings runner in the USA, it received only sporadic screenings across the ITV network, and then invariably late in the midnight hour.

GUEST CAST: Dick Van Dyke.

JASON KING

UK 1972–3 26 x 60m col ITV. A Scroton Production for ITC. US tx 1971 syndicated.

CR *Dennis Spooner, Monty Berman.* **DR** *Roy Ward Baker, Paul Dickson, Cyril Frankel, Jeremy Summers.* **WR** *Various, including Robert Banks Stewart.* **MUS** *Laurie Johnson.*

CAST *Jason King (Peter Wyngarde) Sir Brian (Dennis Price) Ryland (Ronald Lacey) Nicola Harvester (Ann Sharp).*

Spin-off from >*Department S* in which the suave'n'sideburned detective cum novelist went solo on intrigues, these invariably requiring foreign travel and beautiful women (those serving as King's totty included Alexandra Bastedo and Kate O'Mara). Nicola Harvester was King's publisher; Sir Brian and Ryland were the men from the Ministry who blackmailed him (over tax evasion) into working for them. In place of the beguiling baroque plots of *DS*, the show substituted a not altogether successful parodying of fellow ITC actioners. Meanwhile King's dandyish clothes continued to play havoc with early colour cameras.

Shortly after the termination of *Jason King*, actor

Peter Wyngarde's career crashed when he was fined £75 for committing an indecent act with a man in a public lavatory. This only heightened the notoriety Wyngarde had acquired through the recording of an album which was judged, even in the groovy early Seventies, to be so obscene that RCA had to pull it from the shops.

The episodes were: *Wanna Buy a TV Series?/ A Page Before Dying/Buried in the Cold, Cold Ground/A Deadly Line in Digits/Variations on a Theme/As Easy as ABC/To Russia with Panache/*

◆ *Peter Wyngarde as* Jason King; *the character's flamboyant clothing played havoc with early colour cameras.*

*A Red, Red Rose Forever/All That Glisters (Part I)
All That Glisters (Part II)/Flamingos Only Fly on
Tuesdays/Toki/The Constance Missal/Uneasy
Lies the Head/Nadine/A Kiss for a Beautiful
Killer/If It's Got to Go, It's Got to Go/A Thin
Band of Air/It's Too Bad about Auntie/The Stones
of Venice/A Royal Flush/Every Picture Tells a
Story/Chapter I: The Company I Keep/Zenia/An
Author in Search of Two Characters/That Isn't
Me, It's Somebody Else.*

GUEST CAST: Kate O'Mara, John Le Mesurier, Burt
Kwouk, Felicity Kendal, Michele Dotrice, Ralph
Bates, Patrick Troughton, Alexandra Bastedo,
Anne Aston, Stephanie Beacham, Philip Madoc.

JOHNNY STACCATO (AKA STACCATO)

USA 1959–60 27 x 25m bw NBC/ABC.
MCA/Universal. UK tx 1960 ITV.

CR *John Cassavetes.* **PR** *William Freye.* **DR** *John
Cassavetes, Bernard Girard, Robert Parrish,
Joseph Pevney, Boris Sagal, John Brahm, Paul
Henreid.* **WR** *Various, including John Cassavetes.*
MUS *Elmer Bernstein (theme).*
CAST *Johnny Staccato (John Cassavetes) Waldo
(Eduardo Ciannelli) Pianist (John Williams).*

Much criticised on its original US release
for being a carbon copy of >*Peter Gunn*,
this John Cassavetes series actually had a
dynamic style all its own. Cassavetes played

Johnny Staccato, a jazz musician turned private
detective, working out of Waldo's club in
downtown New York and taking whatever cases
came along. The series was noir-ishly shot and lit,
performances were sharp, and the stylish visuals
were underscored by pulsating jazz rhythms. The
theme was composed by Elmer Bernstein, while
scenes in Waldo's club often included
background playing by such jazz luminaries as
Barney Kessel, Red Mitchell, Red Norvo and
Johnny Williams (who later composed the music
for the film *Star Wars* among other high-profile
projects.)

John Cassavetes used the money he earned
from this popular and too-brief series to finance
his directorial début film, *Shadows* (1959). As
with his subsequent movies as director – which
include *Husbands* (1970) and *Gloria* (1980) –
the film was experimental and controversial, and
Cassavetes remains one of the biggest influences
on the landscape of American avant-garde film.
He is probably most familiar, however, for his
starring role in the movie *The Dirty Dozen* (1967)
and as Mia Farrow's betraying husband in
Rosemary's Baby (directed by Roman Polanski,
1968). He died in 1989, aged 60.

Paul Henreid, one of the stars of the classic
movie *Casablanca*, directed the 'Mask of Jason'
episode. Among the guest cast was Gena
Rowlands, who was soon to be Cassavetes' wife.

GUEST CAST: Mary Tyler Moore, Gena Rowlands.

JULIET BRAVO

UK 1980–5 82 x 50m col BBC1. BBC TV.

CR Ian Kennedy Martin. **PR** Terence Williams, Peter Cregeen, Geraint Morris, Colin Shindler. **DR** Various, including Adrian Shergold, Derek Lister, Paul Ciappessoni, Jan Sargent, Carol Wilks, Jonathan Alwyn, Pennant Roberts, Brian Finch, Tristan De Vere Cole. **WR** Various, including Ian Kennedy Martin, Wally K Daly, Susan Pleat, Paula Milne, John Foster, Tony Parker, Ewart Alexander, Don Webb, Tony Charles. **MUS** Derek Groom.

CAST Insp Jean Darblay (Stephanie Turner) Insp Kate Longton (Anna Carteret) Tom Darblay (David Hargreaves) Sgt Joe Beck (David Ellison) Sgt Joe Parrish (Noel Collins) PC Danny Sparks (Mark Botham) PC Brian Kelleher (C J Allen) Chief Insp Perrin (Edward Peel) John Holden (Tom Georgeson) Tom Darblay (David Hargreaves) Div Supt Hallam (James Grout).

Although it came from the creator of actioner >The Sweeney, this Lancashire-based police series was more reminiscent of >Z Cars, being low-key Northern, but full of realistically human drama. The opening episode, 'Fraudulently Uttered', about a charlady stealing the boss's profits (but not for her own benefit), set the tone for the whole series.

What distinguished Juliet Bravo from Z-Cars was that the central figure was a woman police officer, Inspector Jean Darblay (played by Stephanie Turner, one-time Z-Cars WPC, also George Carter's wife in >The Sweeney), and that the series highlighted the sexism she faced from the male officers at the fictional Hartley police station, proving the adage that 'a policewoman's lot is not a happy one'.

In the fourth season Darblay was promoted upstairs and Inspector Kate Longton (Anna Carteret from The Raving Beauties feminist cabaret) took over her post.

Unsurprisingly perhaps, Bravo – which began in the same year as another British policewoman series, >The Gentle Touch – was particularly popular among female viewers. The series' title came from the radio call sign for the Hartley station's woman commander.

GUEST CAST: Karl Howman.

THE KNOCK

UK 1996– 24+ x 60m col ITV. Bronson Knight Productions.

CR Paul Knight, Anita Bronson. **EXEC PR** Sally Head, Jo Wright. **PR** Paul Knight. **DR** Various, including Gerry Poulson, Frank Smith, James Hazeldine. **WR** Various, including Geoffrey Case, Ian Kennedy Martin, Steve Trafford, Stephen Leather.

CAST Katherine Roberts (Alex Kingston) Diane Ralston (Caroline Lee Johnson) Bill Adams (Malcolm Storry) George Andreotti (Enzo Squillino

Jr) Barry Christie (Steve Toussaint) Arnie Reinhardt (Marston Bloom) Kevin Whitwell (Andrew Dunn) Alex Murray (Daniel Brown) Lynn Hickson (Sarah Malin) David Ancrom (Mark Lewis Jones).

Two élite units of London undercover Customs and Excise officers (City & South, Heathrow) hunt down international smugglers.

One of British network ITV's slicker dramas of the Nineties, with the added bonus of novel subject-matter for the cops and robbers format. Plus a discernible budget, enabling location filming in exotic locales (Thailand, South Africa, Russia) and name guest stars. Alex Kingston (later *Moll Flanders* and *ER*) played agent Katherine Roberts in the early episodes. The producer was Paul Knight, who had previously guided the fire-fighter show, *London's Burning*. At its height, the show garnered ratings of over 10 million.

GUEST CAST: Michael Brandon, Cherie Lunghi, Oliver Tobias, Dennis Waterman, Anthony Valentine.

KOJAK

USA 1973–8 112 x 60m, 2 x 120m, 1 x 180m col CBS. A Universal Television Production. UK tx 1974–8 BBC1.

CR Abby Mann. **EXEC PR** Matthew Rapf. **PR** James McAdams, Jack Laird, Chester Krumholz. *DR* Edward M Abroms, Richard Donner, Charles S Dubin, Jerrold Freedman, David Friedkin, Daniel Haller, Jerry London, Russ Mayberry, Sigmund Neufeld Jr, Christian I Nyby II, Joel Oliansky, Ernest Pintoff, Allen Reisner, Telly Savalas, Nicholas Sgarro, Paul Stanley. **WR** Various, including Donald P Bellisario, Ray Brenner, Robert Earll, Jerrold Freedman, Mort Fine, Rift Fournier, Robert Foster, Gene Kearney, Chester Krumholz, Marvin Kupker, Jack Laird, John Meredyth Lucas, Harriet Margulies, James McAdams, Joel Oliansky, Don Patterson, Joseph Polizzi, Eugene Price, Matthew Rapf, Albert Ruben, Bill Schwartz, Robert Swanson, Ross Teel, Michael Wagner. **MUS** Billy Goldenberg (theme).
CAST Lt Theo Kojak (Telly Savalas) Frank McNeil (Dan Frazer) Lt Bobby Crocker (Kevin Dobson) Det Stavros (George Savalas) Det Saperstein (Mark Russell) Det Rizzo (Vince Conti).

'Who loves ya baby?' Until he starred in *Kojak*, the answer for Telly Savalas was 'no one'. He had played the baddie in over 70 films (he first shaved his head for Burt Lancaster's 1962 film *Birdman of Alcatraz*), but it was not until he played the lollipop-sucking, shaven-headed Greek-American cop at the age of 49 that Savalas got famous.

The character audiences fell for world-wide was loud, straight-talking Theo Kojak. A snazzy dresser with fancy waistcoats and an eye for the women, Kojak worked out of New York City's Manhattan South Precinct (the station house of the

⊗ *'Who loves ya baby?' Telly Savalas as the inimitable Kojak, a show which sold world-wide.*

real-life NY 9th Precinct was used for exteriors, as it would be for >*NYPD Blue* in the Nineties) and was a tough, cynical cop for a tough, cynical town. But that was just on the surface – inside he had a tender streak. He cared about his job and he cared about people getting a rough deal and

he was prepared to break the rules if it meant he got justice.

Kojak had a failed marriage and twenty years in the force behind him. His partner in the NYPD when he started out was Frank McNeil, but Frank had worked his way up while Kojak had done things his way, so now Frank McNeil was chief of detectives and his boss. They were still friends, but Frank was never entirely sure about his old pal's methods. Kojak's new partner was young plainclothes detective Lieutenant Bobby Crocker and cuddlesome, easy-going Detective Stavros – played by an actor whose name at first appeared on cast lists as 'Demosthenes' but who was actually Telly's younger brother George Savalas. Police applauded Kojak for being true to life, while anti-violence lobbies complained about the violence, although violence was always a last resort in the series. Extensive use of location footage gave *Kojak* edge and flavour. But what gave the series its huge appeal was Savalas himself. Savalas played the part with gusto and identified strongly with his on-screen persona ('You tell me the difference between Kojak and Telly and I'll tell you the difference between apples and apple pie,' he declared). Unashamedly larger than life himself, he acquired a home in Paul Newman's one-time Beverly Hills estate, a Rolls-Royce Silver Cloud – numberplate TELLY S – and six other foreign sports cars, cut a best-selling LP and got paid $100,000 a week to headline a Las Vegas hotel show. But, just like Kojak, there was another side to Savalas. He was awarded the Purple Heart as a war hero in Korea; he worked as a senior director for ABC News before turning to acting in his thirties, and continued to work behind the camera for *Kojak*, directing episodes of the series.

Theo Kojak made his first appearance in a three-hour Emmy Award-winning TV movie *The Marcus-Nelson Murders*, based on the real-life Wylie-Hoffert homicides). This case established the cop's ethics, as he defended a black Brooklyn kid who had been pushed by the police into confessing to a crime he had not committed. The series was an instant hit, number seven in the ratings in its first season and second only to >*Hawaii Five-O* out of all cop and detective shows. It also sold, duly dubbed for local languages, the world over, including Germany, where it was retitled, with Teutonic idiosyncracy, *The Lion Without a Mane*.

Kojak returned to TV in 1986 for a tranche of TVMs as part of CBS's Mystery Movie package. These were: *Kojak: The Investigation* (1986), *Kojak: The Price of Justice* (1987), *Kojak: Ariana* (1989), *Kojak: None So Blind* (1990). High ratings prompted ABC to spin-off a revived series, in which an ageing Kojak – by now promoted to inspector – worked alongside a bright young assistant called Winston Blake and a secretary called Pamela.

Telly Savalas died in 1994, a year after unsuccessfully suing Universal TV, the makers of *Kojak*, for $6 million – his claim was 25 per cent of the programme's profits.

GUEST CAST: Christopher Walken, Sylvester Stallone (as Detective Rick Daley), Mark Shera, Daniel J Travanti, Veronica Hamel, Richard Gere, José Ferrer, Harvey Keitel, Sharon Gless, Paul Michael Glaser, Robert Mandan.

LADY BLUE

USA 1985–6 1 x 20m, 12 x 45m col ABC. An MGM Production.

CR Robert Vincent O'Neill. **EXEC PR** David Gerber. **PR** Mark Rodgers. **DR** Various, including Gary Nelson, John Florea, Michael Vejar, John D Hancock. **WR** Various, including Robert Vincent O'Neill.

CAST Det Katy Mahoney (Jamie Rose) Chief Det Terry McNichols (Danny Aiello) Sgt Gino Ginelli (Ron Dean) Off Cassidy (Bruce A Young) Capt Flynn (Ralph Foody).

She was deadlier than the male. Detective Katy Mahoney (Jamie Rose, previously Victoria Gioberti-Hogan in sudster Falcon Crest) worked downtown Chicago, .357 Magnum in her sexy manicured hand, eliminating any pimps, drug pushers, rapists and other lowlife unlucky enough to cross her gunsight. Internal Affairs were suspicious, but those she dispatched were always found to have deserved it.

This ultra-violent female cop show was quickly dubbed 'Dirty Harriet' (and rightly so: Rose even admitted to TV Guide that she had rented all the Dirty Harry movies and watched Clint Eastwood's gun moves in order to copy him). For a prime-time TV audience, however, the gratuitous gore was too much to stomach – 56 incidents of violence in one episode alone – and Lady Blue was sent to the TV morgue. The series was filmed on location in Chicago. Danny Aiello played the standard supportive boss. Rose, in a career of true variety, later turned up in St Elsewhere and the cult cheapie movie, Chopper Chicks in Zombietown (dr Dan Haskins, 1989).

LAW & ORDER

USA 1990– 176+ x 60m col NBC. Wolf Films/Studios USA Television/Universal. UK tx 1991– BBC1/Sky 1.

CR Dick Wolf. **EXEC PR** Dick Wolf, Ed Sherin, Rene Balcer. **PR** Jeffrey Hayes, Lewis H Gould, Billy Fox. **DR** Various, including John P Whitsell, E W Swackhamer, Fred Gerber, Ed Sherin, James Hyman, Gilbert Moses, Matt Penn, Gwen Arner, Bill D'Elia, James Frawley, Helaine Head, Peter Levin, Gilbert Moses, Lewis H Gould, Gwen Arner, Bruce Seth Green, Marc Laub, John D Patterson, Peter Levin, Gabrielle Beaumont, Steven Robman, Daniel Sackheim, Kris Tabori, James Quinn. **WR** Various, including Ed Zuckerman, Robert Palm, Michael S Chernuchin, Michael Duggan, Joe Morgenstern, Rene Balcer, Matt Kierne, Shimon Wincelberg, Alec Baldwin. **MUS** Mike Post, Jill Hennessy.

CAST Det Sgt Max Greevey (George Dzundza) Det Sgt Phil Cerreta (Paul Sorvino) Det Michael 'Mike' Logan (Christopher Noth) Det Leonard 'Lennie' Briscoe (Jerry Orbach) Capt Donald Cragen (Dann Florek) Det Reynaldo 'Rey' Curtis (Benjamin Bratt) Lt Anita Van Buren (S Epatha

Merkerson) Asst DA Benjamin 'Ben' Stone (Michael Moriarty) Asst DA Jack McCoy (Sam Waterston) DA Adam Schiff (Steven Hill) Asst DA Paul Robinette (Richard Brooks) Asst DA Abbie Carmichael (Angie Harmon) Asst DA Claire Kincaid (Jillian Hennessy) Dr Elizabeth Olivet (Carolyn McCormick) Det Tony Profaci (John Fiore) Narrator (Steve Morgan).

'In the criminal justice system, the people are represented by two separate yet equally important groups: the police, who investigate the crime; and the district attorneys, who prosecute the offenders. These are their stories.'

👁 Update of >Arrest and Trial, thus devoting the first half of the show to the crime and apprehension of the (alleged) felon, and the second to the ensuing court case.

Atmospherically filmed on location in New York, the show benefited from tight direction and scripting (those contributing, incidentally, included Hollywood actor Alec Baldwin) and gained the just reward of not only a long, long run, but a 1997 Emmy for outstanding Drama. There was a large turn-over of cast, not least because in 1993 network NBC decided that the male exclusiveness of L & O needed to be ended; enter S Epatha Merkerson as Lt Anita Van Buren and Jillian Henessy as Assistant DA Claire Kincaid. Among the longest stayers were Christopher Noth as

Detective Mike Logan, Michael Moriarty as Assistant DA Ben Stone and movie refugee Sam Waterston as Assistant DA Jack McCoy. The original pilot for the show, *Everyone's Favourite Bagman* (with Roy Thinnes, *The Invaders*), was filmed in 1988 for CBS, but when they passed on the show, NBC later shot their own pilot and put *Bagman* in as a first-season episode.
GUEST CAST: Roy Thinnes, Eli Wallach, Daniel Benzali.

LONGSTREET

USA 1971–2 23 x 60m col ABC. Paramount TV. UK tx 1973 ITV.
CR Stirling Silliphant. **EXEC PR** Stirling Silliphant. **PR** Joel Rogosin. **DR** Various, including Leslie H Martinson, Lee Philips, JosephSargent.
WR Various, including Stirling Silliphant.
MUS Billy Goldenburg, Robert Drasnin.
CAST Mike Longstreet (James Franciscus) Niki Bell (secretary) (Marilyn Mason) Duke Paige (Mark Richman) Mrs Kingston (Ann Doram) Li Tsung (Bruce Lee).

👁 The case files of a blind New Orleans private investigator and his Alsatian guide dog, Pax.

Gimmicky Seventies detective show from Stirling Silliphant, starring James Franciscus as the title gumshoe (who lost his wife, as well as his sight, in a bomb explosion triggered by some disgruntled criminals). Mainly memorable for some scintillating chop-chop appearances from Bruce Lee as Longstreet's self-defence instructor, in particular the opening episode, 'The Way of Intercepting Fist'. The series followed a 1970 TVM (90m), directed by Joseph Sargent.

GUEST CAST: Dana Elcar, Lee Meriwether, Marion Ross, Tyne Daly.

LORD PETER WIMSEY

UK 1972–5 21 x 45, 50m col BBC1/ BBC TV/BBC Scotland. US tx 1972–5 PBS.
PR *Richard Beynon, Bill Sellars.* **DR** *Hugh David, Ronald Wilson, Raymond Menmuir, Rodney Bennett, Robert Tronson.* **WR** *Anthony Steven, Bill Craig.*
CAST *Lord Peter Wimsey (Ian Carmichael) Bunter (Glyn Houston/Peter Newark) Detective Inspector Parker (Mark Eden).*

Snobbery with violence. Ian Carmichael played the titled detective in this period mini-series adapted from Dorothy L Sayers stories, with Glyn Houston, followed by Peter Newark, roughing it as Wimsey's manservant, Bunter. The quintet of whodunnits presented were: *Clouds of Witness/The Unpleasantness at the Bellona Club/Murder Must Advertise/The Nine Tailors/Five Red Herrings*. A decade later Wimsey again came to the small screen in *Dorothy L Sayers Mystery* (1987, BBC2 /1987,

WGBH Boston, pr Michael Chapman), but this time played by Edward Petherbridge. This latter version – which adapted a triptych of cases: *Strong Poison/Have His Carcase/Gaudy Night* – was laudably faithful to Sayers, but never quite grabbed the fancy as much as Carmichael's idiosyncratic 'cheer-frightfully-ho' interpretation with its pleasing undertow of Bertie Wooster.

GUEST CAST: Terence Alexander, Peter Bowles, John Junkin, Glyn Houston, Paul Darrow, Russell Hunter, John Welsh, David Wintoul.

MADIGAN

USA 1972–3 6 x 90m col NBC. Oden Productions/Universal TV. UK tx 1973 ITV.
EXEC PR *Dean Hargrove, Frank Rosenberg.* **PR** *Roland Kibbee.* **DR** *Alex March, Boris Sagal, Jack Smight.* **WR** *Various, including William McGovern, Roland Kibbee, Dean Hargrove.*
CAST *Sergeant Dan Madigan (Richard Widmark).*

Spin-off from the 1968 movie of the same title (dr Don Spiegel, wr Abraham Polonsky), with grim-faced Richard Widmark reprising his role as the loner New York homicide cop. For this sextet of cases, Sergeant Madigan several times packed his suitcase for glamorous foreign beats. To forgettable avail. A quintessential NY creation, Madigan always performed best against a cityscape as bleak and embittered as himself. In the USA, Madigan

⊗ *Richard Widmark (left) as grim-faced NY cop*
Madigan, a spin-off from the 1968 movie.

rotated with >*Banacek* and *Cool Million*
(1972–3, starring James Farentino as a P.I. who
charged $1 million a case) as part of NBC's
Wednesday Mystery Movie.

The episodes were: *The Manhattan Beat/The
Midtown Beat/The Lisbon Beat/The London
Beat/The Naples Beat/The Park Avenue Beat.*

THE MAGICIAN

USA 1973–4 1 x 90m, 24 x 60m col NBC.
Paramount TV. UK tx 1974 ITV.

CR Bruce Lansbury. **EXEC PR** Laurence Heath.
PR Paul Playdon, Barry Crane, Alan A Armer.
DR Various, including Marvin Chomsky, Barry
Crane, Alexander Singer, Reza Badiyi, Paul
Krasny, Leslie H Martinson, Sutton Roley.
WR Various, including Walter Brough, Jimmy
Sangster, Joseph Stefano. **MUS** Patrick Williams.

CAST Anthony Blake (Anthony Dorian in pilot) (Bill Bixby) Max Pomeroy (Keene Curtis) Jerry Anderson (Jerry Wallace in pilot) (Jim Watkins) Denis Pomeroy (Todd Crespi) Dominick (Joseph Sirola).

Starred a pre-*Incredible Hulk* Bill Bixby as magician Anthony Blake, who used his illusionist skills to help the innocent. Described by a show character as 'one of the few individuals, in this age of numbness, who can still regard the suffering of a fellow human being as his own', Blake was set on the path of do-goodery by his own false imprisonment for espionage in South America. Among his detecting tricks were a photographic memory and the ability to mirror read. Also seen was Max Pomeroy, Blake's journalist friend, Max's paraplegic son Dennis, and Jerry Anderson, the pilot of Tony's plane, Spirit.

Moderately unusual sleuth show, but as substantial as candyfloss. To Bixby's credit he performed the wizard tricks himself. Joseph Stefano, the screenwriter of Hitchcock's *Psycho*, was among the hired hands in the script department. Those on the guest cast included Brenda Benet, Bixby's then wife.

The episodes were: *Pilot/The Manhunters/The Vanishing Lady/Illusion in Terror/Lightning on a Dry Day/Ovation for Murder/Man on Fire/Lady in a Trap/The Man Who Lost Himself/Nightmare in Steel/Shattered Image/The Illusion of the Curious Counterfeit I/The Illusion of the Curious Counterfeit II/The Illusion of the Stainless Steel Lady/The Illusion of the Queen's Gambit/The Illusion of Black Gold/The Illusion of the Lost Dagger/The Illusion of the Deadly Conglomerate/The Illusion of the Fatal Arrow/The Illusion of the Lethal Plaything/The Illusion of the Cat's Eye/The Illusion of the Evil Spike.*
GUEST CAST: Mark Hamill, William Shatner, Brenda Benet.

MAGNUM PI

USA 1980–8 6 x 120m, 150 x 60m col CBS. Universal TV/TWS Production. UK tx 1981–7 ITV.

CR Donald P Bellisario, Glen A Larson.
EXEC PR Donald P Bellisario, Glen A Larson, Tom Selleck. **PR** Various, including Tom Selleck.
DR Various, including David Hemmings, Peter Medak, Joan Darling, Donald P Bellisario, Bernard Kowalski, Rick Kolbe, Burt Kennedy, Alan Levi, Leo Penn, Russ Mayberry, John Llewelyn Moxey, Harry Harris, Michael O'Herlihy, Roger Young, Robert Loggia, Larry Dohenny, Michael Vejar, Ivan Dixon, Georg Stanford Brown.
WR Various, including Donald P Bellisario, Glen A Larson, Andrew Schneider, Reuben Leder, Tom Selleck, Jeri Taylor, Chris Abbott-Fish.
MUS Various, including Ian Freebairn-Smith, Mike Post, Pete Carpenter.

CAST *Thomas Magnum (Tom Selleck) Jonathan Quale Higgins III (John Hillerman) Theodore 'TC' Calvin (Roger E Mosley) Orville 'Rick' Wright (Larry Minette) Robin Masters (voice) (Orson Welles) Mac Reynolds (Jeff Mackay) Agatha Chumley (Gillian Dobb) Lt Tanaka (Kwan Hi Lim) Ice Pick (Elish Cook Jr).*

'I know what you're thinking, and you're right...'

Tailor-made TV vehicle for muscles-and-moustache actor Tom Selleck, who had caught the eye of Universal TV when playing smug gumshoe Lance White in >*The Rockford Files*. Here Selleck took the role of Thomas Magnum, a rakish Vietnam vet turned private investigator, who had the job of protecting the Hawaiian estate of permanently absent writer Robin Masters; this gave Magnum free use of a red Ferrari 308 GTS (later a 308 Quattrovalvole), as well as a palatial ceiling over his head. Alas, the position at 'Robin's Nest' wasn't quite a sinecure, for alongside the estate's fatal attraction to robbers and trouble-bearing guests there was Masters' crusty British manservant Higgins, who disliked Magnum's freeloading ways and encouraged Doberman pinschers Zeus and Apollo to take bites out of his sun-tanned hide. Aiding Magnum in his bodyguard/security/gumshoe work were wartime buddies TC and Rick, the former now the owner of chopper service Island

⊗ *Tom Selleck as* Magnum PI, *a show tailor-made for the actor after his appearance on* The Rockford Files.

Hoppers, the latter co-owner of the exclusive King Kamehameha Club, a favourite Magnum haunt. (It was a conceit of the show, incidentally, that Magnum, TC and Rick were ex-Navy SEALs.)

Starting with 'Don't Eat the Snow in Hawaii', *Magnum PI* relied heavily – but successfully – on Selleck's sex-appeal and shining talent for comedy, plus (pace >*Hawaii Five-O*) acres of beautiful women in paradise settings. Few noticed *Magnum*'s tendency to recycle plot (the standard *Magnum* model being the friend from the past now in need) or its debt to >*The Rockford Files* (the penchant for parody), and it lasted for eight much-loved seasons before the trigger was pulled. Among the show directors were former actors turned helmsmen, Georg Stanford Brown *(Roots)* and Ivan Dixon *(Hogan's Heroes)*.

⊗ *Rupert Davies as Maigret, the casting of whom Georges Simenon described as 'perfect'.*

SHOW TRIVIA: The guest cast include Jillie Mack, whom Selleck later married / Also on the guest list were three former Rockford actors, Noah Beery Jr, Joe Santos and Stuart Margolin / Series composer Mike Post was at school with Selleck / 'Robin's Nest' was the real-life Ohahu estate of Eve Anderson, and was a former turtle farm / In the course of the eight-year series Magnum was shot eight times.

GUEST CAST: Sharon Stone, Frank Sinatra, Shannen Doherty, Samantha Eggar, Ian McShane, Patrick Macnee, Cesar Romero, Joe Santos, Stuart Margolin, Noah Beery Jr, Miguel Ferrer.

MAIGRET

UK 1960–3 52 x 50m bw BBC. A BBC Television Production/Winwell.
EXEC PR Andrew Osborn. ***PR*** Rudolph Cartier.
DR *Various, including Andrew Osborn, Michael Hayes.* **WR** *Various, including Giles Cooper, Vincent Tilsley, Donald Bull.* **MUS** *Ron Grainer.*
CAST *Chief Insp Jules Maigret (Rupert Davies) Sgt Lucas (Ewen Solon) Mme Maigret (Helen Shingler).*

◉ Classic monochrome series starring Rupert Davies as Georges Simenon's pipe-smoking detective from the Paris Sûreté. Less interested in wielding a magnifying glass than analysing character, Maigret's modus operandi was to watch over the suspects, methodically

133

working through them until the villain of the piece made a fatal error or confessed under the tension. The casting of Davies delighted Simenon (who had sold the TV rights to the BBC ahead of world competition and described Davies as 'perfect' for the part). Davies, however, would later claim, 'I didn't have a life as an actor after I put on his [Maigret's] trilby and struck that match against a wall at the opening of every episode.' In 1963, the final season of *Maigret*, Davies was voted TV actor of the year. Those working in the backroom included designer Eileen Diss, whose sets reeked moody Gallic atmosphere in a style reminiscent of French noir cinema of the Fifties.

Typecast and damned, meanwhile, Davies returned as Maigret to host the 1964 series *Detective* and to feature in a 1969 Play for Today, 'Maigret at Bay'. Davies died three years later, having lived to see a French TV version of Simenon's Maigret stories starring Jean Richard (1967). In 1988 the British HTV company released a 120-minute TVM, *Maigret* (dr Paul Lynch, with a miscast, strangely thin Richard Harris), which was followed by a joint French/Belgian/Swiss production in 1991 with Bruno Cremer as Paris' finest. Another British version, from Granada TV, followed in 1992, with Michael Gambon (*The Singing Detective*) assuming the title role of *Maigret* in a production that interpreted the sleuth as a stolid plodder.

Here Maigret's sidekick, Sgt Lucas, was played by Geoffrey Hutchings, and Madame Maigret by Ciaran Madden/Barbara Flynn. Sponsored by Kronenbourg, the Granada series was filmed in Hungary because it was cheaper and looked more like the Paris of *temps perdu*.

MANCUSO FBI

USA 1989–90 19 x 60m col NBC. A Steve Sohmer Production for NBC. UK tx 1990–91 BBC.
CR *Steve Sohmer* **EXEC PR** *Steve Sohmer, Jeff Bleckner.* **PR** *Jacob Epstein, Ken Solarz.* **MUS** *Dennis McCarthy.*
CAST *Nick Mancuso (Robert Loggia) Eddie McMasters (Fredric Lehne) Jean St John (Randi Brooks) Kristen Carter (Lindsay Frost) Dr Paul Summers (Charles Siebert).*

Veteran FBI agent Nick Mancuso solved international crises in a style all his own and not to the liking of upstart young boss Eddie McMasters. Each week Mancuso resolutely caught lethal public enemies with methods plucked from his past, leaving precious little for tall but passive secretary Jean St John to do. Other series regulars were promising young lawyer Kristen Carter and Mancuso's sometime confidant, forensic expert Dr Paul Summer. Formula stuff, seamlessly made.
GUEST CAST: Denise Crosby

MAN IN A SUITCASE

UK 1967–8 30 x 60m col ITV. An ITC
Production for ATV. USA tx 1968 ABC.

CR *Richard Harris, Dennis Spooner.* **PR** *Sidney Cole.* **DR** *Charles Crichton, Gerry O'Hara, Pat Jackson, Robert Tronson, Freddie Francis, Herbert Wise, Peter Duffell, Don Chaffey, John Glen, Jeremy Summers, Charles Frend.* **WR** *Francis Megahy & Bernie Cooper, Edmund Ward, Philip Broadley, Stanley R Greenberg, Wilfred Greatorex, Jan Read, Roger Parkes, Vincent Tilsley, Reed de Rouen.* **MUS** *Albert Elms, Ron Grainer (title).*

CAST *McGill (Richard Bradford).* **VIDEO** *ITC.*

Bounty hunter McGill, modern adventurer, was an ex-CIA man turned private investigator. Falsely accused of a treasonable offence (failing to stop an eminent scientist defecting to Russia) and kicked out of his job, he was forced to take up a new life and became the *Man in a Suitcase* – a British-based investigator willing to take on any job that paid him $500 a day (plus expenses).

McGill, played by Richard Bradford, was the latest in a string of ATV boss Sir Lew Grade's mid-Atlantic heroes. Grade had been aiming series at the American market with considerable success since >*The Saint*, and was looking for more of the same. McGill neatly fitted the bill. Following close on the heels of ATV's >*The Baron*, McGill was a rugged loner searching Europe for clues to clear his name. His only companions were a battered leather suitcase containing a change of clothes and a gun, and the fear of his shady background catching up with him. Old romances occasionally flickered back into his life, only to be left behind as a new mission called.

Always ready to pull a gun, he would win his fights without so much as taking the cigarette out of his mouth. And he needed to be tough because he could expect no help from the authorities against his never-ending stream of ruthless adversaries. In 'Day of Execution' he faced an unknown assassin's threat to eliminate him; in 'Dead Man's Shoes' he became the target for a group of vicious gangsters; in 'No Friend of Mine' his job as a mercenary in Africa got him sandwiched between white settlers and native Africans; and in 'Three Blinks of the Eyes' he faced the guillotine unless he could find the woman who had hired him to bring her playboy husband to heel.

Man in a Suitcase was a superior thriller series. Thanks to Sir Lew Grade's lust for US sales, some of the best production personnel and guest stars were engaged. Directors included John Glen (now better known as director of the Bond films *For Your Eyes Only, Octopussy* and *A View to a Kill*), Charles Crichton (respected director of comedy films from *The Lavender Hill Mob* and *The Titfield Thunderbolt* to *A Fish Called Wanda*) and

136

Hammer veteran Freddie Francis. Among actor Richard Bradford's later screen appearances was *Hammett* (1983), the Wim Wenders *hommage* to hardboiled inkslinger Dashiell 'Sam Spade' Hammett, in which Bradford in-jokily played a tough-guy detective by the name of – Detective Bradford.

GUEST CAST: Colin Blakely, George Sewell, Robert Urquhart, Donald Sutherland, Judy Geeson, Peter Vaughan, Patrick Cargill, Philip Madoc, Felicity Kendal, Ray McAnally, Edward Fox, Roger Delgado, Rupert Davies, Duncan Lamont.

MANNIX

USA 1967–75 191 x 60m col CBS. Paramount Television. UK tx 1971, 1980–3 ITV.
CR *Richard Levinson, William Link.* **EXEC PR** *Bruce Geller.* **PR** *Ivan Goff, Ben Roberts.* **DR** *Various, including Corey Allen, Michael Caffey, Reza S Badiyi, Richard Benedict, Marvin Chomsky, Barry Crane, Harry Harvey Jr, Alf Kjellin, John Llewellyn Moxey, Paul Krasny, Seymour Robbie, Arnold Laven, Michael O'Herlihy, Allen Reisner, Sutton Roley, Jud Taylor, Bruce Geller, Fernando Lamas.* **WR** *Various, including Richard L Breen Jr, Don Brinkley, Howard Browne, Ric Vollaerts, John Kneubuhl, Robert Pirosh, John Meredyth Lucas, Edward J Lasko, Shirl Hendryx, Robert Lewin, Don M Mankiewicz, James Surtees, Lionel L Siegel.* **MUS** *Lalo Schifrin (theme), Richard Markowitz.*

CAST *Joe Mannix (Mike Connors) Peggy Fair (Gail Fisher) Lou Wickersham (Joseph Campanella) Lt Adam Tobias (Robert Reed) Lt Arthur Malcolm (Ward Wood) Lt George Kramer (Larry Linville) Lt Daniel Ives (Jack Ging).*

Some like 'em tough. Joe Mannix, played with muscular professionalism by Mike Connors, was a private detective of some brains, but more considerable brawn. Initially an operative with the hi-tech Los Angeles agency Intertect, Mannix left after disagreements with boss Lou Wickersham (over Mannix's violent methods) to set up his own solo operation. From season two onwards, Mannix rented a Marlowesque office on the ground floor of his own apartment block at 17 Paseo Verde, with secretarial help from black Peggy Fair (played by Gail Fisher, who won a 1970 Best Supporting Actress Emmy in the role), widowed wife of a former cop buddy. (Part of the series' draw was undoubtedly the thrill of possible miscegenation.) Away from the restraining influence of Wickersham, Korean War vet Mannix was even more routinely involved in fight action and car chases. As his clients found to their relief, there was nothing – absolutely nothing – that scared iron Joe Mannix.

» *Brawn before brains – Mannix starred tough guy Mike Connors as the private detective who was never afraid to use his fists.*

138

Naturally, though, a heart of gold beat beneath the armour-plated exterior. A small child or a pretty girl needed only to ask and Joe Mannix would perform his services for free. His sleuthing efficiency was improved by occasional favours from LAPD Lieutenants Tobias and Kramer (played by Larry Linville, later Frank Burns in M *A *S *H).

Mannix is almost certainly the most violent crime series ever to appear on TV before the Manga animations of the Nineties. Every episode was replete with bloody fisticuffs and deadly gun action. The wonder is not that Mannix was popular – in 1971 it was the top-rated crime show of the season in America – but that it lasted eight years before being cancelled. Those slumming it in the guest cast include Hollywood femme fatale Gloria Grahame ('To the Swiftest, Death', 1971). In 1981 Mike Connors – real name Krekor Ohanion – starred in Today's FBI, the revival of Quinn Martin's >The FBI.

GUEST CAST: Gloria Grahame, Loretta Swit, William Shatner, Tina Louise, Walter Koenig.

MARK SABER

UK 1957–62 135 x 30m bw ITV. Danzigers. US tx 1955–60 ABC/NBC.

PR Edward and Harry Lee Danziger. **WR** Various, including Brian Clemens.
CAST Mark Saber (Donald Gray) Stephanie Ames (Diane Decker) Barney O'Keefe (Michael Balfour) Insp Brady (Patrick Holt) Insp Chester/Insp Parker (Colin Tapley) Bob Page (Robert Arden) Peter Paulson (Neil McCallum/Gordon Tanner) Eddie Wells (Jerry Thorne).

The character of Mark Saber first appeared on the small screen in the US shows Mystery Theatre (1951–2) and Inspector Mark Saber – Homicide Squad (1952–4), where he was played by Tim Conway as a pinstriped British officer seconded to the NYPD. But his most famous incarnation was as a one-armed private detective portrayed by one-armed actor Donald Gray (who had lost an arm during the Second World War), whose movie-idol looks won fans on either side of the Atlantic. Although based in London, Gray's Mark Saber frequently left dowdy native shores for glamorous European locations in pursuit of assorted villains. He was helped in his endeavours by assistants Barney O'Keefe and secretary Stephanie Ames.

Until 1959, that is, when O'Keefe and Ames were unceremoniously dumped, their position as Saber's sidekicks taken by Bob Page, Peter Paulson and ex-thief Eddie Wells. To ring the changes, the show title was changed, confusingly, to Saber of London (the title under which post-1957 episodes of Mark Saber had aired in the US; it initially aired there as The Vise). With the demise of the show, Gray, a former BBC TV announcer, found himself typecast on screen, and worked mainly in radio until his death in 1978.

MARLOWE — PRIVATE EYE

UK 1984 5 x 60m col ITV. A David Wickes Production/London Weekend Television. US tx 1986 HBO.

PR David Wickes. **MUS** John Cameron.

CAST Philip Marlowe (Powers Boothe) Lieutenant Magee (Williams Kearns).

A British-made collection of cases featuring America's most famous fictional detective, Philip Marlowe, here working the mean streets of London as well as LA. The episodes, filmed on location, were: The Pencil/Nevada Gas/Finger Man/The King in Yellow/Smart-Aleck Kill. Powers Boothe's portrayal spiritedly sought to capture Chandler's original concept of Marlowe as a compassionate knight-errant; unfortunately, Humphrey Bogart's world-weary interpretation of Marlowe in the film The Big Sleep had set up audience expectations difficult to shake. Much the same problem had bedevilled an earlier television version of the Marlowe stories, Philip Marlowe (US 1960, 26 x 30m bw), starring the gentlemanly and decidedly underboiled Philip Carey.

Boothe, who had won a 1980 Emmy for Guyana Tragedy: The Story of Jim Jones, took up Marlowe's gumshoes for TV again in 1986 with a further six cases made in Canada, plus a 1989 TVM, Blackmailers Don't Shoot (dr Alan King).

THE MARSHAL

USA 1995 25 x 60m col ABC. Western Sandblast.

CR John Mankiewicz, Daniel Pyne. **EXEC PR** Don Johnson, Aaron Lipstadt, John Mankiewicz, Daniel Pyne. **PR** Gareth Davies, Terry Curtis Fox.

DR Dean Parisot, James Quinn, Tucker Gates, Aaron Lipstadt, Jonathan Sanger. **WR** Various, including Daniel Pyne, John Mankiewicz, Terry Curtis Fox, Jim Leonard, Debra Epstein, Erich Anderson. **MUS** Tim Truman.

CAST Dep US Marshal Winston MacBride (Jeff Fahey) Sally MacBride (Patti Harras) Ollie Mather (Brion James) Felton Lisa (James Persky) Sarah Steenburgen (Elizabeth Russio).

By >The Fall Guy out of >McCloud, with a dash of the Adventures of Briscoe County Jr thrown in for good measure, Film bit-part veteran Jeff Fahey (born in Buffalo, NY, one of thirteen children) played Deputy US Marshal Winston MacBride, the pursuer of fugitives across the US of A, whose self-effacing amiability concealed an implacable dedication to his job. Unusually, MacBride preferred guile to guns and even returned home to a family (wife, plus two daughters) at the end of the case. Sometimes subtly quirky, the crime-action show was executive produced by Don Johnson (>Miami Vice); who turned his hand to direction on the segment 'The Bounty Hunter'.

GUEST CAST: Brian Keith, Pam Grier, Robert Mitchum.

MARTIAL LAW

USA 1998– 19+ x 60m col CBS. CBC/Carlton Cuse/20th Century Fox. UK tx Bravo 1999-
EXEC PR Andre Morgan, Stanley Tong, Calton Cuse. **PR** Jack Clements, Pam Veasey **DR** Various, including Stanley Tong, Deran Sarafian, Greg Beeman, Whitney Ransick **MUS** Mike Post **CAST** Sammo Law (Sammo Hung (aka Sammo Hung Kam-Bo)) Grace Chen ('Pei Pei') (Kelly Hu) Louis Malone (Louis Mandylor) Dana Doyle (Tammy Lauren) Capt Benjamin Winship (Tom Wright) Terrell Parker (Arsenio Hall).

Cop action show, starring Hong Kong movie martial arts legend Sammo Hung. A former pupil of the Peking Opera School (where his classmates included Jackie Chan), Hung played Sammo Law, a Shanghai supercop and combat instructor gone to Los Angeles to search for a missing female undercover colleague, Pei Pei. This temporary assignment turned into a full police exchange, leaving Sammo Law to chop his way through the local criminal fraternity with help of American sidekicks Louis Malone and Dana Doyle, plus the found again Pei Pei. Enemy number one was international supercrook, Lee Hei. The detective element of the hit show was cop TV 'samo, samo', but the martial arts kick-butt

action lit up the small screen, paling into insignificance the featured fight routines of its near genre neighbours >Walker, Texas Ranger; and Kung Fu: The Legend Continues. Aside from Sammo Hung, the featured cast included Louis Mandylor (trained in 'muy thai', Thai Kickboxing) Tammy Lauren (black belt in karate), the vivacious Kelly Hu (brown belt in karate), and former stuntman Tom Wright. The show was overseen by, inter alia, Andre Morgan, who had worked for the Golden Harvest studios making Bruce Lee's famed cycle of martial arts movies, and Stanley Tong, a mainstay Hong Kong action movie director.

But it wasn't all wham bam. Mixed in with the action was a wide vein of comedy, seen not least in the blooper out takes which concluded every episode. And, anyway, the chunky fortysomething Sammo Hung (born 1952, husband of former Miss Hong Kong, Mina Godenzi) was never made to play it purely straight. During the Spring 1999 season talkshow supremo Arsenio Hall was recruited to the cast to play smartmouth LAPD spokesperson Terrell Parker.

Episode list: Shanghai Express/Diamond Fever/Dead Ringer/Funny Money/Cop Out/ Extreme Measuresd/Trackdown/Take Out/How Sammo Got His Groove Back/Bad Seed/Lock-Up/Painted faces/Substitutes/Wildlife/ Breakout/Captive Hearts/Trifecta/Big Trouble/ Nitro Man.

GUEST CAST: Bob Barker, Shanon Lee (Bruce Lee's daughter), James Hong, Marla Gibbs.

MARTIN KANE, PRIVATE EYE

USA 1949–54 120 x 30m bw NBC. An NBC Production.

PR Ed Sutherland, Edward C Kahan, Frank Burns.
MUS Charles Paul.
CAST Martin Kane (William Gargan (1949–51)/ Lloyd Nolan (1951–2)/Lee Tracy (1952–3)/Mark Stevens (1953–4)) Happy McMann (Walter Kinsella) Lt Bender (Fred Hillebrand) Capt Willis (Horace McMahon) Don Morrow (himself) Capt Leonard (Walter Greaza) Capt Burke (Frank Thomas) Sgt Ross (Nicholas Saunder) Lt Grey (King Calder).

The progenitor of TV private eye-dom, *Martin Kane* first appeared on the airwaves played (1949–51) by William Gargan as a debonair wisecracker who worked New York, often in liaison with cop Lieutenant Bender. A frequent hang-out was Happy McMann's tobacco shop – which allowed the hero to happily plug the cigarettes of the show's sponor. By its second season the show had reached number twelve in the Nielsens, although Gargan – a former policeman himself – quit soon after, with the role of Kane passing to Lloyd Nolan, Lee Tracy and Mark Stevens, all of whom projected a tough-guy version of the PI at odds (in the classic hardboiled shamus manner of Dashiell Hammett) with the agency of law enforcement.

In 1954 declining ratings forced *Martin Kane* – the shortened title by which the show had been broadcast since the 1953 season – to hang up his belted raincoat. Later British company Towers of London brought him across the Atlantic to sleuth the streets of the British capital in a series of 39 x 30m bw cases (1958–9, ITV), *Martin Kane, Private Investigator* (syndicated in the USA as *The New Adventures of Martin Kane*). In this incarnation Kane was once again played by William Gargan, with Brian Reece as Superintendent Page, Kane's contact at the Yard.

MATLOCK

USA 1986–95 195 x 60m NBC. A Strathmore Production/Viacom/The Matlock Company. UK tx 1987– ITV.

CR Dean Hargrove. **EXEC PR** Dean Hargrove.
PR Rich Collins. **DR** Various, including Chris Hibler, Russ Mayberry, Nicholas Sgarro, Leo Penn, Burt Brinckerhoff, Bill Duke, Charles Dubin, Michael O'Herlihy, Seymour Robbie. **MUS** Richard DeBenedictis.
CAST Benjamin L Matlock (Andy Griffith) Tyler Hudson (Kene Holliday) Charlene Matlock (Linda Purl) Michelle Thomas (Nancy Stafford) Cassie Phillips (Kari Lizer) Conrad McMaster (Clarence Gilyard Jr) Leanne McIntyre (Brynn Thayer) Asst

DA Julie Marsh (Julie Sommars) Cliff Lewis (Daniel Roebuck) DA Lloyd Burgess (Michael Durrell) Judge Richard Cooksey (Richard Newton).

◈ Andy Griffith as Matlock. *The show was a steal of Perry Mason, but few objected and it enjoyed a long sentence.*

👁 Derivative (of >*Perry Mason*) mystery series about a canny Atlanta defence attorney with a knack of plucking last-minute, trial-winning revelations out of his bag. Andy Griffith played the $250,000-per-case Matlock – with a large jigger of the easy-going Southern charm he had perfected in hick sitcom *The*

Andy Griffith Show (1960–8, CBS) – in a ten-year run, which rarely strayed from formula. But it was pleasant enough for all that. Aiding Matlock in his legal-eagle endeavours (and the detection of the episode's real killer) were daughter Charlene, junior brief Michelle, clerk Cassie and black stock-market whiz-kid Tyler

Hudson, who moonlighted for Matlock & Matlock as a PI.

GUEST CAST: David Ogden Stiers, Scott Bakula, David Carradine, Milton Berle, Robert Culp, David McCallum, William Conrad, Chazz Palminteri, Bill Mumy, Shawn Cassidy, Cameron Mitchell.

MATT HOUSTON

USA 1982–5 68 x 60m col ABC. Matt Houston Company/Largo/Aaron Spelling Productions/ Warner Bros TV. UK tx 1983–7 BBC1.

CR Lawrence Gordon. **EXEC PR** Aaron Spelling. **PR** Michael Fisher. **DR** Various, including Cliff Bole, Hy Averback, Jerome Courtland, Michael Vejar, Peter Crane, Corey Allen, Richard Land,

⊗ Nice work if you can get it. Lee Horsley as playboy PI Matt Houston.

William Crain, Barbara Peters, Charles Picerni.
MUS Dominic Frontiere.
CAST Matt Houston (Lee Horsley) C J Parsons (Pamela Hensley) Lamar Pettybone (Paul Brinegar) Bo (Dennis Fimple) Lt Vince Novelli (John Aprea) Murray Chase (George Wyner) Roy Houston (Buddy Ebsen) Lt Michael Hoyt (Lincoln Kilpatrick) Mama Novelli (Penny Santon) Chris (Cis Rundle) Slim (D D Howard).

Crime caper from the old hit master Aaron Spelling, featuring Matlock 'Matt' Houston, a playboy turned amateur (later pro) peeper. Houston was helped on his new career by beautiful Harvard lawyer friend CJ and obliging police pal Lieutenant Novelli; he was hindered by the lightly comic elements of bickering cowhand employees Bo and Lamar Pettybone (the latter's name was a bit of an in-joke; actor Paul Brinegar had played Wishbone in classic oater series *Rawhide*). In the autumn 1984 season Buddy Ebsen from >*Barnaby Jones* turned up as Houston's retired detective uncle, Roy. The show paraded Mercs and swimming pools full of bathing beauties (Houston's family were oil rich in a Dallas kind of way) but no great suspense sense, despite some extravagantly fantastic touches — such as the case of the killer robot — along the way.
GUEST CAST: Tina Louise, David Hedison, Robert Fuller, George Chakiris.

McCLOUD

USA 1970–7 6 x 60m, 19 x 90m, 21 x 120m col NBC. Universal. UK tx 1972–6 ITV.
CR Herman Miller, Glen A Larson. **EXEC PR** Glen A Larson, Leslie Stevens, Richard Irving. **PR** Michael Gleason, Dean Hargrove, Winrich Kolbe, Ronald Gilbert Satloff, Lou Shaw. **DR** Various, including Glen A Larson, Richard A Colla, Douglas Heyes, Bruce Kessler, Lou Antonio, Nicholas Colasanto, Jerry Paris, Harry Falk, Jimmy Sangster, Russ Mayberry, Hy Averback, Boris Sagal, Noel Black, Jerry Jameson. **WR** Various, including Leslie Stevens, Dean Hargrove, Nicholas Baehr, Sidney Ellis, Robert Hamner, Glen A Larson, Stephen Lord, Michael Gleason, Sy Salkowitz.
MUS Richard Clements.
CAST Deputy Marshal Sam McCloud (Dennis Weaver) Police Chief Peter B Clifford (J D Cannon) Sergeant Joe Broadhurst (Terry Carter) Chris Coughlin (Diana Muldaur) Sergeant Maggie Clinger (Sharon Gless) Sgt Grover (Ken Lynch).

The exploits of a cowboy lawman in the big city, loosely based on the 1968 Clint Eastwood feature *Coogan's Bluff*. Dennis Weaver played Sam McCloud, a New Mexican in New York ostensibly studying the ways and methods of the cops of the 27th Precinct. In fact, Deputy

» *There you go. Dennis Weaver played cowboy-cop McCloud, a spin-off from the 1968 Clint Eastwood movie* Coogan's Bluff.

Marshal McCloud studiously ignored the local modus operandi and treated Manhattan like the Wild West, wore a stetson and cowboy boots, and talked in a homily-laden, down-home-on-the-range manner. Occasionally, he even rode his horse.

McCloud was not a cop show which was very serious about itself; indeed, it usually had its tongue in both cheeks. It also worked the idea of a western-set-in-a-city effortlessly well, with New York's skyscrapers doing a good job as substitute canyons. And a good number of McCloud's cases were uncannily pure frontier: cattle rustling at the meat market, banks robbed by villains in Old West outfits and the like. Leslie Stevens, one of the series' main producers, had a long history in TV westerns (including the creation of *Stoney Burke*), as did Dennis Weaver himself, one-time Deputy Chester from *Gunsmoke*.

The other cast members were J D Cannon as long-suffering Chief Peter B Clifford, Terry Carter as black Sergeant Joe Broadhurst (dragged into constant trouble by McCloud), and Diana Muldaur as McCloud's love interest, Chris Coughlin. Sharon Gless got in some early practice for >*Cagney and Lacey* as Sergeant Maggie Clinger.

The series originated as part of American NBC's Four-in-One series, premiering as the 1969 TVM *McCloud: Who Killed Miss USA?* (dr Richard A Colla), before moving to the Mystery Movie slot in 1971, where it rotated with >*Columbo* and >*McMillan and Wife*. A 1989 reunion TVM, *The Return of Sam McCloud*, was directed by Alan J Levi from Michael Sloan's script.

There you go.

GUEST CAST: John Carradine, Teri Garr, Louis Gossett Jr, John Denver, Cameron Mitchell, Jaclyn Smith, Shelley Winters.

McMILLAN AND WIFE

USA 1971–7 1 x 120m, 39 x 90m NBC. Talent Associates – Norton Simon Inc/Universal TV. UK tx 1972–9 ITV.

CR *Leonard B Stern.* **EXEC PR** *Leonard B Stern.* **PR** *Jon Epstein, Paul Mason, Ted Rich.* **DR** *Various, including Edward M Abroms, Lou Antonio, John Astin, Hy Averback, Harry Falk, Mel Ferber, Leonard J Horn, Lee H Katzin, Alf Kjellin, Barry Shear, James Sheldon, E W Swackhamer, Roy Winston.* **WR** *Various, including Howard Berk, Steven Bochco, Oliver Hailer, Robert Lewin, Leonard B Stern, Don M Mankiewicz.*

CAST *Police Commissioner Stewart 'Mac' McMillan (Rock Hudson) Sally McMillan (Susan Saint James) Sgt Charles Enright (John Schuck) Mildred (Nancy Walker) Agatha (Martha Raye) Sgt Steve DiMaggio (Richard Gilland) Police Chief Paulsen (Bill Quinn) Maggie (Gloria Stroock) Sykes (John Astin) Sgt DiMaggio (Richard Gilliland).*

Like >*Hart to Hart, McMillan and Wife* was a TV crime show which owed much to the Nick and Nora Charles *Thin Man* films of the Thirties and Forties. Hollywood star Rock Hudson,

McMillan and Wife *was the first small screen series for Hollywood legend Rock Hudson.*

in his first small-screen series, played Stewart 'Mac' McMillan, debonair San Francisco Police Chief, whose sexy-but-scatty wife Sally (Susan Saint James) had an uncanny knack of finding corpses in the libraries of the glitzy mansions to which they were invited for cocktails every weekend. Sally usually also found herself

147

kidnapped or in some form of life-threatening danger. The mysteries themselves owed much to the traditional or 'cosy' English whodunnit, but the series' most entertaining quality was the frolicsome relationship between Sally and Mac.

In the USA, *McMillan and Wife* rotated as part of NBC's *Mystery Movie* slot, reaching its highest US Nielsen position, number five, in 1972–3. The show changed format in 1976 when Saint James left over a contract dispute. Her character was killed off in a plane crash, leaving Hudson to detect alone as plain McMillan. Nancy Walker, who did scene-stealing stuff as the McMillans' acid housekeeper, also left at the same time. The magic was gone, and the new version lasted only one season.

John Astin, better known as Gomez from *The Addams Family*, shared the directing duties as well as playing the character Sykes.

GUEST CAST: Kim Basinger, Martin E Brooks (as Deputy DA Chapman), Jackie Coogan, Dabney Coleman, Alan Hale Jr.

MIAMI VICE

USA 1984–9 108 x 60m, 3 x 120m col NBC. A Universal Television Production. UK tx 1985–90 BBC.

CR Anthony Yerkovich, Michael Mann.
EXEC PR Michael Mann, Anthony Yerkovich.
PR Richard Brams, John Nicollella. **DR** Various, including Michael Mann, David Soul, Don Johnson, Lee Katzin, Virgil W Vogel, Paul Michael Glaser, Michael O'Herlihy, Edward James Olmos, Paul Krasny, David Anspaugh, Gabrielle Beaumont, Georg Stanford Brown, Chip Chalmers, Richard A Colla, Alan J Levi, Abel Ferrara, James A Contner, Aaron Lipstadt, Russ Mayberry, John Llewlellyn Moxey, John Wharmby, Alan Myerson, Bil Duke, Richard Compton, Eugene Corr, Colin Bucksey. **WR** Various, including Miguel Pinero. **MUS** Jan Hammer (theme), Rick Conrad, Tim Truman.

CAST Det James 'Sonny' Crockett (Don Johnson) Det Ricardo Tubbs (Philip Michael Thomas) Lt Martin Castillo (Edward James Olmos) Det Gina Navarro Calabrese (Saundra Santiago) Det Trudy Joplin (Olivia Brown) Det Stan Switek (Michael Talbott) Det Larry Zito (John Diehl) Izzy Moreno (Martin Ferrero) Caitlin Davies (Sheena Easton) Caroline Crockett (Belinda Montgomery) Manolo (Tony Azito) Noogie Lamont (Charlie Barnett). **VIDEO** CIC.

Miami Vice was conceived in response to a single two-word memo sent by NBC boss Brandon Tartijoff to creators Yerkovich and Mann. It read: 'MTV Cops'. The resulting series hit the instruction on target: hyper-real colour, pop video editing, Art Deco glitz backdrop, cool

» *Dressed to kill. Philip Michael Thomas (left) and Don Johnson in the glitzy* Miami Vice.

cops, and a throbbing rock soundtrack.

Launching two relative unknowns in starring roles, *Miami Vice* featured a pair of male drug squad cops patrolling the glamorous but sleazy Florida city. Sonny Crockett (Don Johnson, later >*Nash Bridges*), an ex-football star, was the rough-edged, designer-stubbled, bare-ankled vice cop who lived alone (after a failed marriage) save for pet alligator Elvis on a boat called St Vitus Dance; his partner Ricardo Tubbs (Philip Michael Thomas) had come to Miami from New York to search out the Colombian drug dealer who had killed his brother, and stayed. The audience knew little else about the duo save their jobs, but that didn't matter. The inter-racial buddy combo bonded and went undercover on the glamorous beaches and in the seedy back alleys of Miami, tracking pimps, drug-rackets and hookers among the seamy ethnic mix. From then on it was more form than content, but there were few complaints.

Scenes were colour co-ordinated – lime green and hot pink neon, bright white suits for sunshine and sand, pastels for daytime interiors, deep blues and purples for skylines at night. Clothes were from Uomi and Gianni Versace. These were the state-of-the-art production values of the rock video, with hi-tech and rapid edits. If the plots sometimes wore thin, the thickly woven music propelled the viewer on to the next piece of action with a soundtrack that was either specially commissioned or brought in from established stars

to fit the action – among them were tracks by Tina Turner, Lionel Ritchie, the Pointer Sisters and the Rolling Stones. With the top cops driving through the neon cityscape in Crockett's Ferrari Spider (later Testarossa) this was TV as a ride in a fast car with stereo system blaring.

The hipster series was a smash hit, and celebrities not normally seen in TV queued for cameo and guest roles. G Gordon Liddy, the burglar of Watergate infamy, appeared as a real estate agent. Rock gods Little Richard, Leonard Cohen, Iggy Pop and Frank Zappa provided cameos, while British stars making an appearance included Sheena Easton as singer Caitlin, who briefly became Mrs Crockett until she was gunned down by scriptwriters fearful that she would disturb the boys' relationship. As with much of the series, this black/white friendship was more fashion than social statement and there was no subversion involved – Crockett was always in control, leader of the two-man team. That said, at least a black man was in a lead role in a major weekly series, and former *Hair!* star Thomas emerged as TV's first black male sex symbol.

But the glossy accessories and props took their toll on budgets. To attain the lush look Michael Mann was spending $1.2 million per episode. He was amply rewarded with a top ten hit in the first two seasons and fifteen Emmy nominations in the series' first year. But then NBC programmed it against >*Dallas*, and Miami Vice proved no match for the other high-life series. By its fifth and final season it had fallen to 53rd place and the series was cancelled.

Executive producer Michael Mann meanwhile took his distinctive style on to >*Crime Story* before heading to the big screen with such flics as *Manhunter* (1986), a tense thriller that, long before *Silence of the Lambs*, had Dr Hannibal Lecter as its hero, *Last of the Mohicans* (1992) and *Heat* (1995).

GUEST CAST: Bruce Willis ('No Exit', 1984), Joan Chen, Keye Luke, Iggy Pop, Little Richard, Sheena Easton, John Turturro, Dennis Farina, John Santucci, Pam Grier (as Valerie Gordon), Eartha Kitt, Little Richard, Frankie Valli, Peter Sellars, Melanie Griffiths, Julia Roberts, Liam Neeson, Brad Dourif, Wesley Snipes, Helena Bonham Carter, G Gordon Liddy ('Phil the Shill', 1985), Jan Hammer, Leonard Cohen, Bianca Jagger, Frank Zappa, Giancarlo Esposito.

MICKEY SPILLANE'S MIKE HAMMER

USA 1984–7 1 x 120m, 46 x 60m col CBS. Columbia Pictures TV. UK tx 1984–6 ITV.
EXEC PR Jay Bernstein. **PR** Lew Gallo. **DR** Various, including John Nicolela, Bernard Kowalski, Paul Krasny, Michael Preece, James Frawley, Leo Penn, Stacy Keach. **MUS** Earle Hagen.
CAST Mike Hammer (Stacy Keach) Velda (Lindsay Bloom) Capt Pat Chambers (Don Stroud) Ozzie

the Answer (Danny Goldman) Asst DA Lawrence D Barrington (Kent Williams) Jenny the Bartender (Lee Benton) Moochie (Ben Powers) Ritchie (Eddie Barth) Hennessey (Edie Fagan) The Face (Donna Denton).

Hammer by name, Hammer by nature. The cases of a New York private dick, so tough a guy he never had to remove the cigarette from his mouth while pulverising the villain to pulp.

Comic-strip-like trash, based on Spillane's lurid novels, though updated to the 1980s. Not for the weak stomached; if Hammer wasn't pounding the faces of the bad guys he was giving them lead injections from his pistol, 'Betsy'. Voluptuous secretary Velda headed the parade of smoke-voiced babes whose 'hips waved a happy hello' (to borrow Spillane's best line) through every episode. On the detecting job, the wisecracking Hammer – a Vietnam vet in this new scenario – received assistance from snitch Ozzie and NYPD contact, Captain Pat Chambers.

Production of the show was halted, somewhat ignominiously for a detective caper, when actor Stacy Keach (brother of director James, Jane Seymour's spouse) was imprisoned in Britain's Reading Gaol for drugs offences.

Keach wasn't the first actor to portray Hammer on TV. That honour went to Darren McGavin (*Kolchak: The Night Stalker*) in Revue's series for syndication in the USA (1957–60, 78 x 30m bw).

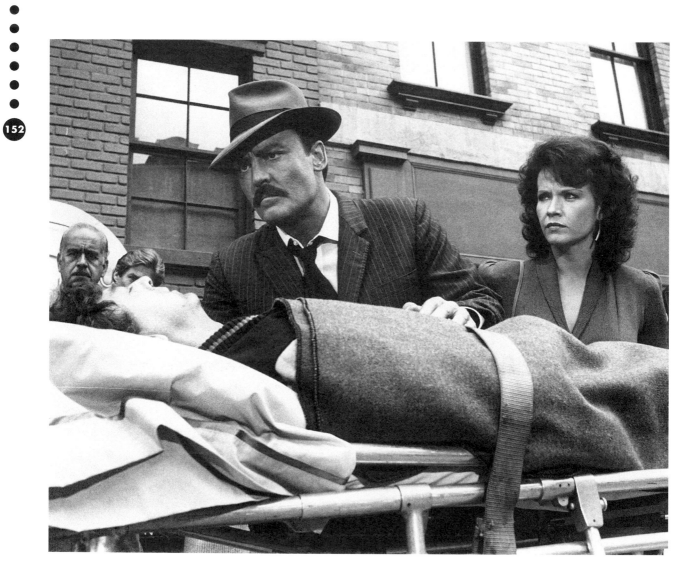

⊗ *Stacy Keach in* Mickey Spillane's Mike Hammer; *the actor was jailed mid production for drugs offences.*

GUEST CAST: Barbara Bain, Sharon Stone, Ray Liotta, Emma Samms, Delta Burke, Barbara Bosson.

MIDNIGHT CALLER

USA 1988–91 60 x 60m col NBC. December 3rd/Lorimar. UK tx 1989–91 BBC1.

CR *Richard Diello.* **EXEC PR** *Robert Singer.* **PR** *John F Perry.* **DR** *Various, including Thomas Carter, Peter Levin, Mimi Leder, Eric Laneuville, Rob Bowman, Fred Gerber, James Quinn.* **WR** *Various,* including Richard Diello, Stephen Zito, David Israel, Robert Singer, Randall Zisk, John Schulian, Chris Carter. **MUS** Brad Fiedel (theme), Peter D Kaye.

CAST Jack Killian (Gary Cole) Devon King (Wendy Kilbourne) Billy Po (Dennis Dun) Lt Carl Zymack (Arthur Taxier) Deacon Bridges (Mykel T Williamson) J J Killian (Jack's father) (Peter Boyle) Nicolette 'Nicky' Molloy (Lisa Eilbacher).

'This is your host Jack Killian on KJCM 98.3 FM. Goodnight, America, wherever you are ...'

Jack Killian was a San Francisco cop who accidentally killed his partner during a shoot-out. Devastated and morose, Killian took to the bottle – until the wealthy Devon King encouraged him to take a job with her KJCM radio station as 'The Nighthawk', host of a night-time call-in show. Aside from listening to the problems of his myriad callers, humanitarian Killian became personally involved in their plight, taking to the streets himself to investigate every kind of crime (up to, and including, murder) of which they informed him. Not infrequently, the cases touched on heavy social issues, such as child abuse and AIDS. Lieutenant Zymack was Killian's still friendly ex-boss in the SFPD, while Billy Po was his sidekick at the radio station. When King became pregnant she sold KJCM, and Nicky Molly took over as station boss.

Moody TV, it was bewitchingly evocative both of late-night radio and the strange world of the sleepless nocturnal city. Actor Gary Cole's later CV also included another quality crime series, >American Gothic. Among the screenwriters was Chris Carter, later to devise The X-Files and >Millennium.

GUEST CAST: Richard Bradford, Roger Daltrey, G Gordon Liddy.

MILLENNIUM
USA 1996– 59 x 50m col FTV. Ten Thirteen Productions/20th Century Fox. UK tx 1996– Sky 1.
CR Chris Carter. **EXEC PR** Chris Carter, Glen Morgan, James Wong. **PR** Thomas J Wright, Chris Johannessen. **DR** Various, including Cliff Bole, Thomas J Wright, David Nutter, Winrich Kolbe, Allen Coulter, Jim Charleston, Dwight Little, Randall Zisk, Ron Pridy, Peter Markle, John Peter Kousakis. **WR** Various, including Chris Carter, Chris Johannessen, Frank Spotnitz, Ted Mann, Glen Morgan, James Wong, Darin Morgan.
MUS Mark Snow.
CAST Frank Black (Lance Henriksen) Catherine Black (Megan Gallagher) Jordan Black (Brittanny Tiplady) Lara Means (Kirsten Cloke) Det Bob Geibelhouse (Stephen J Lang) Peter Watts (Terry O'Quinn) Lt Bob Bletcher (Bill Smitrovich) Special Agent Emma Hollis (Klea Scott) Asst DA Andy McClaren (Stephen E Miller).

'This Is Who We Are ...'

Detective drama from *The X-Files* creator Chris Carter. Virtually tailor-written for mesmerising, craggy-faced actor Lance Henriksen (*Aliens, Omen II, Terminator*), it featured him as an ex-FBI agent who joined an undercover law enforcement project in Seattle, called The Millennium Group, dedicated to battling serial killers and psycho-criminals as the new millennium approached. The twist was that Henriksen's Frank Black had the psychic ability to enter his quarry's mind ('I put myself in his head. I become the horror.') Black's wife, meanwhile, was the subject of a sicko's looming intentions – and was exited, a tragedy for which Black blamed the Group, which, it had transpired, was a less than clear-cut Good Thing. Also prominent in the cast were Black's daughter Jordan (another psychic), and

Lifeless in Seattle – Frank Black examines another cadaver in creeper 'tec series Millennium.

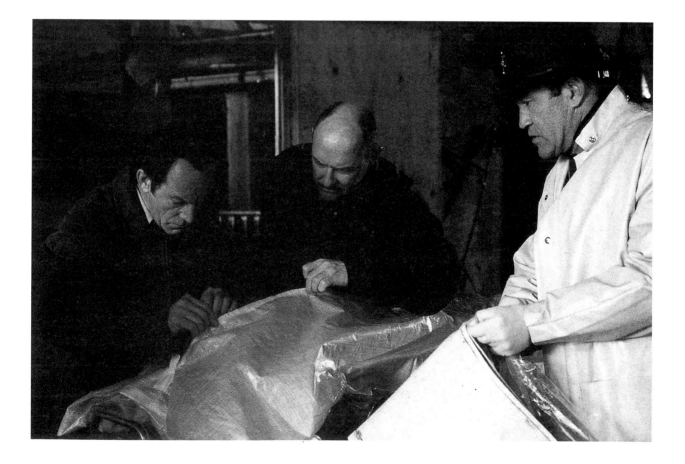

Black's fellow ghoul-chasers, Peter Watts and forensic scientist Lara Means. Although it trod the same dark and foreboding ground as >*Twin Peaks* and the movie *Seven*, it did so with semi-decent shock value and the occasional harrowing scene. The turn-off was the pseudo mind-reading babble, sounding like the Society of Psychics' weekly meet. The show won the 1997 People's Choice Award for Best New Drama.

SHOW TRIVIA: Although Carter wanted Henriksen for the part of Black, Fox wanted William Hurt – but Hurt declined because he would not do TV / Some of the serial killer characters were based on real-life psychos, Henry Dieon in 'Paper Dove' being a composite of Ed Kemper and Herbert Mullins / Darrin McGavin, who guest starred as Black's father, played the lead in the Sixties fright-night classic, *Kolchak: The Night Stalker*, the show which inspired *The X-Files*.

GUEST CAST: Sean Six, C C H Pounder, Brad Dourif, Darrin McGavin, Stefan Arngrim, Doug Hutchinson (as the Polaroid man), Kim Patten.

MISS MARPLE

UK 1984–92 16 x 50m, 1 x 115m, 3 x 110m, 1 x 100m col BBC1. BBC TV/Arts and Entertainment Network/Network 7. US tx WGBH Boston 1986–92

PR Guy Slater, George Gallacio. **DR** Silvio Narizzano, Roy Boulting, David Giles, Guy Slater, Julian Amyes, John Davies, Mary

 Joan Hickson as Miss Marple, *the Queen of English TV whodunnitry. Hickson died in 1998 aged 92.*

McMurrary, David Tucker, Martyn Friend, Christopher Petit, Norman Stone. **WR** T R Bowen, Julia Jones, Alan Plater, Ken Taylor, Jill Hyem. **MUS** Ken Howard, Alain Blaikey. **CAST** Miss Jane Marple (Joan Hickson) Chief Inspector Slack (David Horowitz).

Agatha Christie's busybody sleuth from quaint St Mary Mead – first met in the 1930 novel, *Murder at the Vicarage* – was interpreted on the screen by numerous fine thespians (including Margaret Rutherford) before Joan Hickson assumed the role in this occasional joint UK/US/Australian series. The pieces were consummately crafted (Ray Boulting and Chris Petit were among the directors), while Hickson's tea-sipping, slighted hunched gentility was Marple as written by Christie. Indeed, Christie had once watched Hickson act (as Miss Pryce) in her 1946 play *Appointment with Death*, causing her to write to the actress: 'I hope you will play my dear Miss Marple.' She did, definitively so.

For the production, Nether Wallop in Hampshire doubled as 1930s St Mary Mead. There were twelve TV cases (ranging from feature-length one-parters to three-parters of 50 minutes) before Hickson OBE retired. She died in 1998, aged 92.

The cases were: *The Body in the Library/The Moving Finger/A Murder is Announced/A Pocketful of Rye/Murder at the Vicarage/Sleeping Murder/At Bertram's Hotel/Nemesis/4.50 from Paddington/A Caribbean Mystery/They Do It with Mirrors/The Mirror Crack'd from Side to Side.*

GUEST CAST: Timothy West, Peter Davison, Paul Eddington, George Baker, Maurice Denham, Donald Pleasence, Joss Ackland, Barry Newman.

THE MOD SQUAD

USA 1968–73 123 x 60m col ABC. An Aaron Spelling Production for ABC. UK tx 1970–2 ITV. **CR** Buddy Raskin. **EXEC PR** Aaron Spelling, Danny Thomas. **PR** Tony Barrett, Harve Bennett, Sandor Storm. **DR** Various, including George McCowan. **WR** Various, including Tony Barrett. **MUS** Earle Hagen.

CAST Pete Cochran (Michael Cole) Julie Barnes (Peggy Lipton) Linc Hayes (Clarence Williams III) Capt Adam Greer (Tige Andrews).

Keep the faith, baby. Along with >*Miami Vice* arguably the detective show most clearly the product of its age. In the case of *The Mod Squad*, the groovy end of the Sixties/ beginning of the Seventies.

Whilst on probation wealthy Beverly Hills drop-out white teen Pete (crime: stealing a car), black Afro-headed teen Linc (arrested during the LA Watts riots) and blonde teen Julie (a runaway from her San Francisco prostitute mother) are approached by Captain Greer of the LAPD and recruited as undercover cops to go into the youth counter-culture and apprehend the bad guys – the adults who prey on the credulous young.

Utterly contrived, but undeniably hip (conveniently forgetting, for a moment, that the

❯❯ *Hey man, that's cool. The Mod Squad were hippie cops – and carried beads not guns.*

show was a prime example of the Sixties youth movement being co-opted by The Establishment). Pete, Linc and Julie might have been acting for 'The Man' but, hey, they wore beads, said flowery things like 'Baby', and didn't carry guns. Sometimes the cast even managed to act convincingly, with Peggy Lipton (later to crop up as Norma, the manageress of the diner in >*Twin Peaks*) winning a 1971 Best Actress Golden Globe. And creator Buddy Raskin himself had once been a police detective in a special youth squad which had infiltrated the Fifties jazz-reefer scene. Even the trademark episode ending – with the camera, suspended on a crane, panning away from the three until they were just out of focus, and then freezing – was cool.

They don't make 'em like that any more.

Well they do, actually, but shouldn't. A 1979 reunion movie, *Return of the Mod Squad* (120m), viewed badly because, removed from the social context of the flower-power years, it made little sense and for much embarrassment. A 1999 movie (with just Clarence Williams III appearing from the original cast) was destined to fare no better.

The episodes were: *The Teeth of the Barracuda/Bad Man on Campus/My, What a Pretty Bus/When Smitty Comes Marching Home/ You Can't Tell the Players Without a Programme/ A Time to Love, A Time to Cry/Find Tara Chapman/The Price of Terror/A Quiet Weekend in the Country/Love/Twinkle, Twinkle, Little Starlet/The Guru/The Sunday Drivers/Hello Mother, My Name is Julie/Flight Five Doesn't Answer/Shell Game/Fear is the Bucking Horse/ A Hint of Darkness, A Hint of Light/The Uptight Town/A Reign of Guns/A Run for the Money/ Child of Sorrow, Child of Light/Keep the Faith, Baby/Captain Greer, Call Surgery/Peace Now – Arly Blau/A Seat by the Window/The Girl in Chair Nine/My Name is Manolete/An Eye for an Eye/Ride the Man Down/To Linc with Love/ Lisa/Confrontation!/Willie Poor Boy/The Death of Bill Hannachek/A Place to Run, a Heart to Hide In/The Healer/In This Corner, Sol Albert/ Never Give the Fuzz an Even Break/The Debt/ Sweet Child of Terror/The King of Empty Cups/ A Town Called Sincere/The Exile/Survival House/ Mother of Sorrow/The Deadly Sin/A Time for Remembering/Return to Darkness, Return to Light/ Call Back Yesterday/Should Auld Acquaintance Be Forgot/Long Road Home/See the Eagles Dying/Who Are the Keepers, Who Are the Inmates/'A' is for Annie/The Song of Willie/ Search and Destroy/Just Ring the Bell Once/ Welcome to the Human Race, Levi Frazee/A Far Away Place So Near/A Time of Hyacinths/The Judas Trap/Fever/Is There Anyone Left?/A Short Course in War/Kicks Incorporated/A Bummer for RJ/The Hot, Hot Car/Suffer, Little Children/Is That Justice?, No, It's Law/A Double for Danger/ Welcome to Our City/The Comeback/We*

Spy/The Price of Love/The Sentinels/Cricket/ Home is the Streets/Survival/Colour of Laughter, Colour of Tears/The Medicine Men/The Sands of Anger/The Poisoned Mind/Exit the Closer/ Whatever Happened to Linc Hayes?/And a Little Child Shall Bleed Them/The Loser/Death of a Nobody/Feet of Clay/I Am My Brother's Keeper/Deal with the Devil/Kill Gently, Sweet Jessie/Shockwave/No More Oak Leaves for Ernie/The Cave/The Wild Weekend/The Tangled Web/Outside Position/Bid George/The Connection I/The Connection II/The Thunder Makers/Yesterday's Ashes/A Gift for Jenny/Taps, Play It Louder/Eyes of the Beholder/Good Times Are Just Memories/Corbey/Can You Hear Me Out There?/ Another Final Game/Crime Club/ The Twain/Belinda/End of Little Miss Bubble Gum/Kristie/Sanctuary/Run, Lincoln, Run/Don't Kill My Child/Death in High Places/Put Out the Welcome Mat for Death/Scion of Death/The Night Holds Terror/Cry Uncle/And Once for My Baby.

GUEST CAST: David Cassidy, Martin Sheen, Margot Kidder, Sammy Davis Jr, Tyne Daly, Cameron Mitchell, Andy Griffith, Bruce Foxworth, Bobby Sherman, Diana Muldaur, Meg Foster, Richard Dreyfuss, Marion Ross, Noam Pitlik.

MOONLIGHTING

USA 1985–9 1 x 120m, 66 x 60m col ABC.
Picturemaker Productions. UK tx 1986–9 BBC2.
CR *Glenn Gordon Caron.* **EXEC PR** *Glenn Gordon Caron.* **PR** *Jay Daniel.* **DR** *Various, including Allan Arkush, Sam Weisman, Christian I. Nyby II, Kevin Connor, Burt Brinckerhoff, Peter Werner, Will Mackenzie, Dennis Dugan, Paul Krasny, Paul Lynch.* **WR** *Various, including Glenn Gordon Caron.* **MUS** *Lee Holdridge and Al Jarreau (theme), sung by Al Jarreau.*
CAST *Maddie Hayes (Cybill Shepherd) David Addison (Bruce Willis) Agnes Dipesto (Allyce Beasley) Herbert Viola (Curtis Armstrong) Virginia Hayes (Eva Marie Saint) Alex Hayes (Robert Webber) MacGilicuddy (Jack Blessing).*
VIDEO *V-COL/ABC.*

The epitome of post-modern TV, *Moonlighting* starred two beautiful people and tricksy self-referential technique. For all its crime plots and action, it ladled on romantic comedy with one old-fashioned and enduring question: 'Will they or won't they?'

This glamorous series – which rescued Cybill Shepherd's flagging career and shot Bruce Willis to Hollywood stardom – was one of ABC's few major hits in the mid Eighties, replete with in-jokes as well as detective elements. The plot revolved around cool one-time international model Maddie Hayes who, after being swindled by embezzlers,

decides to turn the small detective agency among her assets from tax-dodge to profit-making concern. Along with the newly named Blue Moon Detective Agency she inherits brash, lascivious, wisecracking private eye David Addison, whom she promotes to partner. Together they became LA's unlikeliest detective team and their love–hate relationship was the stuff of the show. Sexual chemistry sparked on screen. He lusted and wolf-whistled after her, but elegant Maddie resisted –

⊗ Moonlighting *was a show from the same stable as* Remington Steele. *Actor Bruce Willis (pictured) beat 3000 other hopefuls to the part of David.*

until the end of the second season, that is, when the producers and the two characters gave in to the inevitable with a bed scene generating massive advance publicity and correspondingly huge ratings. Receptionist Miss Dipesto also added her own daffy, special charm to the proceedings.

There was considerable cross-over between the stars and their on-screen characters (although if Shepherd's off-screen statements were to be believed, this did not stretch to the sexual chemistry). Cybill Shepherd was indeed an ex-model (in 1968 she was Model of the Year) and came to *Moonlighting* as one-time star of feature film *The Last Picture Show* (1971) and NBC's Texan rancher series *The Yellow Rose* (1983–4). Willis had previously landed only one role as a crook in *Miami Vice* and turned up among 3,000 hopefuls to read for the part of David Addison with a punk haircut, khaki army trousers and three earrings. He was the last to read and he got the part.

The show's aficionados loved it for its quirkiness and knowing games with TV conventions. One episode, for example, dealing with an unsolved Forties mystery, was shot in black-and-white. Another, 'Atomic Shakespeare', was written in iambic pentameters. Most featured one style-trick or another – asides to camera, shows within a show or comments on the show itself before the story began. The series pleased male and female audiences alike, and won the ratings battle with the male-appeal show *Riptide* scheduled against it by NBC.

Inspired by the 1940 film *His Girl Friday*, *Moonlighting* was created by Glenn Gordon Caron (previous credits as producer-writer included *Breaking Away*, >*Remington Steele* and *Taxi*) and was produced by his own company, Picturemaker Productions. Its much publicised production and personality problems – there was a three-way running battle between Shepherd, Willis and Caron that forced its creator off the show – only added a frisson for its devoted audience. Episodes often ran over budget and over time and repeats were frequent during the regular season. *Moonlighting* was hastily cancelled in 1989. This proved no hardship to Bruce Willis, however, whose future was secure in movie stardom with lead roles in such flicks as the *Die Hard* cycle. Shepherd, meanwhile, went missing off the radar until she did a Roseanne Barr and emerged in a sitcom based around herself, *Cybill* (1995–8).

The episodes were: *Moonlighting/Gunfight at the So-So Corral/Read the Mind – See the Movie/The Next Murder You Hear/Next Stop Murder/The Murder's in the Mail/Brother, Can You Spare a Blonde?/The Lady in the Iron Mask/Money Talks – Money Walks/The Dream Sequence Always Rings/My Fair David/Knowing Her/Somewhere Under the Rainbow/Portrait of Maddie/Atlas Belched/Twas the Episode Before Christmas/The Bride of Tupperman/North by North Dipesto/In God We Strongly Suspect/Every Daughter's Father/Witness for the Execution/Sleep Talkin' Guy/Funeral for a Door Nail/Camille/The Son Also Rises/The Man Who Cried Wife/Symphony in Knocked Flat/All*

162

Creatures Great ... and Not/Big Bill on Mulberry Street/Atomic Shakespeare/It's a Wonderful Job/The Straight Poop/Poltergeist II – Diepesto Nothing/Blonde on Blonde/Sam & Dave/It's Maddie's Turn to Cry/I am Curious/To Heiress Human/A Trip to the Moon/Come Back, Little Shiksa/A Tale in Two Cities/Cool Hand Dave I/Cool Hand Dave II/Father Knows Last/Los Dos Dipesto/Fetal Attraction/Tracks of My Tears/ Eek! A Spouse/Maddie Hayes Got Married/ Here's Living With You, Kid/And the Flesh was Made Word/Womb with a View/Between a Yuk and a Hard Place/The Color of Maddie/Plastic Fantastic Lovers/Shirts and Skins/Take My Wife, For Example/I See England, I See France/Those Lips, Those Lies/Perfecto/When Girls Collide/In 'n Outlaws/Eine Kleine Nacht Murder/Lunar Eclipse.

GUEST CAST: Orson Welles, Peter Bogdanovich, Pat Boone, Ray Charles, Whoopi Goldberg, John Goodman, Brad Dourif, Richard Belzer, Barbara Bain, Pierce Brosnan.

M SQUAD

USA 1957–60 115 x 30m bw NBC. Latimer Productions/Revue Studios/Universal TV UK tx 1959–60 ITV.

EXEC PR Richard Lewis. **PR** John Larkin. **DR** Various, including Robert Altman, John Brahm, Bernard Girard, Sidney Lanfield, David Butler, Allen H Miner, Don Weis, Don Taylor, Don Medford, Robert Ellis Miller. **WR** Various, including Jack Laird. **MUS** Count Basie ('Theme from M Squad'), John Williams, Stanley Wilson.
CAST Lt Frank Ballinger (Lee Marvin) Capt Grey (Paul Newlan).

There have been hundreds of crime shows set in the naked city of Chicago, and this Fifties cop series was one of them. Lee Marvin starred as Lieutenant Frank Ballinger, the top detective in the élite plainclothes homicide team that was 'M Squad', the role creating at one punch Marvin's screen persona as a heavy. The show achieved popularity, largely on the free ride of Marvin's magnetism and some muscular, thick-ear action, but had little else to distinguish it and is always destined to be viewed as the warm-up for Quinn Martin's similar, but superior, >The Untouchables. The jazz theme from season two onwards was composed by Count Basie, while tyro helmsman Robert Altman was among those on the directors' roster.

GUEST CAST: Robert Fuller, DeForest Kelley.

MURDER ONE

USA 1995-7 31 x 60m col ABC. Steven Bochco Productions/20th Century Fox. UK tx 1996-7 Sky Movies, BBC2.
CR Steven Bochco, Charles H Eglee, Channing Gibson. **EXEC PR** Steven Bochco, Charles H Eglee, Michael Fresco. **PR** Various, including Joe

Ann Fogle, Ann Donahue, Geoffrey Neigher, Marc Buckland. **DR** *Various, including Charles Haid, Michael Fresco, Nancy Savoca, Jim Charleston, Adam Nimoy, Elodie Keene.* **WR** *Various, including Charles H Eglee, Steven Bochco, Geoffrey Neigher, Charles D Holland, Gay Walch, Channing Gibson, David Milch, Doug Palau.* **MUS** *Mike Post.*
CAST *Theodore Hoffman (Daniel Benzali) Justine*

Appleton (Mary McCormack) Chris Docknovich (Michael Hayden) Lisa Gillespie (Grace Phillips) Arnold Spivak (J C MacKenzie) Richard Cross (Stanley Tucci) Det Arthur Polson (Dylan Baker) Lila Marquette (Vanessa Williams) Louis Heinsbergen (John Fleck) David Blaylock (Kevin Tighe) Miriam Grasso (Barbara Bosson) Annie Hoffman (Patricia Clarkson) Neil Avedon (Jason Gedrick) Aaron Mosley (DB Woodside) Donald Cleary (Jim Beaver) Roger Garfield (Gregory Itzin) Francesca Cross (Donna Murphy).

⊗ Dylan Baker, Barbara Bosson and Grace Phillips make the case in Murder One.

>From multiple-Emmy winner Steven Bochco (>*Hill Street Blues, LA Law,* >*NYPD Blue*), the first serialised law drama to follow a single case for an entire season. Hot on the heels of two real-life, long-running trials – the Menendez brothers and OJ Simpson – the show took a gamble on art imitating life, hoping to engross a newly law-literate audience. Lest following one case for six months proved arduous for viewers, however, Bochco cannily sugared the pill with a heady mix of Hollywood, drugs, prostitution, and under-age sex: 'You've got your naked fifteen-year-old victim, you've got your presence of drugs, your rumours of sexual depravity and your gorgeous older sister and former alleged prostitute …' as character Chris Docknovich succinctly stated in episode one. And from grainy whip-pan *vérité* to mannered freeze-frame and slow motion the camerawork helped push up the tension.

Intricately exploring every aspect of the high-profile murder, *Murder One* boasted a tough team of largely unknown actors led by the series' star – shaven headed Daniel Benzali as celebrity attorney Theodore 'Teddy' Hoffman. A theatrical performer citing Laurence Olivier as his hero, the Brazilian-born Benzali honed his craft on the British stage (Trevor Nunn's Royal Shakespeare Company, Hal Prince's *Evita*, Andrew Lloyd Webber's *Sunset Boulevard*). Once in Hollywood, a recurring role in *LA Law* was followed by a performance as a mob attorney in *NYPD Blue*

powerful enough to land him the plum role in *Murder One*. Benzali's other past screen credits included a villainous appearance in the 1985 James Bond film *A View to a Kill,* and it was the blend of avenging angel and Machiavellian villain that gave this spockeared, hawk-eyed man his fascination, his search for truth and justice inevitably compromised by the sleaze and corruption of his clients and milieu.

The world of Hoffman & Co ran the gamut of LA life from media, witnesses and jurors to the team of legal experts: insecure, cuticle-biting attorney Arnold Spivak, veteran investigator David Blaylock, receptionist Lila Marquette (played by Vanessa Williams recently of *Melrose Place*), intrepid legal assistant Louis Heinsbergen, boyish associate Chris Docknovich, and ambitious attorney Justine Appleton. The maestro's main support on the case came from Lisa Gillespie, the wide-eyed innocent-but-smart attorney (Grace Phillips beat big names such as Claudia Schiffer to the job).

Ranged against Hoffman were veteran prosecuting attorney Miriam Grasso played by five-time Emmy nominee Barbara Bosson, Bochco's wife of twenty-six years, and the vengeful Detective Arthur Polson whose ambition to best Hoffman was spiked by a still-smouldering grudge from an earlier case.

Prime suspects, celebrities both, were wealthy Los Angeles philanthropist Richard Cross, owner of the luxurious LA apartment in which the fifteen-year-old girl was found and lover of women including the victim's older sister, and Hollywood brat and heartthrob Neil Avedon, a young star with questionable sexual tastes, initially acting big but later running scared.

Sentiment was never too far away in this would-be mainstream production: music, titles and Hoffman's wife and young daughter at home all added a little schmaltz to the show. Fine performances lending a darker, everyone-has-secrets atmosphere and a plot with more twists and turns than an Eszterhas movie gave it a vicelike grip. Even so, when scheduled across America against ratings-topping hospital drama *ER* poor audiences meant the plug was pulled after episode seven and it was relaunched in a different slot seven weeks later. In Britain, the BBC and Sky paid a record £250,000 for the series and scheduled it more wisely.

A second series followed, although with Anthony LaPaglia's James Wyler replacing Benzali's Hoffman (judged a miss by US network ABC) as lead lawyer and a new format of 3 consecutive trials. A mini-series, *Murder One: Diary of a Serial Killer* issued forth in 1997.

GUEST CAST: Joe Spano, Robert Pine

MURDER, SHE WROTE

USA 1984–96 263 x 60m, 2 x 120m col CBS. Universal TV. UK tx 1985–96 ITV.

CR *Peter S Fischer, Richard Levinson, William Link.* **EXEC PR** *Peter S Fischer, Richard Levinson.* **PR** *Douglas Benton, Angela Lansbury, Todd London, Robert Van Scoyk.* **DR** *Various, including John Astin, Walter Grauman, Jerry Jameson, Peter Crane, John Llewellyn Moxey, Anthony Pullen Shaw, Vincent J McEveety, Seymour Robbie, Allen Reisner, David Hemmings, Chuck Bowman, Kevin Corcoran, Michael J Lynch.* **WR** *Various.* **MUS** *Various, including Bruce Babcock, Richard Markowitz, Lance Rubin.*

CAST *Jessica Fletcher (Angela Lansbury) Sheriff Amos Tupper (Tom Bosley) Dr Seth Hazlett (William Windom) Sheriff Mort Metzger (Ron Masak) Grady Fletcher (Michael Horton) Mayor Sam Booth (Richard Paul) Dennis Stanton (Keith Michell) Lt Perry Catalano (Ken Swofford) Robert Butler (James Sloyan) Dr Raymond Auerbach (Alan Oppenheimer) Dep Andy Broom (Louis Herthum) Eve Simpson (Julie Adams).*

Popular US mystery series, unmistakably a steal of Agatha Christie's >*Miss Marple*. British-born actress Angela Lansbury (who had even played Marple in the 1980 movie *The Mirror Crack'd*) starred as silver-haired Jessica Fletcher, a best-selling authoress of detective stories. She was never short of inspiration, since

165

166

her relatives and friends were victims of murder or framed for same at a prodigious rate – even in her quiet home town of Cabot Cove, Maine, a sort of St Mary Mead-by-the-Sea. Since in one sort of crime show the cops are hopeless plods – in *MSW* it was Sheriff Amos, played by Tom Bosley from *Happy Days* – Fletcher was obliged to use her amateur sleuthing skills to find whodunnit. (In 'Magnum on Ice' she even saved the sun-tanned hide of Hawaiian private dick *>Magnum PI*.) Also seen was Sheriff Metzger (who took over from Amos when Bosley went off to star in his own TV crime series, *>Father Dowling Mysteries*), Mayor Sam Booth, reformed jewel thief Dennis Stanton, chess-playing friend Dr Seth Hazlett, and Fletcher's tax accountant nephew, Grady. In 1991 Fletcher moved to New York to teach criminology, returning home to Cabot Cove – and corpses galore – at the weekend.

The cases, which began with the 120-minute TVM *The Murder of Sherlock Holmes*, were merely cryptic puzzles made televisual, entirely bereft of adequate characterisation or intellectual substance. But a pleasant enough way to while away a sleepy hour on the evening couch. And Lansbury's pleasure in her character was winningly evident, although not quite winning enough to garner an Emmy, despite almost annual nominations. (She did receive four Golden Globes for her performance as Fletcher, to stack on the chimney-piece next to her sixteen Tonys for Broadway work.) A reunion movie, *Murder, She Wrote: South By Southwest*, aired in 1997.

By way of a footnote, Lansbury was the granddaughter of the 1930s British Labour Party leader, George Lansbury, and sister of screenwriter Bruce, the creator of *>The Magician*.

GUEST CAST: Sonny Bono, Barry Newman, Doug McClure, Karen Black, Milton Berle, John Astin, Melissa Sue Anderson, Morgan Brittany, Jenny Agutter, Richard Bradford, Michael Ansara, Shirley Jones, Tom Selleck, Robert Stack, Adam West, David Ogden Stiers, John Saxon, David Soul, Cesar Romero, Michael Brandon, Edd Byrnes, Loretta Swit.

THE NAKED CITY

USA 1958–62 39 x 25m, 99 x 55m bw ABC. Shelle Productions/Screen Gems/A Columbia Pictures TV Production. UK tx 1962–3 ITV (57 episodes).

CR Mark Hellinger, Stirling Silliphant.
EXEC PR Herbert B Leonard. **PR** Charles Russell.
DR Various, including Buzz Kulik, Arthur Hiller, Elliott Silverstein, Stuart Rosenberg, William Conrad, Laslo Benedek, Lamont Johnson, Jack Smight, Paul Wendkos, William A Graham, Tay Garnett, Harry Harris, Walter Grauman, Robert Ellis Miller, William Beaudine, John Brahm.
WR Various, including Stirling Silliphant, Herbert Leonard, Gene Roddenberry, W R Burnett,

Howard Rodman, Jay Dratler. **MUS** Nelson Riddle, Billy May and Milton Raskin (theme).
CAST Det Lt Dan Muldoon (John McIntire) Det Jim Halloran (James Franciscus) Janet Halloran (Suzanne Storrs) Lt Mike Parker (Horace McMahon) Det Adam Flint (Paul Burke) Libby (Nancy Malone) Ptlm/Sgt Frank Arcaro (Harry Bellaver).

A police procedural out of the >Dragnet school of grainy urban realism, The Naked City had numerous famous leading players – principally John McIntire, also a master of Wagon Train – but the real star of the series was the vast metropolitan city which formed its backdrop: New York. Filmed with a hard, street look, the show made much use of the Big Apple's varied locales, from downtown Manhattan to Staten Island, as veteran cop Muldoon taught new boy Halloran lessons on how to catch the city's massed petty villainry. Unlike Jack Webb's Dragnet, The Naked City did not pretend that all cops were angels in blue clothing, but recognised them as fallible human beings, sometimes little better than the crooks.

Cast changes were numerous. Muldoon's car crashed into a petrol tanker and he was killed in a blaze of glory when McIntire wanted out of the series before the end of the first season (the episode 'The Bumper'), and the role of old hand was taken by Lieutenant Mike Parker. After a sixteen-month break the series returned in 1960 – as the abbreviated Naked City – in a sixty-minute format, with tighter, deeper scripts and a new young sidekick for the tough Parker in the shape of Adam Flint (played by Paul Burke, later Congressman Neal McVane in Dynasty), boyfriend of Libby.

The series was based on a 1948 feature Naked City directed by Jules Dassin, itself inspired by the 1945 book of NY photographs, Naked City, by Weegee (Arthur Felig). As developed for TV by Mark Hellinger, the show made a particular feature of bizarre episode titles, notable among them 'Howard Running Bear Is a Turtle', 'The Day It Rained Mink' and 'Today the Man Who Kills Ants Is Coming'. It also gave early parts to a wealth of the not yet famous, such as Dustin Hoffman, Robert Redford, Bruce Dern, Robert Duvall and Peter Falk.

The famous end-line of each episode, intoned by the narrator, has passed into legend. 'There are eight million stories in the Naked City. This has been one of them.'
GUEST CAST: George C Scott, Robert Redford, Robert Duvall, Dustin Hoffman, Peter Falk, Telly Savalas, Bruce Dern, Rocky Graziano, Walter Matthau, Eli Wallach.

NASH BRIDGES

USA 1996– 76 x 60m col CBS. Carlton Cuse Productions/Don Johnson Company/Rysher Entertainment. UK tx 1997– Sky 1.

CR Don Johnson, Hunter S Thompson. **EXEC PR** Carlton Cuse, John Wirth. **PR** Jed Seidel, Don Johnson. **DR** Various, including Jim Charleston, David Carson, Colin Bucksey, Chuck Bowman, Adam Nimoy, Tucker Gates, Peter Werner, Robert Mandel, Neal Israel **WR** Various, including John Wirth, Reed Steiner, Glenn Mazzara, Shawn Ryan. **MUS** Eddie Jobson ('I Got a Friend in You' theme), Elia Csmiral.

CAST Insp Nash Bridges (Don Johnson) Joe Dominguez (Richard 'Cheech' Marin) Lisa Bridges (Annette O'Toole) Harvey Leek (Jeff Perry) Evan Cortez (Jaime Gomez) Nick Bridges (James Gammon) Cassidy Bridges (Jodi Lyn O'Keefe) Michelle Chan (Kelly Hu) Caitlin Cross (Yasmine Bleth) Kelly Weld (Serena Scott Thomas) Lt A J Shimamura (Cary-Hiroyuki Tagawa).

👁 After careering around >*Miami Vice* in a Ferarri, actor Don Johnson waited a decade then careered around *Nash Bridges* in a yellow 1971 Hemi 'Cuda (plate: GQ13685). The mitigating circumstance? Johnson played Nash Bridges, a glamorous inspector with the

« *Don Johnson as* Nash Bridges, *a show dreamed up by the star and gonzo journalist Hunter S Thompson.*

élite Special Investigations Unit of the San Francisco PD, who had to chase what a super-cop had to chase. The similarities with *Miami Vice* didn't end at cool cars; whereas in *Vice* Johnson's Crockett lived on a boat, in *Nash Bridges* his character got to work out of one; for most of the show's run the SIU headquarters was a boat at North Pier. And, naturally, Bridges' home life was the usual one of a TV cop: wrecked. Bridges had no less than two ex-wives (caterer Lisa and society gal Kelly), with a daughter, troublesome teen Cassidy, by the former. Sharing Bridges' sumptuous apartment was his father, Nick, a hard-drinking ex-longshoreman who had become rich(ish) through a long-forgotten real-estate deal but was in the early stages of Alzheimers. On the cop job, Bridges was partnered routinely by Joe Dominguez (played by Richard 'Cheech' Marin, no less, from the famed 'Cheech and Chong' comedy duo), an ex-PI turned SIU cop (who liked to supplement his earnings with half-cooked scams, such as marketing his personal recipe for Salsa, running a gay club, etc). Harvey Leek – the name, of course, intended to suggest, ever so unsubtly, geek – was the SIU's computer and surveillance expert, a Sixties leftover who adored the Grateful Dead, and wore a black armband in tribute to the Dead's deceased Jerry Garcia. Womanising Evan Cortez was a younger model of Bridges himself.

The show apparently derived from an idea of

Johnson's and the gonzo journalist Hunter S Thompson. Certainly, Mr Thompson donated a cameo appearance as a restaurant piano player in the first episode. Much of the way in which the show used the hilly backdrop of `Frisco, meanwhile, was reminiscent of the Karl Malden/Michael Douglas classic, >*The Streets of San Francisco*. The executive producer of *Bridges* was Carlton Cuse, who was also the mainstay behind >*Martial Law* and *The Adventures of Brisco County Jr.*

Oh, and Bridges' gun? A Colt .38, 1911 issue.

GUEST CAST: Philip Michael Thomas, David L Lander.

NERO WOLFE

USA 1981 14 x 60m col NBC. Paramount TV. UK tx 1983 ITV.

EXEC PR *Ivan Goff, Ben Roberts.* **DR** *Various, including Michael O'Herlihy, Ron Satlof, George McCowan, Herbert Hirschman, Bob Kjelljan.* **WR** *Various, including Peter Nesco, William Ware, Stephen Downing, Lee Sheldon, Seeleg Lester, Alfred Hayes, Dick Nelson, Peter Alan Fields, Gerald Sandford.* **MUS** *John Addison.* **CAST** *Nero Wolfe (William Conrad) Archie Goodwin (Lee Horsley) Saul Panzer (George Wyner) Insp Cramer (Allan Miller) Fritz Brenner (George Voskovec) Theodore Horstman (Robert Coote).*

 Televersions of Rex Stout's stories featuring his orchid-loving, sedentary-living (in a NY brownstone) amateur detective.

More fatman detective work for William Conrad (>*Cannon*). Lee Horsley played Archie, Nero's legman. Also on his immenseness's staff were cook Fritz, gardener Horstman and Archie's own sidekick, Saul Panzer.

The episodes were: *The Golden Spider/Death on the Doorstep/Before I Die/Wolfe at the Door/ Might as Well be Dead/To Catch a Dead Man/ In the Best of Families/Murder by the Book/What Happened to April/Gambit/Death at the Double/The Murder in Question/The Blue Ribbon Hostage/Sweet Revenge.*

GUEST CAST: Christine Belford, Darren McGavin, Linden Chiles, Delta Burke.

THE NEW ADVENTURES OF CHARLIE CHAN

UK 1957–9 39 x 30m bw ITV. ITC. US tx 1957 syndicated.

EXEC PR *Leon Fromkess.* **PR** *Sidney Marshall, Rudolph Flotnow.* **CAST** *Charlie Chan (J Carrol Naish) Barry Chan ('Number One Son') (James Hong) Insp Duff (Rupert Davies) Insp Marlowe (Hugh Williams).*

'Don't talk too much. Words are like sunbeams the more they are condensed the deeper they burn.' Charlie Chan

ITC half-hour series which transferred Earl Derr Biggers' famous Oriental proverb-uttering detective (from Hawaii) to London, where he pursued complex cases with the help of eager-pup 'Number One Son'.

A show so terrible that it made for fascinating viewing. Although J Carrol Naish was not the first Caucasian to be yellowed-up for the role of Chan (being preceded by, among others, Warner Oland and Sidney Toler in the cinema), by the late Fifties the device was becoming transparently racist. It did not help that Naish himself appeared so ill at ease in the role. Or that the show was stagily shot and made. A pre->*Maigret* Rupert Davies appeared as the Yard's Inspector Duff, while the part of Number One Son went to American-Asian actor James Hong, already on the career ladder that would take him to *Blade Runner*, *Chinatown* and *Big Trouble in Little China* among 450 other films and TV shows.

A kiddie cartoon version of the Chan saga, *The Amazing Chan and the Chan Clan*, was released by Hanna-Barbera in 1972, with Keye Luke (Master Po in Kung Fu) as the voice of Chan. The character was originally modelled by Biggers on a real person, Honolulu police detective Chang Apana.

The episodes were: *Your Money or Your Wife/ Secret of the Sea/The Lost Face/Blind Man's Buff/The Great Salvos/The Counterfeiters/Death of a Don/Charlie's Highland Fling/The Patient in Room 21/The Rajput Ruby/Final Curtain/Death at High Tide/Circle of Fear/Exhibit in Wax/ Backfire/Patron of the Arts/Hamlet in Flames/ Dateline – Execution/The Sweater/The Noble Art of Murder/Three Men on a Raft/No Holiday for Murder/No Future for Frederick/Safe Deposit/ Voodoo Death/The Expatriate/Airport Murder Case/The Hand of Hera Dass/The Chippendale Racket/The Invalid/The Man in the Wall/ Something Old, Something New/The Man with a Hundred Faces/Point of No Return/A Bowl by Cellini/Without Fear/Kidnap/Rhyme or Treason/ Three for One.*

THE NEW BREED

USA 1961 36 x 60m bw ABC. A Quinn Martin Production/Selmur productions. UK tx 1963 ITV.

EXEC PR Quinn Martin.

CAST Lt Price Adams (Leslie Nielsen) Capt Keith Gregory (Byron Morrow) Sgt Vince Cavelli (John Beradino) Ptlm Joe Huddleston (John Clarke) Ptlm Pete Garcia (Greg Roman).

Quinn Martin 60-minute actioner starring Leslie Nielsen as Lieutenant Price Adams, head of the LAPD's élite Metro Squad. The gimmick was that Adams and his ops were a 'new breed' of policemen, equipped with the latest electronic hardware. The Canadian Nielsen – his brother Eric was sometime Deputy Prime

171

Minister of Canada – later mercilessly spoofed his fearless Price Adams persona in the comedy series *Police Squad!* (1982) and its *Naked Gun* movie knock-ons.

The episodes were: *No Fat Cops/Prime Target/Death of a Ghost/To None a Deadly Drug/The Compulsion to Confess/'Till Death Us Do Part/The Butcher/Wave Goodbye to Grandpa/Sweet Bloom of Death/The Valley of the Three Charlies/Lady Killer/Blood Money/I Remember Murder/The All-American Boy/Cross the Little Line/To Sell a Human/Care is No Cure/ Policemen Die Alone I/Policemen Die Alone II/ Mrs Weltschmerz/Wings for a Plush Horse/How Proud the Guilty/The Torch/All Dead Faces/The Deadlier Sex/Edge of Violence/Echoes of Hate/ The Man with the Other Face/Thousands and Thousands of Miles/Hail, Hail, the Gang's All Here/My Brother's Keeper/A Motive Named Walter/Wherefore Art Thou, Romeo?/Judgement at San Belito/So Dark the Night/Walk This Street Lightly.*

GUEST CAST: Gloria Grahame, Telly Savalas, Peter Fonda, Charles Bronson.

NYPD BLUE

USA 1993– 120+ x 50m col ABC. Steven Bochco Productions. UK tx 1994– C4.
CR *Steven Bochco, David Milch, Gregory Hoblit.*
PR *Steven Bochco, David Milch, Burton Armus, Robert J Doherty, Leonard Gardner, Ted Mann,* David Mills. **DR** *Various, including Gregory Hoblit, Daniel Sackheim, Michael M Robin, Donna Deitch, Charles Haid, Mark Tinker, Elodie Keene, Paris Barclay, Kathy Bates, Adam Nimoy, Eric Laneuville, Dennis Dugan, Lesli Linka Glatter, Davis Guggenheim, Randall Zisk.* **WR** *Various, including Steven Bochco, David Milch, Ann Biderman, Channing Gibson, Charles H Eglee, Ted Mann, Rosemary Breslin, David Mills, Gardner Stern, Larry Cohen, Bill Clark, Nicholas Wootton, Leonard Gardner, Michael R Perry, Stephen Gaghan.* **MUS** *Mike Post, Danny Lux.*
CAST *Det John Kelly (David Caruso) Det Andy Sipowicz (Dennis Franz) Lt Arthur Fancy (James McDaniel) Laura Kelly (Sherry Stringfield) James Martinez (Nicholas Turturro) Det Bobby Simone (Jimmy Smits) Det Greg Medavoy (Gordon Clapp) Asst DA Sylvia Costas (Sharon Lawrence) Donna Abandando (Gail O'Grady) Det Danny Sorenson (Rick Schroder) Off Janice Licalsi (Amy Brenneman) Off Abby Sullivan (Paige Turco) Asst DA Leo Cohen (Michael Silver) Det Diane Russell (Kim Delaney) Det Jill Kirkendall (Andrea Thompson) Desk Sgt Vincent Agostini (Vincent Guastaferro) Det Adrianne Lesnick (Justine Miceli) IAB Sgt Martens Scott (Allan Campbell) Andy Sipowicz Jr (Michael deLuise) Zone Commander Haverill (James Handy) Dolores Mayo (Lola Glaudini) Gina Colon (Lourdes Benedicto) John Irvin (Bill Brochtrup) Off James Shannon (James McBride) Benita Alden (Melina Kanakaredes).*

Jimmy Smiths (left) and Dennis Franz (centre), the stars of the Emmy-laden NYPD Blue.

Police procedural out of the >*Dragnet* school of New York *vérité*. Created by TV wunderkind Steven Bochco (>*Hill Street Blues*, >*Cop Rock*, *LA Law*), in association with sometime Yale professor of English Literature David Milch (*Hill Street Blues*), *NYPD Blue* was notably bleaker than Bochco's other law-based shows, although leavened by judicious doses of schmaltz. The romantic liaisons and work-time abrasions of its 15th Precinct squad occupied almost as much screen time as the crime case in weekly question, leading to its dubbing as 'Thirtysomething with handcuffs'. The principal protagonists were sensitive ginger-haired detective John Kelly, who earned his detective shield at 28 (but at the cost of his marriage to attorney Laura), and his long-term partner, the permanently sweating Andy Sipowicz (scene-stealingly played by Vietnam vet Dennis Franz,

173

>*Hill Street Blues*, >*Beverly Hills Buntz*).

In each episode romance, comradeship or competition in the precinct was interwoven with socially-aware storylines such as wife-battering in the tenements, or racism on the streets. Yet, what held the attention, if not churned the stomach, was the camera work – tight, tense, jerky, hand-held, allowing the viewer a full sense of the precinct's pressures. Further authenticity was achieved by grainy half-lighting, ear-straining sound and the use of Bill Clark, a former NYPD detective, as story consultant. Most of the exterior shooting was done on location, with the real-life 9th Precinct stationhouse on 321 East 5th Street in NY standing in for the fictional 15th's exterior (>*Kojak*, incidentally, had also used the 9th for exteriors).

The show received a record-breaking 26 Emmy nominations at the end of its first season (winning six: Outstanding Lead Actor for Franz, Writing, Directing, Editing, Art Direction, Casting). In series two a new member was introduced into the 15th Precinct: Detective Bobby Simone, played by Emmy-winning Jimmy Smits (Victor Sifuentes in *LA Law* and the co-lead in the pilot for >*Miami Vice*), who took over as Sipowicz's partner when Caruso was ruthlessly written out of the show in 'Dead and Gone'. (Caruso, to studio ire, had quit for movieland; in the world of *NYPD Blue*, his character was fingered in a corruption probe after having helped

clear Mob-compromised lover Officer Licalsi of a murder.) The new pairing of Franz and Smits was as nuanced and watchable as the old one – perhaps no surprise, since Smits was Bochco's original choice for the role of Kelly – with an antagonistic start (Simone telling Sipowicz to 'kiss my French-Portuguese ass') giving way to a modus vivendi, symbolised by a joint singalong to 'Duke of Earl'. The other squadroom regulars were: streetwise young Detective James Martinez (Nicholas Turturro, brother of John Turturro, star of *Barton Fink*), who increasingly took over some of John Kelly's caring, sharing mantle; the by-the-book precinct commander, Lieutenant Arthur Fancy (*Malcolm X*); self-destructive, allergy-plagued Greg Medavoy (Gordon Clapp, co-star of the cult movie *Return of the Secausus Seven*); the voluptuous but sensitive clerk Donna Abandando; and rising Assistant DA Sylvia Costas (who later married Sipowicz).

In 1998 Jimmy Smits left the show, allegedly because he had tired of playing second banana to Franz; certainly David Milch had stacked all the best stories on to Franz's Sipowicz, a character reputedly based on his own father. With Simone out of the 'One-Five' squadroom, Detective Danny Sorenson was promoted to narrative front rank, his relationship with Franz helped by a shared background as Army vets and Sorenson's passing resemblance to the late Andy Sipowicz Jr.

GUEST CAST: David Benzali, David Schwimmer (Josh '4B' Goldstein), Tom Towles, Wendie Malick, Barbara Bosson, Johnny Cocktails, Anthony Head, Dan Castellaneta, Joe Sabatini, Peter Boyle, Giancarlo Esposito.

THE ODD MAN

UK 1962–3 24 x 60m bw ITV. A Granada Television Network Presentation.
CR Edward Boyd. **PR** Stuart Latham. **DR** Various, including Derek Bennett, Stuart Latham, John Llewellyn Moxey, Eric Price. **WR** Various, including Edward Latham.
CAST Steve Gardiner (Edwin Richfield) Judy Gardiner (Sarah Lawson) Chief Insp Gordon (Moultrie Kelsall) Det Sgt Swift (Keith Barron) South (Christopher Quinee) Chief Insp Rose (William Mervyn).

Offbeat Sixties thriller from Edward Boyd (who would later create >The Corridor People), which featured East London actor Edwin Richfield as Steve Gardiner, a theatrical agent and part-time PI who became enmeshed in macabre cases. Also featured were Detective Sergeant Swift, Chief Inspector Gordon, Gardiner's wife and her mysterious mute killer, South. During the second season of this Hitchcockian-like TV crime series, Inspector Rose entered the narrative, to be eventually spun off to the more conventional detective show It's Dark Outside (1964–5, 16 x 60m bw, ITV), which featured a yet-to-be-famous Oliver Reed in its cast and a number one hit in Jackie Trent's 'Where Are You Now?' theme. It also generated a further knock-on with Mr Rose (1968, 25 x 60m col, ITV).
GUEST CAST: Donald Sutherland.

PACIFIC BLUE

USA 1996– 57+ x 60m col NBC. North Hall Productions. UK tx 1996– Sky 1.
CR Bill Nuss. **EXEC PR** Bill Nuss, Gary Nardino. **DR** Various, including Mickey Dolenz. **WR** Various, including David Kemper, Emily Skupov, T Treas, M Zand, Tom Szollisi. **MUS** Christopher Franke
CAST Lt Anthony Palermo (Rick Rossovich) Off T C Callaway (Jim Davidson) Off Chris Kelly (Darlene Vogel) Off Victor Del Torro (Marcos Ferraez) Off Cory McNamara (Paula Trickey) Bobby Cruz (Mario Lopez) Elvis (the bike mechanic) (David L Lander) Russ Granger (Jeff Stearns).

Eco-friendly mix of >CHiPS and Baywatch in which an élite squad of beach police patrolled Santa Monica on … bikes. Inevitably, there was a certain amount of unintentional Keystone cops comedy in the sight of pumping-kneed cops chasing baddies in Ferraris, though few adolescent males – with a screenful of babes and a thumping rock soundtrack – found a free hand to file a complaint. Staple show director was Mickey Dolenz of The Monkees, who also

176

appeared on screen as 'Mayor Mickey Dolenz'.
GUEST CAST: Brian Keith.

PARIS

USA 1979–80 13 x 60m col CBS. MTM. UK tx
1980–1 ITV.
CR Steven Bochco. **EXEC PR** Steven Bochco.
PR Gregory Hoblit, Edward De Blasio. **DR** Georg
Stanford Brown, Arnold Laven, Jackie Cooper,

⊘ *Admired for its blonde babes and bicycle-riding
beach cops, Pacific Blue was a particular hit with
adolescent males.*

Jack Starrett, Alex March, Alexander Singer, Jerry
McNeely, Alf Kjellin, Bruce Paltrow, Victor Lobl,
Alan Rachins. **WR** Steven Bochco, Edward De
Blasio, Burton Armus, Del Reisman, Irv Pearlberg,
Larry Alexander, Jack Gillis, David Solomon,
Michael Kozoll. **MUS** Fred Karlin.

CAST *Det Capt Woodrow 'Woody' Paris(James Earl Jones) Barbara Paris (Lee Chamberlain) Willie Miller (Mike Warren) Dep Chief Jerome Bench (Hank Garrett) Stacey Erickson (Cecilia Hart) Ernie Villas (Frank Ramirez) Charlie Bogart (Jake Mitchell).*

Steven Bochco police show (preceding >*Hill Street Blues* by two years) and also the first American prime-time cop series to star a black actor. This was James Earl Jones (born Todd Jones), who played Woody Paris, detective head of the LAPD's élite Metro Squad and part-time criminology professor at UCLA. Stories also incorporated the main man's home life – unusually so for cop TV – and his marriage to Barbara, a nurse. Even excusing the sometime beta-level scripts and palpable air of uncertain direction, Jones' personal charisma and likeably thoughtful character should have made for a long run; that Paris lasted only thirteen episodes suggested that white America was not yet ready for an Afro-American male in a leading weekly cop part. Perhaps the best episode, one in which the show articulated moral questions with consummate scripting and played them out with fine acting, was Bochco's own 'Dead Men Don't Kill', in which a convicted killer (Georg Stanford Brown from *Roots*; he also, incidentally, directed on *Paris*) is proved innocent by Paris – but, almost incredibly for prime-time, there was no last-minute reprieve, only a graphic and harrowing scene in which Brown's character was gassed to death.

As an indictment of capital punishment, TV has rarely done it better. For that episode alone, *Paris* deserves a blessed memory. It also has a place of distinction in the evolution of TV, since on the set of *Paris* came together many – Bochco, Michael Kozoll, James B Sikking, Michael Warren, Taurean Blacque, Kiel Martin and more – who would go on to make, and star in, the seminal >*Hill Street Blues*.

The episodes were: *Pilot/Dear John/Pawn/ Friends and Enemies/Once More for Free/Dead Men Don't Kill/Burnout/Decisions/Fitz's Boys/ The Price is Right/The Ghost Maker/Pay the Two Bucks/America the Beautiful.*

GUEST CAST: Vic Morrow, Georg Stanford Brown, James B Sikking, Bruce Weitz, Jonathan Frakes, Michael Warren, Kiel Martin, Joe Spano, Michael Conrad, Taurean Blacque, Barbara Babcock.

PERRY MASON

USA 1957–66 270 x 60m bw, 1 x 60m col
CBS. Paisano Productions. UK tx 1961–7
BBC1. cr Erle Stanley Gardner.
EXEC PR *Gail Patrick Johnson, Arthur Marks.*
PR *Art Seid, Sam White, Ben Brady, Herbert Hirschman.* **DR** *Various, including Christian Nyby, Gerd Oswald, Ted Post, Jerry Hopper, William D Russell, Arthur Marks, Bernard L Kowlaski, Francis D K Lyon, Earl Bellamy, Don Weis, Irving J Moore,*

Richard D Donner, Jack Arnold, Jesse Hibbs. **WR** Various, including Erle Stanley Gardner, Jonathan Latimer, Stirling Silliphant, Stanley Niss, Gene Wang, Robert C Dennis, Seeleg Lester, Jackson Gillis, Edward Lasko, Robert Leslie Bellem, Samuel Newman, Robb White, Philip Saltzman. **MUS** Bernard Herrmann (theme), Richard Shores, Fred Steiner, Barney Kessel. **CAST** Perry Mason (Raymond Burr) Della Street (Barbara Hale) Paul Drake (William Hopper) DA Hamilton Burger (William Talman) Lt Arthur Tragg (Ray Collins) David Gideon (Karl Held) Lt Anderson (Wesley Lau) Lt Steve Drumm (Richard Anderson) Sgt Brice (Lee Miller) Terence Clay (Dan Tobin). **VIDEO** Columbia House.

A hugely successful series that made a star of Raymond Burr as Perry Mason, stalwart and near-invincible criminal lawyer. An early and staunchly reliable show, with high production values, Perry Mason ran in black-and-white for nine years, only venturing into colour for the final one of its 271 episodes. A large part of Perry Mason's appeal was its predictability. Plots ran roughly thus: a murder would be investigated by trilby-hatted Lieutenant Arthur Tragg who, with District Attorney Hamilton Burger, would build a watertight case. The accused then went to Perry Mason, who would investigate the case along with devoted secretary Della Street and private detective Paul Drake.

Every episode ended in a courtroom trial, and every trial ended either with the witness yielding to Mason's dogged examination or with assistant Paul Drake rushing a vital piece of evidence into the courtroom in the nick of time – leaving Mason's adversary DA Hamilton Burger eternally thwarted, and Perry, Della and Paul to enjoy a leisurely post-mortem of their victory after the final commercial. (If they celebrated with wine, this would have only been appropriate; Raymond Burr was a keen vintner, and eventually sold the wine from his California yard commercially – 'a case worth investigating' as the ad line had it.) When Mason lost one case because a defence witness refused to reveal vital information, thousands of viewers' letters signalled the level of audience dissatisfaction.

Television's longest-running lawyer series was based on lawyer-novelist Erle Stanley Gardner's scores of novels featuring the defence attorney. Created in the 1933 novel, The Case of the Velvet Claws, the character was adapted for radio in a CBS series running from 1943 to 1955, which was as much soap opera as detective series. Three movie adaptations by Warner Bros – The Case of the Howling Dog (1935), The Case of the Black Cat (1936) and The Case of the Stuttering Bishop (1937) – were

» Raymond Burr as Perry Mason; the show has run continuously in syndication in the USA.

poorly received, primarily because Warners tried to recast Mason as a kind of debonair wiseacre in the *Thin Man* mould. Gardner, unhappy with the radio and big-screen versions, opted to be creator for the TV series and was closely involved in every aspect, from casting through to a cameo role as judge in the final episode, 'The Case of the Final Fadeout'. Among the principal writers of the teleplays was another ace crime-writer, Jonathan 'Headed for a Hearse' Latimer.

Burr, who had played a succession of baddies in Hollywood, was originally screen-tested for the part of Burger, but asked to try out as Mason as well. Gardner spotted him and the rest is history. Burr took his part seriously; he spent six months sitting in court studying real-life attorneys, and consulted throughout the series with six Superior Court judges before delivering his speeches. He was even awarded an Honorary Doctor of Law degree by a law college in Sacramento. The role also won him a Outstanding Actor in a Dramatic Series Emmy in 1959 (Barbara Hale picked up a Outstanding Supporting Actress Emmy in the same awards), and the same prize in 1961.

The original *Perry Mason*, with its clean characters welcome in every living-room, is one of TV's most enduring series. It has never stopped running in syndication in the US and is a staple of television world-wide. CBS attempted to revive the series in 1973 as *The New Adventures of Perry Mason*, with Monte Markham in the title role

leading an entirely new cast, but it failed to pick up an audience and was cancelled mid-run. In 1985 NBC aired a reunion movie, *Perry Mason Returns*, once more starring Burr and bringing back Barbara Hale as Della (other regular cast members had since died; Hale's real-life son, William Katt, took over as Paul Drake Jr, with David Ogden Stiers (*M*A*S*H*) as new courtroom adversary Michael Reston). This led to a series of feature-length Perry Mason movies (1986–93): *The Case of the Shooting Star/The Case of the Notorious Nun/The Case of the Murdered Madam/The Case of the Sinister Spirit/The Case of the Scandalous Scoundrel/The Case of the Lost Love/The Case of the Lady in the Lake/The Case of the Avenging Ace/The Case of the Musical Murder/The Case of the All-Star Assassin/The Case of the Lethal Lesson/The Silenced Singer/The Case of the Poisoned Pen/ The Case of the Desperate Deception/The Case of the Defiant Daughter/The Case of the Ruthless Reporter/The Case of the Fatal Fashion/The Case of the Maligned Mobster/The Case of the Glass Coffin/The Case of the Heartbroken Bride/The Case of the Reckless Romeo/The Case of the Fatal Framing/The Case of the Killer Kiss/ The Case of the Skin-Deep Scandal/The Case of the Telltale Talk Show Host.*

Incidentally, while *The New Adventures of Perry Mason* had been trying to find viewers, Raymond Burr was already playing another much-loved television crime-fighter. From 1967 to 1975 he was busy as wheelchair-bound Robert Ironside, special consultant to the San Francisco Police Department, in NBC's >Ironside.

GUEST CAST: Erle Stanley Gardner, Frankie Laine, Mary Ann Mobley, Lee Meriwether, Keye Luke, James Coburn, Angie Dickinson, Ryan O'Neal, Bette Davis, Burt Reynolds, Robert Redford, Lee Van Cleef, Fay Wray, Adam West, Werner Klemperer, Ivan Dixon, Barbara Eden, Bill Mumy, George Takei, Barbara Bain, Noah Beery, Alan Hale Jr, Leonard Nimoy.

THE PERSUADERS!

UK 1971–2 24 x 60m col ITV. A Tribune Production. US tx 1971–2 ABC.

CR Robert S Baker. PR Robert S Baker, Terry Nation, Johnny Goodman. DR Basil Dearden, Roy Ward Baker, Roger Moore, Leslie Norman, Val Guest, Peter Hunt, Gerald Mayer, Sidney Hayers, Peter Medak, David Green, James Hill. WR Brian Clemens, Terry Nation, Terence Feely, John Kruse, Michael Pertwee, Tony Williamson, Milton S Gilman, Donald James, Tony Barwick, David Wolfe, Walter Black, Peter Yeldham, Harry H Junkin, Donald James, Val Guest. MUS John Barry (theme), Ken Thorne, Tony Hatch, Jackie Trent, David Lindup.

CAST Lord Brett Sinclair (Roger Moore) Danny Wilde (Tony Curtis) Judge Fulton (Laurence Naismith). VIDEO ITC.

Schlock. But enjoyable schlock. *The Persuaders!* was a barely disguised attempt by Sir Lew Grade, head of ITC, to follow up the transatlantic success of >*The Saint* by giving them more of the same under a different name. The small difference was that the suave English adventurer (played by Roger Moore, naturally, here wearing his self-designed safari suits) in *The Persuaders!* was called Lord Brett Sinclair – and this time out he had a friend, one Danny Wilde (Tony Curtis) from New York.

Sinclair and Wilde, so the premise went, were as different as London gin and Coca-Cola. Sinclair had been to Harrow and Oxford; Wilde had grown up in the Bronx and graduated from the University of Life. Only latterly had he made a million in the oil business. Initially antagonists, the two playboys were brought together at a Riviera party by retired Judge Fulton and blackmailed into co-operating as international fighters against crime. And so they wandered through 24 glossy international jet-set episodes seeking thrills – and girls, girls, girls. (Those who served heroically as screen adornments included Joan Collins, Catherine Schell, Susan George, Nicola Pagett, and Diane Cilento in the episode 'A Death in the Family', a spoof by Terry Nation of *Kind Hearts and Coronets*.) What saved the series from the great TV scrap-heap were good scripts, John '007' Barry's 'dum dum di dum dum' theme, and a sparky, amusing relationship between Sinclair

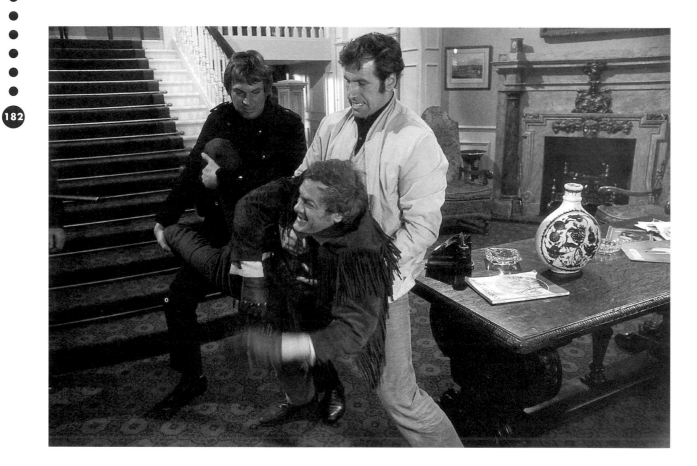

and Wilde, incessant rivals – especially when pursuing the female guest stars – as well as friends.

Despite this, and high production values – each episode cost £100,000, while the directors' list included such names as Val Guest (When Dinosaurs Ruled the Earth), Basil Dearden (The Blue Lamp) and Peter Hunt (On Her Majesty's Secret Service) – the series failed to sell in the one country it was made for – the USA. The ABC network cancelled it after just 24 episodes (130

Be-tasselled Danny Wilde (Tony Curtis) is apprehended for crimes against fashion in The Persuaders!

had been scheduled) following poor ratings. It was judged too jokey for American tastes and Curtis's Wilde, with his bomber jackets and leather gloves, was considered something of a stereotype of the 'poor', unsophisticated Yankee cousin. The series did enormous business elsewhere, though, was dubbed into over twenty languages, and is still a staple of European networks.

The series entered the news in 1999 when Roger Moore filed a lawsuit against Carlton of the UK, who had recently purchased the ITC library, alleging that his share of the re-run rights had not been agreed.

The episodes were: *Overture/The Gold Napoleon/Take Seven/Greensleeves/ Powerswitch/The Time and the Place/Someone Like Me/Anyone Can Play/The Old, the New and the Deadly/Angie, Angie/Chain of Events/ That's Me Over There/The Long Goodbye/The Man in the Middle/Element of Risk/A Home of One's Own/Five Miles to Midnight/Nuisance Value/The Morning After/Read and Destroy/A Death in the Family/The Ozerov Inheritance/To the Death, Baby/Someone Waiting.*

GUEST CAST: Anouska Hempel, Nicola Pagett, Susan George, Sinead Cusack, Carmen Munroe, Lionel Blair, Nina Baden-Semper, Joan Collins, Denholm Elliott, Roger Delgado, Lois Maxwell, Duncan Lamont, Terry Thomas, Hannah Gordon, Shane Rimmer, Bernard Lee, Larry Storch, George Baker, Catherine Schell, Diane Cilento.

PETER GUNN

USA 1958–61 110 x 30m bw NBC/ABC. A Spartan Production.

CR *Blake Edwards.* **PR** *Blake Edwards.* **DR** *Various, including Gene Reynolds, Blake Edwards, Lamont Johnson, Robert Altman, Alan Crosland Jr.* **MUS** *Henry Mancini (theme).*

CAST *Peter Gunn (Craig Stevens) Edie Hart (Lola Albright) Lt Jacoby (Herschel Bernadi) 'Mother' Hope Emerson ((season one)/Minerva Urecal (season two) Leslie (maître d') James) Lanphier Emmett (Bill Chadney).*

Peter Gunn was one of the first (along with >*77 Sunset Strip*) of a rash of new-style PI shows with a cool new feel in the late Fifties. Their featured breed of gumshoe had the best of both worlds – plush offices uptown with a list of glamorous clients and, for their night-time haunts, lowlife sleazy jazz clubs where they drank in the atmosphere and music of the beatnik era.

Detective Peter Gunn's well-appointed office was at 351 Ellis Park Road, Los Angeles, and his spare time was spent over at 'Mother's' jazz club watching his blonde girlfriend take the stage as resident singer. On the way to getting his clients out of trouble or cracking a case, Gunn might find himself with a fight on his hands, but this man was as laid-back as he was well-groomed and always came out on top – even if he did need the help of his friend Police Lieutenant Jacoby. Original jazz themes by Henry Mancini punctuated the action and helped create the contemporary mood (as well as providing RCA with two memorable and very successful albums). The slick, successful series ran for over 100 episodes and spawned a number of imitators including Pete Kelly's *Blues* and >*Johnny Staccato*.

184

Peter Gunn helped to launch the glittering career of creator-producer Blake Edwards, whose other TV series in the Fifties were the similarly jazz-influenced *Mr Lucky* (also with music by Mancini) and *Dante's Inferno*. His feature film credits include *Breakfast at Tiffany's*, *A Shot in the Dark*, the other *Pink Panther* movies, *10* and *Victor/Victoria*. He returned to TV in 1991–2 as executive producer of the sitcom *Julie*, which starred his wife Julie Andrews. Edwards and Stevens teamed up again in 1967 to make the unsuccessful movie *Gunn*.

GUEST CAST: Diahann Carroll, John McIntire.

PETROCELLI

USA 1974–6 1 x 90m, 45 x 60m col NBC. A Paramount Television Production. UK tx 1978–9 BBC1.

CR *Sidney J Furie, Harold Buchman, E Jack Newman.* **EXEC PR** *Thomas L Miller, Edward J Milkis, Ralph Riskin.* **DR** *Various, including Richard Donner, Jerry London, Irving J Moore, Leonard Katzman, Joseph Pevney, Robert Scheerer, Bernard McEveety, Vincent J McEveety, Don Weis, Russ Mayberry, Don Taylor, Herschel Daugherty, James Sheldon, Paul Stanley, Allen Reisner.* **WR** *Various.* **MUS** *Lalo Schifin.*
CAST *Tony Petrocelli (Barry Newman) Maggie Petrocelli (Susan Howard) Peter Ritter (Albert Salmi) Lt John Ponce (David Huddleston) Asst DA Frank Kaiser (Michael Bell).*

'I'm Tony Petrocelli, but please, you can call me Tony.'

Knock-on from the 1970 movie *The Lawyer*, with Barry Newman reprising his role as Italian-American attorney Anthony Petrocelli, but here giving up the big city to practise law in the Southwestern town of San Remo. Usually, Petrocelli performed his services gratis, leaving his wife and himself in trailer-living penury. Cowhand Pete Ritter was hired on as investigator.

Above average intelligence crime show, with a likeably human hero. (He spent many an episode assuring blue-collar types, 'That's a great job! Your mother will be proud of you whatever you do.') It notched up a respectable number of viewers at home and abroad – 21.7 million at its 1979 British peak. 'In view of this, your honour, I move that the charges against my client be dropped.'

GUEST CAST: Harrison Ford, Stefanie Powers, William Shatner, Julie Kavner.

PICKET FENCES

USA 1992–6 1 x 120m, 86 x 60m col NBC. CBS Television. UK tx 1995–7 Sky 1.
EXEC PR *David E Kelley, Michael Pressman.* **PR** *Alice West.* **DR** *Various, including Ron Lagomarsino, Kris Tabori, Dan Lerner, Lou Antonio, Michael Pressman, Tom Moore, Joan Tewkesbury, Tom Skerritt, Richard Masur.*

CAST *Sheriff Jimmy Brock (Tom Skerritt) Dr Jill Brock (Kathy Baker) Maxine Stewart (Lauren Holly) Kimberly Brock (Holly Marie Combs) Matthew Brock (Justin Shenkarow) Judge Henry Bone (Ray Walston) Douglas Wambaugh (Fyvush Finkel) Kenny Lacos (Costas Mandylor) Ginny Weedon (Zelda Rubinstein) Carter Pike (Kelly Connell) Myriam Wambaugh (Erica Yohn) Howard Buss (Robert Cornthwaite) Father Gary Barrett (Roy Dotrice).*

Picket Fences was the anti->*Twin Peaks* of US television. Set in the humdrummingly normal small town of of Rome, Wisconsin, it starred Tom Skerritt (previously Evan Drake in *Cheers*) as shining-badged local sheriff Jimmy Brock and Kathy Baker as Brock's physician wife, Jill. Of course, Rome had more than its fair share of way-out crimes – including bizarre murders and spontaneous human combustion – but it was never a mired pool steeped in evil à la *Twin Peaks*, and Skerritt and his officers tended to solve crimes with a distinctly quirky modus operandi. Conjure Capra's *It's A Wonderful Life, Northern Exposure* and old-time sheriff-sitcom *The Andy Griffith Show* to the mind's eye, then you have it. It was also made to double-Emmy-winning standards (Outstanding Drama in 1993 and 1994), with Skerritt securing the Lead Actor Emmy in 1993 and Kathy Baker Lead Actress Emmys in 1993, 1995 and 1996. Ray Walston, who played

⌃ Picket Fences *was exec-produced by David E Kelley, aka Mr Michelle Pfeiffer*

Judge Bone, took Outstanding Supporting Actor Emmys in 1995 and 1996. The show's executive producer was David E Kelley (husband of Michelle Pfeiffer, >*B.A.D. Cats;* she also guested on *Picket Fences*), previously of LA Law and later the hand which created the ditzy *Ally McBeal.*
GUEST CAST: Louise Fletcher, Efrem Zimbalist Jr, Michelle Pfeiffer, James Coburn, Robert Foxworth, Louis Gossett Jr, James Earl Jones, Paul Winfield.

PLAYERS

USA 1997 16 x 60m col. NBC. Universal
TV/Wolf Films/NBC Studios.
CR Reggie 'Rock' Bythewood, Ice-T, Dick Wolf,
Shaun Cassidy **EXEC PR** Dick Wolf, Ed Zuckerman
PR Kevin G. Cremin, Randy Anderson, Robert
Lloyd Lewis, Clyde Phillips, Michael Vittes.
DR Jace Alexander (I), Allan Arkush, Richard
Compton, Frederick King Keller, Jefery Levy,
Donald Petrie, James Quinn (I), Michael Vittes.
MUS Mike Post.
CAST Isaac 'Ice' Gregory (Ice-T) Alphonse Royo
(Costas Mandylor) Charles 'Charlie' O'Bannon
(Frank John Hughes) Christine 'Chris' Kowalski
(Mia Korf) Ginny (Marta Martin).

The 'players' were a trio of ex-cons paroled
from prison under a radical new plan to
lend the FBI the street smarts of con artists.
Transformed into a team of FBI operatives, the
three proceeded to use the skills they had honed
on the wrong side of the law to help fight crime,
and to keep themselves out of the Federal pen.
The partners were called on to deal with situations
the Bureau couldn't handle by legitimate means
and they didn't follow the same rules as the G-
men. But their authority had limits. If they didn't
stay on the straight and narrow each of them
owed the Bureau of Prisons nineteen years and six
months.

Rapper/actor/author Ice-T (New Jack City),

real name Tracy Morrow, father of the 'gangsta'
rap which spawned the careers among others of
N.W.A. and Snoop Doggy Dogg, played Isaac
'Ice' Gregory charmer, brain man and head of the
gang; Costas Mandylor (Picket Fences), played
Alphonso Royo, handsome, smooth talking ladies
man and master of disguises from gay
photographer to saucy Latina, and Frank John
Hughes (>Law and Order, New York Undercover)
played Charles 'Charlie' O'Bannon, computer
genius with so many phobias there weren't labels
to cover them, as well as the ability to reprogram
FBI files and broadcast fake basketball scores.
Mia Korf (Chicago Hope) was a strong, sceptical
FBI special agent, control officer and contact for
the three undercover operatives.

Series creators included Shaun Cassidy, also
creator of cult hit >American Gothic. Dick Wolf,
creator and executive producer, also created Law
and Order and New York Undercover and
executive produced >Miami Vice. Music was
supplied by cop TV show composer extraordinaire
Mike Post whose credits include >The Rockford
Files, 1974, >CHiPs, 1977, >Magnum PI,
1980, >Hill Street Blues, 1981, >The A-Team,
1983, >LA Law, 1986, >Law and Order, 1990,
and >Murder One, 1995 (for which he won an
Emmy in 1996). Despite the calibre of its
originators, however, this was a short-lived series.
A kind of latter day >Mod Squad, the concept
was almost as old as the flickering screen. Ice-T

was without doubt the star of the show, and his presence alone lent the series a cult following. But *Players* was light-hearted, tongue-in-cheek stuff low on violence and his fans usually demanded more hip and heavy fare. Week one had good viewing figures. By week four the series had dropped to 93rd place in the Nielsen rankings. Hammy, predictable with over the top performances (Ice T as a rapping cowboy and a fake winning lottery ticket plotline) the episode led the way to an early cancellation of the show. Eighteen episodes were made, only sixteen broadcast. Those who loved it laid the blame at NBC's door for under-promotion. But maybe it was the strain of producing all those episodes sporting 'con' in the title.

Episode titles: *Pilot; Con Law; In Concert; Con Artist; Contact Sport; Con Amore; Rashacon; Three of a Con; Mint Condition; Confidence Man; Con-traband; Con-tinental; Wrath of Con; Con-strained; Con-spiracy; Contamination; (Con-undrum, Con-Vivants,* unaired).

GUEST CAST: Jon Polito, Mitch Pileggi

POLICE STORY

USA 1973–88 15 x 120m, 2 x 90m, 87 x 60m col NBC/ ABC (season six, 1988). Screen Gems/
Columbia Pictures Corporation (US)/David Gerber Productions.UK tx 1974–80 ITV.
CR *Joseph Wambaugh.* **EXEC PR** *David Gerber.*
PR *David Gerber, Liam O'Brien.* **DR** *Various, including Corey Allen, John Badham, Vince Edwards, Lee H Katzin, Alex March, Gary Nelson, Seymour Robbie, Barry Shear.*
WR *Various, including Joseph Wambaugh.* **MUS** *Jerry Goldsmith, Richard Markowitz.*

Created by Joseph Wambaugh, former LAPD detective turned best-selling crime novelist, this anthology series was pitched on realism. With Wambaugh acting as consultant and authenticity monitor, storylines ranged from the day-to-day detail of the policeman's lot to its high-octane thrills and dangers. Care was taken that the officers' home lives and problems, from marital strains to forced retirement, prevailed.

Two episodes of *Police Story* spun off series of their own. 'The Gamble', March 1974, starred Angie Dickinson as policewoman Lisa Beaumont; by autumn that year Dickinson was starring in >*Police Woman,* complete with the more easily marketed name of Pepper Anderson. 'The Return of Joe Forrester', starring Lloyd Bridges, aired as a 90-minute special in 1975 and the following autumn became >*Joe Forrester,* with Lloyd Bridges reprising his role. Episodes were self-contained, but occasionally characters recurred. These included Tony Lo Bianco as Tony Calabrese and Don Meredith as Bert Jameson, either as partners or separately, and James Farentino as Charlie Czonki.

187

The title 'Police Story' was also used by an earlier US anthology show, which ran for one season in 1952 (16 x 30m bw, CBS), dramatising real-life cases. It was narrated by Norman Rose.

GUEST CAST: Angie Dickinson, Lloyd Bridges, Michael Ansara, Ken Olin, Jan-Michael Vincent, Desi Arnaz Jr, Tina Louise, Ron Masak, Robert Englund, Cheryl Ladd, Joe E Tata, Ed Asner, Robert Culp.

POLICE SURGEON

UK 1960 12 x 30m bw ITV. ABC TV.

PR *Julian Bond, Leonard White.* **DR** *Various, including Guy Verney, Don Leaver.* **WR** *Various, including Julian Bond.*

CAST *Dr Geoffrey Brent (Ian Hendry) Inspector Landon (John Warwick).*

Short-lived tape series set in London's Bayswater, featuring a young police surgeon, Dr Geoffrey Brent, who was unable to resist turning investigator on his cases.

So-so crime show, but assured of a place in the TV annals as the origin of famed spy caper *The Avengers*, since actor Ian Hendry carried on his white coat and magnifying glass – under the new name of Dr David Keel – into that show's opening episodes.

Police Surgeon was also title for a US series (1972, syndicated) about a doctor attached to a police emergency unit who, like Hendry's Brent,

had the sleuthing habit. Sam Groom played the said Dr Simon Locke. The concept of a medical detective, of course, was most successfully exploited by >*Quincy ME*.

GUEST CAST: Harry H Corbett, Geoffrey Palmer, Michael Crawford.

POLICE WOMAN

USA 1974–8 91 x 60m col NBC. A Columbia Pictures Television Production. UK tx 1975–9 ITV.

CR *Robert Collins.* **EXEC PR** *David Gerber.*
PR *Douglas Benton, Edward De Blasio.*
DR *Various, including Robert Collins, Robert Vaughn, Corey Allen, Alvin Ganzer, Alt Kjellin, Herschel Daugherty, David Moessinger, John Newland.* **WR** *Various, including Robert Collins.*
MUS *Morton Stevens.*

CAST *Sgt Suzanne 'Pepper' Anderson (Angie Dickinson) Lt Bill Crowley (Earl Holliman) Det Joe Styles (Ed Bernard) Det Pete Royster (Charles Dierkop) Cheryl (Nichole Kallis) Lt Paul Marsh (Val Bisoglio).*

Police Woman first aired on 26 March 1974 as 'The Gamble', an episode for Joseph Wambaugh's successful show >*Police Story*, with Angie Dickinson (aka Angeline Brown) playing policewoman Lisa Beaumont. The pilot achieved good ratings, and the series started up in October of the same year, with Dickinson's

⊗ *Angie Dickinson in* Police Woman, *a spin-off from Joseph Wambaugh's anthology show* Police Story.

character undergoing a name change to the spicier Pepper Anderson. It set a trend in female cops and made a star of Angie Dickinson.

Although *Police Woman* featured an early leading part for a woman in a traditionally male preserve, it milked star Dickinson's looks and femininity for all they were worth. (The peep-show shot of Dickinson descending a staircase in the opening credits has passed into TV legend.) A sexy, brassy blonde, Sergeant Pepper Anderson was an undercover agent for the criminal conspiracy department of the Los Angeles Police Department. Working on a vice squad team that

190

included two other undercover cops, Detectives Joe Styles and Pete Royster, she was required to pose as anything from a prostitute to a gangster's girlfriend – frequently in short skirts or fishnet tights. The team reported directly to Lieutenant Bill Crowley (Earl Holliman).

But the show was not all high heels. Anderson's personality was rounded out by occasional visits to autistic younger sister Cheryl in the first season, while overall the show managed to retain something of the *vérité* spirit of its originating series. One month before filming, Dickinson, along with other cast members, went to the Hollywood Division police station to absorb the atmosphere and found herself in the midst of a real-life gun drama ending in the murder of an armed attacker.

Dickinson later starred in another NBC crime series, >*Cassie and Company* (1982), in which she played Cassie Holland, a beautiful Los Angeles private detective. Her earlier roles included the part of Mary McCauley in the CBS adventure series *Men into Space* (1959–60), the story of the US government's space programme as seen through the eyes of Air Force Colonel Edward McCauley. Writer, director and creator Robert Collins also worked on *Marcus Welby MD*, >*Police Story* and >*Serpico*.

GUEST CAST: Robert Vaughn, Ron Masak, Kelley Miles, David Birney, Robert England, Lisa Hartman.

PRIME SUSPECT

UK 1991–99 x 120m, 3 x 110m col. Granada TV. US tx 1995–6 WGBH Boston.
CR Lynda La Plante. **PR** Don Leaver, Paul Marcus, Brian Park, Lynn Horsford, Sally Head.
DR Various, including Christopher Menaul, John Strickland, David Drury, Sara Pia, John Madden, Philip David. **WR** Various, including Lynda La Plante, Allan Cubbitt, Eric Deacon, Guy Hibbert, Guy Andrews, Paul Billing. **MUS** Stephen Warbeck.
CAST DCI/Supt Jane Tennison (Helen Mirren) DS Bill Ottley (Tom Bell (1, 3)) DCS Mike Kernan (John Benfield (1, 2, 4)) DI Muddiman (Jack Ellis (1, 2, 4)) DI Richard Haskons (Richard Hawley (1, 2, 4)). **VIDEO** Granada.

'Look, I know what you've heard about me – "That bloody Jane Tennison, she'll come storming into your nick, the balls of your best officers trailing from her jaws, spraying people with claret, calling people Masons, threatening resignation"– well I just wanted to tell you I'm not a complete maniac.' Detective Chief Inspector Jane Tennison

Relentlessly gripping cycle of police thrillers from Lynda La Plante focusing on the shackles of sexism that bound the career of ambitious Metropolitan CID officer Jane Tennison, as she pursued high-profile crimes beginning with serial prostitute-murder in the 1991 two-parter, *Prime Suspect*. Such was its success, that the chain-smoking, not-so-gentle-touch Tennison was back in *PS 2* a year later (macabre buried corpse in a racially antagonised black backstreet), while *PS 3* saw her transferred from Southampton Row to Soho's vice squad and a case of paedophilia. *PS 4* saw a change of format to a series of three separate 120-minute films *(The Lost Child, Inner Circles, The Scent of Darkness)*, their common link being that they more fully explored the way professional women – the emblematic Tennison – (mis)use power as well as experience it. For *PS 5* Tennison (based on real-life policewoman DCI Jackie Malton) was demoted to Manchester where the confession by a twelve-year-old boy to the murder of a small-time drug-dealer opened up a dizzying vista of police corruption. Much of the series' continuing success was down to actress Helen Mirren (born Ilyena Mironoff, daughter of a Tsarist colonel), recognised not least by a 1996 Outstanding Actress Emmy.

GUEST CAST: Zoë Wanamaker *(PS 1)*, Colin Salmon (as DS Oswalde, *PS 2*), Peter Capaldi *(PS 3)*, Craig Fairbrass (as DI Burkin, *PS 1 & 2*), John McArdle (as DCS Ballinger, *PS 5*), Julia Lane (as DI Devanny, *PS 5*), David O'Hara (as DS Jerry Rankin, *PS 5*), Christopher Fairbank *(PS 3)*, Ciaran Hinds *(PS 3)*, Adrian Lukis *(PS 4)*, Ralph Fiennes *(PS 1)*, Noel Dyson *(PS 1 & 2)*, Tom Wilkinson *(PS 1)*, Mossie Smith *(PS 4)*.

THE PROFESSIONALS

UK 1977–83 57 x 60m col ITV. Avengers Mark I/LWT.

CR *Brian Clemens.* **EXEC PR** *Brian Clemens, Albert Fennell.* **DR** *Various, including Douglas Camfield, William Brayne, Charles Crichton, Anthony Simmons, Peter Medak, Martin Campbell, Pennant Roberts, Tom Clegg, Chris Burt, Gerry O'Hara, David Wickes, Raymond Menmuir, John Crome, Dennis Lewiston, Dennis Abey, Ray Austin, Francis Megahy, Benjamin Wickers, Christopher King, Ferdinand Fairfax, Ernest Day, Chris Burt, Ian Sharp.* **WR** *Various, including Brian Clemens, Dennis Spooner, Gerry O'Hara, Ted Childs, Ronald Graham, Tony Barwick, Christopher Wickling, Roger Marshall.* **MUS** *Laurie Johnson.* **CAST** *William Andrew Philip Bodie (Lewis Collins) Ray Doyle (Martin Shaw) George Cowley (Gordon Jackson) Murphy (Steve Alder) Betty (Bridget Brice).* **VIDEO** *The Video Collection.*

Macho crypto-fascism or clever spoof on thick-ear police actioners? History is still in judgement on *The Professionals*, the Seventies hit series from Brian Clemens (previously one of the movers and shakers of *The Avengers*), although the interim evidence suggests the worst. Bodie and Doyle were action-men members of fictitious Criminal Intelligence 5 (CI5), a crack British anti-terrorist police unit headed by gruff limping boss, George 'The Cow' Cowley. Bodie was ex-SAS,

Doyle an ex-East End cop, Cowley formerly of MI5: Episodes consisted mainly of Cowley barking orders (not terribly convincingly, as for most viewers he was was still the butler Hudson from period soap *Upstairs, Downstairs*), much rushing around in bubble-permed Doyle's Ford Capri, followed by bouts of pistol-in-the-face, door-kicking violence.

The show topped the ratings in 1981, and drew plaudits from the National Viewers and Listeners Association for its lack of swearing and sex. However, it was dogged by criticism over its violence quotient, and one episode had to be pulled completely. (The unaired segment, 'The Klansman', was a well-meaning piece of anti-

Bodie (left) and Doyle in quintessential macho mode in 70s actioner The Professionals.

racism, which proves the difficulty of pigeon-holing the show.) Eventually the show's leads tired of the gratuitous mayhem themselves, with Martin Shaw (later *The Chief*), in a belated display of taste, dismissing his character as a 'violent puppet'. (Shaw forbade repeats until 1992.) To their credit, however, Shaw and Collins (formerly the drummer with Sixties popsters *The Mojos*) did their own muscular stuntwork, and at no small cost; between them they sustained 27 stitches, three broken ankles and a fractured collar-bone.

Even if not tongue-in-cheek itself, *The Professionals* has been remorselessly sent up by others, Keith Allen's *The Bullshitters* being one parody among many.

It may have been risible but, over twenty years after *The Professionals* first smacked on to the small screen, the show was revived by David Wickes, a former *Professionals* director. None of the originals appeared in the 1998 revival, leaving it to the ubiquitous Edward Woodward (>*The Equalizer*) to head the new team as boss Harry Malone. Colin Wells, Kal Weber and Lexa Doig also starred in what was known in Germany, amusingly enough, as *The Professionals – The Next Generation*.

GUEST CAST: Steven Berkoff, Ed Bishop, Pierce Brosnan, Charles Dance, Maurice Denham, Karl Howman, Patricia Hodge, Michael Praed, Pamela Stephenson, David Suchet, Gabrielle Drake, Tony Osoba, Art Malik, Christopher Ellison.

PROFILER

USA 1996 31+ x 60m col NBC. A Sander-Moses Production.

CR *Cynthia Saunders.* **EXEC PR** *Kim Moses, Ian Sander, Stephen Kronish.* **PR** *Charles Holland, Anthony Santa Croce.* **DR** *Various, including Jack Bender, Tucker Gates, John D Patterson, Dan Lerner, Kevin Hooks, James Whitmore, Ian Sander, Lewis Teague, John Harrison Sarah Pia Anderson, Matt Penn.* **WR** *Various, including Cynthia Saunders, Nancy Miller, Steve Fekes, George Geiger.* **MUS** *Angelo Badalamenti (theme), Danny Lux.*

CAST *Dr Sam Waters (Ally Walker) Chloe Waters (Caitlin Wachs) Bailey Malone (Robert Davi) George Fraley (Peter Frechette) Angel Brown (Erica Gimpel) Grace Alvarez (Roma Maffia) Frances Malone (Heather McComb) John Grant (Julian McMahon) Jack Dennis (Christopher Marcus) Payton (Shiek Mahmud-Bey) Donald Lucas (Mark Rolston) Nick 'Coop' Cooper (A Martinez).*

Suspense show starring Ally Walker (from *When You Were Sleeping*) as Dr Sam Waters, a forensic psychologist with the Violent Crimes Task Force, a federal agency which aided the FBI and other law enforcement bodies on difficult murder cases – mad bombers, serial killers, ritualistic murderers on American Indian reservations and the like. A recurring plot element

194

⊗ *Robert Vaughn as Harry Rule in* The Protectors; *the show was produced by Gerry 'Thunderbirds' Anderson.*

was Waters' search for the anonymous serial killer 'Jack', who had murdered her husband. And was now lying in wait for her. The theme was by Angelo Badalamenti of >*Twin Peaks*.

GUEST CAST: David Carradine, Richard Roundtree, Talia Balsam, James Coburn, Larry Wilcox, Kim Darby.

THE PROTECTORS

UK 1972–4 52 x 30m col ITV. A Group Three Production for ITC. US tx syndicated.

CR *Lew Grade.* **PR** *Gerry Anderson, Reg Hill.*
DR *John Hough, Don Chaffey, Jeremy Summers, Roy Ward Baker, Cyril Frankel, Harry Booth, Michael Lindsay-Hogg, Robert Vaughn, Don Leaver, Charles Crichton, David Tomblin.*
WR *Terence Feely, John Goldsmith, Brian Clemens, Donald James, Ralph Smart, Lew*

Davidson, Jesse and Pat Lasky, Donald Jonson, Tony Barwick, Sylvia Anderson, Dennis Spooner, Terry Nation, John Kruse, Trevor Preston, Anthony Terpiloff, Shane Rimmer, David Butler, Robert Banks Stewart. **MUS** John Cameron; theme, 'Avenues and Alleyways' by Mitch Murray and Peter Callander, performed by Tony Christie. **CAST** Harry Rule (Robert Vaughn) Contessa Caroline di Contini (Nyree Dawn Porter) Paul Buchet (Tony Anholt) Suki (Yasuko Nagazami) Chino (Anthony Chinn). **VIDEO** ITC.

The Protectors: a world-wide, freelance crime-fighting team which hired out its services to whichever government, business or wealthy individual could afford them. Robert Vaughn *(The Man from UNCLE)* played cool professional Harry Rule, based in London. New Zealand actress Nyree Dawn Porter (Irene in *The Forsyte Saga*) played the Contessa di Contini, a wealthy British noblewoman and widow who ran a high-class detective agency, specialising in art and antiques theft, from her luxury villa in Rome, and whose wardrobe lent a touch of *The Avengers'* style to the series. Tony Anholt played Frenchman Paul Buchet, the youngest of the three, a swinging Parisian whose suave charms attracted a stream of beautiful women. Created by Sir Lew Grade for an international market, *The Protectors* went for the Bond touch with star names, exotic locations and fast cars. Its trio of crime-fighters pitted their wits against challenges, kidnappings and diplomatic problems in Rome, Paris, Salzburg, Venice and the Mediterranean. Formula plots included jail-springing, Nazi criminals, jewel thefts, Russian scientists, Vietnam War veterans and atomic secrets.

Other characters, for the first season only, included Eastern martial arts experts Suki, Harry's au pair and judo expert (and large phwoar factor for the audience – woof, woof), plus Chino, the Contessa's Oriental driver and karate expert. From the second season, *The Protectors* were considered able to fend for themselves.

The Protectors was produced by Gerry Anderson, creator of supermarionation series *The Thunderbirds* and *Stingray,* and as well as Anderson's wife Sylvia its writers included Terry Nation, Dennis Spooner, Brian Clemens and Terence Feely. Directors were equally eminent. Series star Robert Vaughn tried his hand behind the camera for 'It Could Be Practically Anywhere On the Island', and other regular directors included Charles Crichton and Michael Lindsay-Hogg. Vaughn's later credits include *The Lieutenant, Washington Behind Closed Doors* (coincidentally also starring *Girl from UNCLE* Stefanie Powers), *Backstairs at the White House* and TV movies *The Woman Hunter, Centennial, City in Fear* and *The Day the Bubble Burst.* **GUEST CAST:** Patrick 'Dr Who' Troughton, Patrick Magee, Eartha Kitt, George Baker, Jeremy Brett.

195

PUBLIC EYE

UK 1965–75 28 x 60m bw, 59 x 60m col ITV. An ABC Weekend Network Production/Thames Television.

CR Roger Marshall, Anthony Marriott. **EX PR** Lloyd Shirley, Robert Love. **PR** Don Leaver, John Bryce, Richard Bates, Michael Chapman, Kim Mills, Robert Love. **DR** Various, including Don Leaver, Robert Tronson, Kim Mills, Jonathan Alwyn, Laurance Bourne, Guy Verney, Quentin Lawrence, Patrick Dromgoole, Dennis Vance, Douglas Camfield, Bill Bain, David Wickes, Richard Knights, Piers Haggard. **WR** Various, including Roger Marshall, Martin Worth, Terence Frisby, Robert Holmes, Julian Bond, Jack Trevor Story, Robert Banks Stewart, Trevor Preston, James Doran, Brian Finch, Richard Harris, Michael Chapman. **MUS** Robert Earley.

CAST Frank Marker (Alfred Burke) Det Insp Firbank (Ray Smith) Ron Gash (Peter Childs).

Frank Marker was the prototype seedy British private investigator (>Hazell and >Shoestring were among his screen heirs). He worked out of dingy offices, wore a grubby white raincoat that would have embarrassed Columbo and earned a pittance – £6 per day plus expenses. A classic foot-slogger employed on unusually realistic cases (missing persons, thefts, divorce work, blackmail), Marker was the quintessential loner; as actor Alfred Burke said of his character, 'Marker doesn't want anything, except to be left alone.' Only towards the very end of the series did he enjoy the company of other characters, namely Ron Gash, a PI who wanted partnership with Marker, manipulative Detective Inspector Firbank, and landlady Helen Mortimer (Pauline Delany).

Unlike the American and mid-Atlantic private eyes of the time, Marker was far from invincible, and was several times duped by his clients. In the 1968 episode 'Cross That Palm when We Come to It' he was even caught in possession of stolen jewellery – and went to prison (outraged fans wrote demanding his release). At first Marker was based in London, but later moved on to Birmingham and Brighton. But the cases remained the believable all the same.

It is said that Alfred Burke (later >The Borgias) was cast as Marker because, thin and 46 years old, he looked less like a private detective than anyone else who auditioned for the part (he started his acting career as a villain in British films). Certainly, Burke's world-weary, bruised-looking performance was essential to Public Eye's success. It was also Burke who came up with the name Marker. The character had originally been titled Frank Marvin, which was way too suggestive of tough-guy American gumshoes to have suited the shambling figure who walked the seedy streets of Britain.

GUEST CAST: Brian Blessed, Colin Baker.

QUINCY ME

USA 1976–83 5 x 120m, 143 x 60m col NBC.
Glen A Larson Productions. UK tx 1977–85.
CR *Glen Larson, Lou Shaw.* **EXEC PR** *Glen Larson.*
PR *Lou Shaw, Peter Thompson, Michael Star,*
Robert F O'Neil. **DR** *Various, including E W*
Swackhamer, Paul Krasny, Ron Satlof, Daniel
Petrie, Michael Vejar, Rod Holcomb, Leslie H
Martinson, Georg Fenady, Alvin Ganzer. **WR**
Various, Michael Sloan, Jack Klugman, Jeri Taylor,
Sam Egan, Steve Greenberg, Robert Crais,
Michael Braverman. **MUS** *Glen A Larson (title*
theme).
CAST *Dr R Quincy ME (Jack Klugman) Sam*
Fujiyama (Robert Ito) Danny Tovo (Val Bisoglio) Lt
Frank Monahan (Garry Walberg) Dr Robert Astin
(John S Ragin) Diane (waitress) (Diane Markoff)
Lee Potter (Lynette Mettey) Dr Emily Hanover (Anita
Gillette).

Dr R Quincy was a widowed medical
examiner with the Los Angeles County
Coroner's Office, who had a habit of amateur
sleuthing. This was useful, since the corpses that
came his way had a habit of being the victims of
murder – not that the cops ever saw this. After all,
there were no obvious signs on the cadaver. It
took a great forensic ME – someone like Quincy,
for instance – to see the tell-tale marks of foul play
and then go out and find whodunnit.

The show stemmed from the *Mystery Movie*

⊗ *Jack Klugman as* Quincy ME, *a show which, like
numerous other US crime-time hits, began life as a
Mystery Movie.*

slot, but subtly changed format over the seasons
until it became, at the end, more medical drama
(with Quincy putting everything from child abuse
to an outbreak of botulism under his microscope)
than crime show. In the meantime, actor Jack
Klugman made the green-clad, raucous-voiced
Quincy as beloved a TV character as his Oscar
Madison in *The Odd Couple*. Among the
supporting cast were Robert Ito as Quincy's
sidekick Sam Fujiyama, Val Bisoglio as Quincy's

restaurateur friend Danny, and John S Ragin as Dr Astin, Quincy's pompous boss at the coroner's office. Anita Gillette played Dr Emily Hanover, the psychiatrist who later became Quincy's wife. The name of the boat on which Quincy lived, incidentally, was Fiji.

GUEST CAST: Cameron Mitchell, Tyne Daly, Jonathan Frakes, John McIntire, June Lockhart, Jamie Lee Curtis, Sondra Blake, Julie Adams, Robert Foxworth.

RANDALL AND HOPKIRK (DECEASED)

UK 26 x 60m 1969–71 col ITV. An ITC Production. USA tx 1973 syndicated.

CR Dennis Spooner. *PR* Monty Berman. *DR* Cyril Frankel, Ray Austin, Paul Dickson, Leslie Norman, Jeremy Summers, Roy Ward Baker, Robert Tronson. **WR** Ralph Smart, Mike Pratt & Ian Wilson, Ray Austin, Tony Williamson, Donald James, Gerald Kelsey. mus Edwin Astley. *CAST* Jeff Randall (Mike Pratt) Marty Hopkirk (Kenneth Cope) Jean Hopkirk (Annette Andre) Inspector Large (Ivor Dean). **VIDEO** ITC.

'There's something different about this pair of private eyes . . . one of them is dead!' ran the billing for this typically oddball Spooner/Berman collaboration featuring flesh-and-blood PI Jeff Randall and his ghostly partner Marty Hopkirk.

The scene for this unnatural pairing was set in episode one, 'My Late Lamented Friend and Partner'. Jeff and Marty were partners in detective agency Randall and Hopkirk, until Marty was run down and killed by a car. Grieving Jeff went to his buddy's grave to pay his respects and instead found his ghostly friend paying him a visit to make sure that his killer would be tracked down. Marty made the mistake of staying in the earthly world too long and unwittingly violated an ancient curse: 'Cursed be the ghost who dares to stay and face the awful light of day.' The result was that Marty was forced to roam the earth for a hundred years, and Jeff had to endure the company of an invisible partner. The resulting detective-comedy series had plenty of high-speed action, good storylines and a neat gimmick, with Hopkirk, in an immaculate white suit that symbolised his other-worldliness, visible only to Randall and viewers (although the occasional ghost hunter, psychic or drunk could glimpse him too).

Randall and Hopkirk's was a love–hate relationship. Hopkirk's talents for eavesdropping or slipping through walls could be a considerable asset ('He's standing behind the door with a bottle in his hand' was a typical piece of advice). On the other hand, the long-suffering Randall regularly took the rap for his spiritual companion's actions and got beaten up, thrown down stairs or hospitalised for 'talking to himself'. Hopkirk also

⊗ *Mike Pratt and Kenneth Cope in oddball crime caper* Randall and Hopkirk (Deceased).

proved to be a jealous ghost around his widow Jean, who took on a job at Jeff's office.

The best episodes were those with ingenious plots making full use of Hopkirk's supernatural possibilities. In 'But What a Sweet Little Room' written by Ralph Smart, for instance, a greedy financial advisor lured wealthy widows into a sealed room where they were gassed as they

helplessly watched him dig their graves through the window. Invisibility also enabled Marty to besport himself at such places as the Queen's tea party or on the pitch at Wembley.

Production values may not have been the highest, with obvious use of stand-ins for location work and some poor editing, but *Randall and Hopkirk* could be spooky and fun and did not deserve its abysmal reception in the States where its syndication under the title *My Partner the Ghost* failed miserably to attract an audience.

The show was remade in 1999 with 'top comedy duo' Vic Reeves and Bob Mortimer in the lead part of the PI and his ghostly partner.

GUEST CAST: Frank Windsor, Peter Vaughan, Philip Madoc, Anton Rodgers, Brian Blessed, George Sewell, Roger Delgado, Ronald Lacey.

REMINGTON STEELE

USA 1982–7 91 x 60/120m col NBC. An MTM Production. UK tx 1983–4 BBC1/C4.

CR Michael Gleason, Robert Butler.
EXEC PR Michael Gleason. **PR** Glenn Gordon Caron, Gareth Davies, Lee Zlotoff. **DR** Various, including Seymour Robbie, Leo Penn, Don Weis, Peter Medak, Will Mackenzie, Rocky Lang, Christopher Hibler, Gabrielle Beaumont, Burt Brinckerhoff, Robert Butler, Sidney Hayers.
WR Various, including Michael Gleason, Brian Clemens, Glenn Caron, Lee Zlotoff, Susan Baskin, Jeff Melvoin, John Wirth, Brad Kerr, Rick Mittleman, Richard DeRoy. **MUS** Henry Mancini, Richard Lewis Warren.
CAST Laura Holt (Stephanie Zimbalist) Remington Steele (Pierce Brosnan) Mildred Krebs (Doris Roberts) Bernice Foxe (Janet DeMay) Murphy Michaels (James Read) Tony Roselli (Jack Scalia) Daniel Chalmers (Efrem Zimbalist Jr).

'Try this for a deep, dark secret. The great detective Remington Steele, he doesn't exist … I invented him. I always loved excitement so I studied and apprenticed and put my name on an office but absolutely nobody knocked down my door. A female investigator seemed so feminine, so I invented a superior, a decidedly masculine superior. Suddenly there were cases around the block.' Laura Holt's voice-over introduction to Remington Steele episodes

When LA private eye Laura Holt, played by Stephanie Zimbalist, has trouble attracting clients because of her sex, she creates a fictitious male boss, Remington Steele. And lo, shortly afterwards, a mysterious handsome stranger turns up claiming to be Remington Steele. Holt (somewhat improbably) makes him a partner, and together they cleverly solve cases. In between flirting and reparteeing wittily, that is. Murphy and Bernice were the agency employees, later replaced by ex-IRS official Mildred Krebs (who only had eyes for Remington).

Generally watchable, lighter-than-air detective show with comedy undertones, one in a long line of such dating back to >The Thin Man. The punning episode titles (eg, 'Thou Shalt Not Steele', even 'Steele Waters Run Deep') however, were excruciatingly unfunny. Producer Glenn Gordon Caron later tinkered with the show formula, lessening the detection and heightening the romantic comedy element, to create Moonlighting. There was a hint of substance underneath Remington Steele – the problems of a

Zimbalist's father Efrem (>*77 Sunset Strip*, >*The FBI*) occasionally appeared as Daniel Chalmers, Steele's mentor.

GUEST CAST: Sharon Stone ('Steele Crazy After All These Years', 1983), Tom Baker, Keye Luke, Lewis Arquette, Conrad Janis, Geena Davis, Delta Burke, Jonathan Frakes, Susan Strasberg, Tracy Scoggins.

RENEGADES

USA 1983 6 x 60m col ABC. Paramount TV.
EXEC PR *Lawrence Gordon.* **PR** *Chuck Gordon.*
CAST *Bandit (Patrick Swayze) Eagle (Randy Brooks) Tracy (Tracy Scoggins) JT (Paul Mones) Gaucho (Fausto Bara) Dancer (Robert Thaler) Dragon (Brian Tochi) Lt Marciano (James Luisi) Capt Scanlon (Kurtwood Smith).*

Renegades was an Eighties make-over of >*The Mod Squad* – nothing more, and perhaps something less. Bandit, Eagle, Tracy, JT, Dancer, Gaucho and Dragon were a big-city street gang who were given the choice by Lieutenant Marciano of going to jail for crimes committed or becoming an undercover police unit in the teen scene. To no great narrative surprise they chose option B. Captain Scanlon was the old-style cop who thought it all a bad idea.

As did most viewers, and only six episodes were made. Ex-ballet pupil Patrick Swayze at least found the show useful work on his way up the celebrity ladder, while the ever reliable Tracy

⊗ NBC's detective show Remington Steele *launched Pierce Brosnan to celebrity. And the role of 007 on the big screen.*

woman professional in a man's world – yet it never came through. Its legacy, of course, was to make the name of Brosnan, Pierce Brosnan, who eventually succeeded to the shoes of the big screen's 007. Before *Remington Steele*, the Irish actor's noticeable screen work had been largely confined to the US mini-series *The Manions of America*.

Scoggins (a former Elite model) looked good in street grunge.

The series was preceded by a 1982 TVM of the same name (dr Roger Spottiswoode, wr Rick Husky and Steven E De Souza).

RICHARD DIAMOND, PRIVATE EYE

USA 1957–60 77 x 30m bw CBS/NBC. Four Star.

CR *Blake Edwards.* **PR** *Mark Sandrich.*
DR *Various, including Leigh Jason, Roy Del Ruth, Tom Gries, Hollingsworth Morse, Alvin Ganzer.*
WR *Various, including Richard Carr, David T Chantler, John Robinson, Ed Adamson.*
CAST *Richard Diamond (David Janssen) Lt McGough (Regis Toomey) Karen Wells (Barbara Bain) Lt Pete Kile (Russ Conway) Sam (Mary Moore (aka Mary Tyler Moore)/Roxanne Brooks) Sgt Alden (Richard Devon) Sgt Riker (Bill Erwin) Laura Renault (Hillary Brooke).*

Created by Blake Edwards, private investigator Richard Diamond was a fixture on radio between 1949 and 1952, where he was voiced by Hollywood's Dick Powell. Other commitments prevented Powell from portraying the character when the time came for his incarnation on TV, so Powell suggested the young David Meyer in his stead – but also got Meyer to change his name to Janssen.

As seen on TV, Diamond was a suave ex-New York cop, whose old friend and former boss Lieutenant McGough was a mine of help. Diamond remained two seasons in NY, before transferring to LA for the show's golden age. Here he gained a girlfriend, Karen Wells (Barbara Bain, later *Mission: Impossible*), and tootled around in a convertible with a car phone. This enabled him to speak constantly to his answering service, Sam, who – a neat gimmick this – was only ever seen from the waist down. A million men fell for her legs, although the producers took umbrage when the unnamed actress concerned revealed her face and modelled hosiery for the *TV Guide*. The actress was one Mary Moore, soon to become Mary Tyler Moore and world famous for her role in the sitcoms *The Dick Van Dyke Show* and *The Mary Tyler Moore Show*.

Meanwhile, back at the lot, Moore was replaced as Sam by Roxanne Brooks and the show continued through another two action-oriented seasons. Laura Renault was the old-time movie actress with a penchant for finding Trouble and constantly needing Diamond's help. The newly minted David Janssen, of course, made a career out of playing PIs and cops on TV, later starring in >*Harry O* and *O'Hara, US Treasury* (1971–2, 52 x 60m col, CBS, executive produced by Jack 'Dragnet' Webb), as well as the man-on-the-lam classic, *The Fugitive*. In syndication, *Richard Diamond* was sometimes transmitted as *Call Mr D.*

The episodes were: *The Mickey Farmer Case/ Custody/Escape from Oak Lane/The Homicide Habit/Picture of Fear/Hit and Run/The Big Score/The Chess Player/The Torch Carriers/The Pete Rocco Case/Venus of Park Avenue/The Merry-Go-Round Case/The Space Society/The Dark Horse/The Pay-off/Double Jeopardy/ Arson/The Ed Church Case/Chinese Honeymoon/Rodeo/The George Dale Case/A Cup of Black Coffeee/Juvenile Jacket/Short Haul/Pension Plan/Another Man's Poison/The Purple Penguin/Lost Testament/The Percentage Takers/Widow's Walk/The Bungalow Murder/ One Foot in the Grave/Snow Queen/The Sport/ Pack Rat/Body of the Crime/Soft Touch/ Boomerang Bait/Matador Murder/Murder at the Mansion/Marineland Mystery/Charity Affair/ Two for Paradise/Crown of Silla/Jukebox/Echo of Laughter/The Limping Man/The Hideout/ Rough Cut/Family Affair/Design for Murder/The Hoodlum/Act of Grace/The Bookie/The Client/The Runaway/No Laughing Matter/The Messenger/The Counselor/The Image/The Adjustor/Marked for Murder/The Caller/One Dead Cat/Dead to the World/Seven Swords/ The Fine Art of Murder/The Popskull/And Whose Little Baby Are You?/Fallen Star/Coat of Arms/ Double Trouble/The Lovely Fraud/Accent on Murder/East of Danger/Running Scared/The Mouse.*

RICHIE BROCKELMAN, PRIVATE EYE

USA 1978 5 x 60m col NBC. Universal TV.

CR Stephen J Cannell, Steven Bochco.
EXEC PR Stephen J Cannell, Steven Bochco.
PR Peter S Fischer. **DR** Various, including Hy Averback. **WR** Various, including Stephen Cannell.
MUS Mike Post, Pete Carpenter.
CAST Richie Brockelman (Dennis Dugan) Sharon (Barbara Bosson) Sgt Ted Coopersmith (Robert Hogan) Mr Brockelman (father) (John Randolph).

Spin-off from >*The Rockford Files* starring Dennis Dugan as the private eye who didn't look like one. Owing to his absurdly youthful visage and demeanour, Brockelman – who was in fact a 23-year-old college graduate – was never taken seriously by the cops or the villains, which gave him the edge over both. And, like Uncle Jim Rockford himself, Richie had a glib tongue, useful for extricating himself from those unpleasant situations in which television PIs oft-times find themselves. Playing Brockelman's secretary was Barbara Bosson (wife of wunderkind producer Steven Bochco), with Robert Hogan as Sergeant Coopersmith, Brockelman's disbelieving contact at the local police department. The show was preceded by a 1976 TVM (90m), while another TVM, made from edited-down episodes, later aired as *The Diary of Richie Brockelman.*

203

The episodes were: *The Framing of Perfect Sydney/Junk It To Me Baby/A Title on the Door and a Carpet on the Floor/A Pigeon Ripe for Plucking/Escape from Caine Abel.*

204

THE ROCKFORD FILES

USA 1974–80 113 x 60m, 5 x 120m, 1 x 90m col NBC. Roy Huggins-Public Arts/Cherokee Productions/Universal TV. UK tx 1975–82 BBC1.

CR *Roy Huggins, Stephen J Cannell.*
EXEC PR *Stephen J Cannell, Meta Rosenberg.*
PR *Juanita Bartlett, David Chase, Charles Floyd Johnson, Lane Slate.* **DR** *Various, including William Wiard, Corey Allen, Lou Antonio, Dana Elcar, Reza S Badiyi, Stephen J Cannell, Lawrence Dohenny, Ivan Dixon, Reza S Badiyi, James Coburn, Winrich Kolbe, Jeannot Swarc, Russ Mayberry, Richard Crenna, James Garner, Bruce Kessler, Stuart Margolin, Vincent McEveety, Juanita Bartlett, Christian I Nyby II, Joseph Pevney, Charles S Dubin, Meta Rosenberg, Jerry London, Bernard Kowalski, Arnold Laven.* **WR** *Various, including Juanita Bartlett, Stephen J Cannell, David Chase, Gordon Dawson, Howard Browne, John Thomas James (aka Roy Huggins), Robert Hamner, Edward J Lasko, Eric Kaldor, Mitchell Lindemann, Leroy Robinson, Jo Swerling, Rogers Turrentine, Shel Williams.* **MUS** *Mike Post and Pete Carpenter (theme), Richard DeBenedictis, Artie Kane.*

CAST *James Scott 'Jim' Rockford (James Garner) Joseph 'Rocky' Rockford (Noah Beery Jr) Sgt Dennis Becker (Joe Santos) Beth Davenport (Gretchen Corbett) Evelyn 'Angel' Martin (Stuart Margolin) John Cooper (Bo Hopkins) Lt Doug Chapman (James Luisi) Gandy Fitch (Isaac Hayes) Lt Alex Diehl (Tom Atkins) Off Billings (Luis Delgado) Capt McEnroe (Jack Garner) Lance White (Tom Selleck) Rita Capkovic (Rita Moreno) LJ (Al Stevenson).*

'This is Jim Rockford. At the tone leave your name and message. I'll get back to you.'

For someone who is a soldier hero in real life (two Purple Hearts in the Korean War), James Garner has an ironic affinity for cowardly conniving roles on screen: Bret Maverick in *Maverick*, the sheriff in the Burt Kennedy *Support Your Local* … western features – and Jim Rockford, only and eponymous operative of the Rockford Detective Agency, Los Angeles.

Every fictional peeper needs a gimmick and Rockford's – aside from his endearing antipathy to gunplay (he kept his revolver in a biscuit barrel) – was that he was an ex-con, wrongly imprisoned for five years in San Quentin. Consequently, he was no great lover of the police, despite a friendship of sorts with LAPD Sergeant (later 'lootenant') Dennis Becker, and specialised in cases that had them dead-ended. He charged

⊗ *James Garner (born Baumgarner) in the sublime*
The Rockford Files.

$200 a day ('plus expenses') but was usually
cheated out of his fee by clients who were less
honest than he. Rockford lived alone in a
beachfront trailer, which doubled as an office. He
didn't have a secretary, only an answerphone.

Despite Rockford's desire to avoid trouble,
hardly an episode of this wry, atmospheric PI
show went past without Jim being beaten up by
enormous heavies, giving car-chase in his Gold
Pontiac Firebird, or landing in deep jail-sort

schtuck, and having to be bailed out by attorney
girlfriend Beth Davenport. Not infrequently,
Rockford was led astray by former cell-mate Angel
Martin, a petty criminal of zilch moral fibre but
many half-baked scams. (The part was played
brilliantly by Stuart Margolin, who won
Outstanding Supporting Actor Emmys in 1979
and 1980.) Rockford's other less than upstanding
acquaintances included disbarred lawyer John
Cooper and tough guy Gandy Fitch, played by
soul man Isaac (*Shaft*) Hayes. Meanwhile,
Rockford's retired trucker father, 'Rocky' (Noah
Beery Jr, *Circus Boy, Hondo*), badgered his boy
to take up a safer, more honest line of work.

It is often forgotten that Rockford was a good
detective – or at least got results. He employed
dubious means, tricking, bribing and
impersonating (he carried a portable printing
press, to make fake ID cards for every occasion),
but always got his man.

The series came to an abrupt end when Garner
quit for health reasons, having damaged his legs
doing his own stuntwork for the *Files*' six seasons.
It was never an enormous ratings success – only
once breaking into the top twenty in the USA –
but few crime shows have ever found better
teleplays, characters or performances. *The
Rockford Files* was made by Roy Huggins (who
also created *Maverick*) as a vehicle for Garner,
who acted the part of the line-shooting gumshoe
to a 1977 Outstanding Leading Actor Emmy.

In the final season of the show, Tom Selleck appeared as the irritatingly perfect PI Lance White. The exposure led to the actor being cast six months later as >Magnum, PI. The show had previously spun off another gumshoe caper, *Richie Brockelman, Private Eye* (starring Dennis Dugan, 1978 NBC).

Of course, everything successful under TV heaven has a second life and in 1994, twenty years after the première of the original *Rockford Files*, Garner returned as Jim Rockford in a tranche of TVMs. To date, these have been: *The Rockford Files: I Still Love LA* (1994)/*The Rockford Files: A Blessing in Disguise* (1995)/*The Rockford Files: Friends and Foul Play* (1996)/*The Rockford Files: If the Frame Fits …* (1996)/*The Rockford Files: Murder and Misdemeanours* (1997).

GUEST CAST: Robert Donley, Bill Mumy, Lindsey Wagner (as Sara Butler), Abe Vigoda, James Woods, Sharon Gless, Paul Michael Glaser, Dana Elcar, Rob Reiner, John Saxon, Louis Gossett Jr, Michael Lerner, Larry Hagman, Sharon Acker, Lauren Bacall.

THE RUTH RENDELL MYSTERIES

UK 1987– 45 x 60m, 2 x 90m, 2 x 120m col ITV. TVS/Meridian. US tx 1990 Arts & Entertainment.

EXEC PR *Graham Benson.* **PR** *John Davies, Neil Zeiger.* **DR** *Various, including Don Leaver, Mary McMurray, Sandy Johnson, Herbert Wise, Sandy Johnson, Bill Hays, John Gorrie.* **WR** *Various, including Clive Exton, Geoffrey Case, Trevor Preston, George Baker, Roger Marshall, Ruth Rendell, Guy Hibbert, John Brown, Peter Berry, Robert Smith.*

CAST *Det Chief Insp Wexford (George Baker) Det Insp Mike Burden (Christopher Ravenscroft) Dora Wexford (Louie Ramsay) Jenny Burden (née Ireland) (Diane Keen) Sgt Barry Vine (Sean Pertwee) Det Sgt Martin (Ken Kitson) Sheila Wexford (Deborah Poplett).*

Ruth Rendell's bucolic Inspector Wexford (played by florid-faced TV veteran George Baker) of Kingsmarkham was first introduced to TV in 1987's 'Wolf to the Slaughter', beginning a two-decade procession of stately whodunnits which, if never quite >Inspector Morse, adequately filled their prime-time slot.

The hick-talking but deep-thinking Wexford was helped in his investigations into the gruesome murders which so often gripped his sleepy southern English market town by widower Detective Inspector Mike Burden (a character well named, for his grieving, put-upon air never departed even when he was later remarried, to history teacher Jenny). There was further copperly help from Sergeant Vine and Detective Sergeant Martin. Also seen was Wexford's spouse Dora (played by Baker's real-life wife, Louie Ramsay).

The TV tales were dramatised from Rendell's Wexford novels until these ran out (Baker was one of those who contributed new stories). Confusingly the series was changed into a general Rendell anthology in the mid 1990s. It was not until 1996, after a three-year absence, that Wexford himself recommended TV investigations with the 'Simisola' case.

SHOW TRIVIA: The character was dreamed up by Rendell while she was on holiday in Ireland, hence 'Wexford' after the Eire county / The show was filmed in the town of Romsey, Hampshire.

GUEST CAST: Peter Capaldi, Cherie Lunghi, Sharon Maughan, Dorothy Tutin, Amanda Redman, Sylvia Sims, Patrick Malahide.

THE SAINT

UK 1962–9 71 x 60m bw, 47 x 60m col ITV. An ATV Production for New World/A Bamore Production for ITC. USA tx 1967–9 NBC.

CR Robert S Baker, Monty Norman. **PR** Robert S Baker, Monty Norman. **DR** Various, including John Ainsworth, Peter Yates, Roger Moore, Jeremy Summers, Robert S Baker, Leslie Noman, Roy Baker, Freddie Francis, Alvin Rakoff, John Moxey, Ray Austin, John Gilling, Robert Asher.
WR Various, including Gerald Kelsey, Terry Nation, Harry W Junkin, John Knise, Norman Borisof, Ian Stuart Black, Julian Bond, Michael Cramoy, Lewis Davidson, John Gilling, Richard Harris, Robert Holmes, Michael Winder, Leigh Vance, Dick Sharples, Donald James. **MUS** Edwin Astley.
CAST Simon Templar, 'The Saint' (Roger Moore) Chief Inspector Teal (Ivor Dean). **VIDEO** ITC.

'… a roaring adventurer who loves a fight … a dashing daredevil, imperturbable, debonair, preposterously handsome, a pirate or a philanthropist as the occasion demands.'

Thus novelist Leslie Charteris defined his most famous creation, Simon Templar, aka 'The Saint' because of his initials and his penchant for helping those (especially damsels) in distress. The character – whose visiting card depicted a stick figure with a halo – first appeared in the 1928 novel *Meet the Tiger* and after becoming a sensation in publishing, comics, on the radio and big screen (played by George Sanders), it was only natural that he would progress to TV. Initially, Charteris himself tried to produce a television version of *The Saint* (with David Niven as the romantic hero), but the project only came to fruition under the guidance of TV tycoon Lew Grade, who considered it ideal for a slick, mid-Atlantic package. Patrick McGoohan (*Danger Man*, *The Prisoner*) was offered the title part but turned it down because *The Saint* womanised too much for his taste, so it was offered to London ex-cardigan model Roger Moore, already well known to audiences in both

⊘ *Playing* The Saint *made former cardigan-model Roger Moore one of the richest men in TV.*

the UK and USA for his lead roles in *Ivanhoe* and *Maverick*. It turned out to be a good choice: Moore played *The Saint* with a memorable dry style, perfect coiffure, a quizzical arch of his eyebrows, and a wink in his eye.

The TV episodes – initially all adapted from Charteris's stories – were entertaining action-capers in which The Saint roved up-market British and exotic foreign locales (Paris, Rome, Nassau,

Athens, Miami), meeting and beating kidnappers, blackmailers, thieves and murderers. The fight sequences, if inevitable, were excellently choreographed. In Britain, The Saint drove around in a yellow Volvo P1800, with a number plate ST 1, a prop much admired by Sixties audiences. (The same make of car features in the cult Steve McQueen film *Bullitt,* 1968, the first American movie by ex-Saint director Peter Yates.)

Whatever the setting, every episode involved a beautiful girl; among the actresses featured over the years were Honor Blackman ('The Arrow of God'), Jane Asher ('The Noble Sportsman'), Julie Christie ('Judith'), and Gabrielle Drake ('The Best Laid Plans'). Kate O'Mara appeared in different guises on some four occasions. Apart from The Saint himself, the only other recurring character was Chief Inspector Teal, invariably referred to by Templar in dismissive tones as 'Scotland Yard's finest'. It was Teal's lot to turn up at the often ruthless denouement to find himself once again outsmarted by the modern-day Galahad-with-a-gun.

In 1966, filming of *The Saint* switched to colour. Consequently, the budget – the series was the most expensive of its time – in other areas was tightened. Some of the glamour and expensive props went (the radiated, giant ant in 'The House on Dragon's Rock' ranks amongst the lowliest of model creatures ever to appear on screen), but the show continued its triumphant commercial progress. Some estimates put the earnings from world sales as high as £370 million. (Since Roger Moore owns the rights to the 47 colour episodes this makes him a man of some wealth.)

A 1978–9 rehash of the series, *Return of the Saint* (24 x 60m col, ITC; transmitted in the US on CBS, 1979–80) featuring Ian Ogilvy as the suave hero, blessed with perfect taste in all things, was execrable. As was a 1997 movie, *The Saint*, starring a miscast Val Kilmer (dr Philip Noyce).

GUEST CAST: Oliver Reed, Lois Maxwell, Peter Bowles, Sylvia Sims, Burt Kwouk, Willoughby Goddard, Julie Christie, David Prowse, Warren Mitchell, Honor Blackman, Jane Asher, Gabrielle Drake.

SERPICO

USA 1976–8 15 x 60m col NBC. Paramount TV. UK tx 1977 BBC1.

CR *Robert E Collins.* **EXEC PR** *Emmett G Lavery.* **PR** *Don Ingalls.* **DR** *Various, including Art Fisher, Reza Badiyi, David Moessinger, Michael Caffey, Robert Michael Lewis, Robert Markowitz, Paul Stanley, Robert E Collins.* **MUS** *Robert Drasnin, Elmer Bernstein.*

CAST *Frank Serpico (David Birney) Lt Tom Sullivan (Tom Atkins).*

Short-run police show, which trod slightly different ground from the 1973 film *Serpico* (starring Al Pacino). Here loner cop Frank Serpico was less concerned with rooting out corruption in the NYPD's 22nd Precinct than in pursuing murderers – your basic prime-time TV crime. For the record, Serpico's badge number was 21049, and both movie and TV series were derived from the story of the real-life police crusader of the title.

77 SUNSET STRIP

USA 1958–64 205 x 60m bw ABC. A Warner Bros Production. UK tx 1958–64 ITV (ABC, Anglia).

CR *Roy Huggins.* **EXEC PR** *William T Orr, Jack Webb (season six).* **PR** *Howie Horwitz, William Conrad, Fenton Earnshaw, Harry Tatelman, Joel Rogosin.* **DR** *Various, including Budd Boetticher, Leslie H Martinson, William Conrad.* **WR** *Various.* **MUS** *Mack David, Jerry Livingston.*

CAST *Stu Bailey (Efrem Zimbalist Jr) Jeff Spencer (Roger Smith) Gerald Lloyd Kookson III ('Kookie') (Edd Byrnes) Roscoe (Louis Quinn) Suzanne Fabray (Jacqueline Beer) J R Hale (Robert Logan) Rex Randolph (Richard Long) Hannah (Joan Staley) Lt Gilmore (Byron Keith).*

A hip, humorous series with flashy action that ushered in a rash of copycat, new-style private eye shows. *77 Sunset Strip* was set in the glamorous world of Hollywood, with detective partners who were smart in both senses – they had college degrees and they were up-market.

Efrem Zimbalist Jr (son of concert violinist Efrem Zimbalist and opera star Alma Gluck, father of >*Remington Steele* star Stephanie Zimbalist) starred as Stu Bailey, cultured former OSS officer and expert in languages. An Ivy League PhD, he had set out to become a college professor but turned PI instead. His partner was Jeff Spencer, also a former government agent, who had a degree in law. Both men were judo experts. They worked out of an office at number 77 on Hollywood's world-famous Sunset Strip and their cases took them to all the glamour spots of the world.

Other regulars included Roscoe the racetrack tout and Suzanne the beautiful French switchboard operator. But it was the proto-beatnik teenage would-be private eye and parking-lot attendant who worked at posh restaurant Dino's next door who shot the series into the top ten. Constantly combing his glossy, duck-tailed hair and speaking in what was called 'jive talk', Gerald Lloyd Kookson III – 'Kookie' to his friends – helped Stu and Jeff out on their cases and stole the show. Teenage girls went wild for Kookie (Edd Byrnes) and his fan mail reached 10,000 letters a week. A glossary was issued for those who wanted to learn his language, which included such young dude phrases as 'let's exitville' (let's go), 'out of print' (from another town), 'piling up the Z's' (sleeping), 'a dark seven' (a depressing week) and 'headache grapplers' (aspirin) – all

Kookie lend me your comb... Roger Smith (left), Efrem Zimbalist Jr (centre) and Edd Byrnes were the stars of Warner's 77 Sunset Strip.

soon copied by youth world-wide.

Kookie even had a smash hit record with 'Kookie, Kookie, Lend Me Your Comb', a duet with Connie Stevens, star of detective series >*Hawaiian Eye*. The *77* show spawned a number of records: the theme music from the show became a best-selling album, while stars Efrem Zimbalist Jr and Roger Smith, both lured into record contracts after Byrnes' success, bombed miserably.

Kookie, a kind of 'Fonzie' of the Fifties, fast

began to overshadow the principals. At one point Byrnes walked out, angry at his secondary role. He was swiftly brought back and promoted to a fully fledged partnership in the agency by the 1961–2 season. J R Hale took over the job of parking-lot attendant at Dino's.

By 1963 the novelty had worn off and ratings were declining. Drastic changes were made. Jack Webb (>*Dragnet*) was brought in as producer, William Conrad (>*Cannon*) was brought in as principal director, Efrem Zimbalist Jr became a freelance investigator travelling the world on no-expense-spared chases, and money was lavished on guest stars and top writers. But it didn't help, and the series left the screens in 1964, with a blaze of imitators close behind it.

77 Sunset Strip, which won the 1960 Golden Globe for Best Drama show, was introduced by two pilot TV movies – *Anything for Money* (1957, 60m, ABC) and *Girl on the Run* (1958, 90m, ABC) – both starring Efrem Zimbalist Jr. His other TV credits include >*The FBI, Maverick* and >*Remington Steele.*

The creator of the series, action-adventure producer and writer Roy Huggins, was also responsible for *Maverick, Colt 45, The Fugitive,* >*The Rockford Files* and *City of Angels.* As executive producer his credits include *Alias Smith and Jones,* >*Baretta* and >*Toma.*

GUEST CAST: Brian Keith, DeForest Kelly, Mary Tyler Moore, Gena Rowlands, Lee Van Cleef.

SHAFT

USA 1973–4 7 x 90m col CBS. MGM TV. UK tx 1974–5 ITV.

CR *Ernest Tidyman.* **EXEC PR** *Allan Balter.*
PR *William Reed Woodfield.* **DR** *Ivan Dixon, John Llewellyn Moxey, Alexander Singer, Nicholas Colasanto, Harry Harris, Lee Philips, Allen Reisner, Lawrence Dobkin.* **WR** *William Reed Woodfield, Allan Balter, Ellis Marcus, Ken Kolb.*
MUS *Isaac Hayes (theme), Johnny Pate.*
CAST *John Shaft (Richard Roundtree) Lieutenant Al Rossi (Ed Barth).*

'Who is the man who fights for his brother man? Shaft!'

Richard Roundtree reprised his film role as tough black New York private eye John Shaft, in this calculated TV venture into blaxploitation. Unfortunately, the series toned down Shaft's ethnicity (they gave him a white friend, Lieutenant Al Rossi), his b-a-a-dass nigger-with-attitude violence, his conquests with the ladies and his flamboyant clothes to the point where he became unconscionably square. The cases too were tepid. The only hang-overs from the Shaft movies – and the only decent things about the series – were Isaac Hayes' Oscar-winning theme and Roundtree's boppy, muscular walking style.

Shaft the TV series lasted for only seven

⚐ *Trevor Eve as the 'private ear' of Radio West, Shoestring.*

episodes, being rotated in its original US transmission with >*Hawkins* as part of The New CBS Tuesday Night Movie. Nicholas Colasanto, the late 'Coach' of *Cheers*, directed the episode 'The Killing'. Roundtree's subsequent TV work has included *Roots* and *Outlaws*.

The series and movies were developed from the 1970 novel, *Shaft*, by Ernest Tidyman.

The episodes were: *The Enforcers/The*

Killing/The Kidnapping/Cop Killer/The Capricorn Murders/The Murder Machine.
GUEST CAST: Robert Culp, Richard Jaekell, Don Matheson, Tony Curtis, Darren McGavin, Clu Galager.

SHOESTRING

UK 1979–80 21 x 50m col BBCl. BBC TV.
CR *Robert Banks Stewart.* **PR** *Robert Banks Stewart.* **DR** *Various, including Paul Ciapessoni, Douglas Camfield, Mike Vardy.* **WR** *Various, including Robert Banks Stewart, John Kruse, Peter King, William Hood, Terence Feely.* **MUS** *George Fenton.*
CAST *Eddie Shoestring (Trevor Eve) Don Satchley (Michael Medwin) Erica Bayliss (Doran Godwin) Sonia (Liz Crowther).* **VIDEO** *BBC.*

👁 Eddie Shoestring was a computer expert who suffered a nervous breakdown and during convalescence decided on a new career as a gumshoe. An early detecting success at the studios of England's Radio West led to an invitation by station manager Don Satchley (played by Michael Medwin, *The Army Game*) to host a radio phone-in show where people told Shoestring their problems, which the 'private ear' would duly investigate. In a departure from the usual PI show format, Shoestring's cases were uniformly believable, the result of difficulties faced by 'ordinary people'. They were nonetheless interesting viewing, and pulled in audiences of 25 million.

Trevor Eve played the unkempt, Cortina Estate-driving Shoestring to perfection, giving the character an almost tangible air of vulnerability. Although largely unknown on the small screen before *Shoestring*, Eve had been a Gold Medal winner at RADA and appeared in several leading stage plays, including the role of Paul McCartney in *John, Paul, George, Ringo and Bert*. Aside from Eve and Michael Medwin, the other regular performers were Doran Godwin as Erica Bayliss, lawyer and Shoestring's landlady, and Liz Crowther (daughter of comedian Leslie) as Radio West receptionist, Sonia. The episode 'The Farmer Had a Wife' marked one of the very first screen appearances (if fleeting) of Daniel Day Lewis, cast as a DJ.

The series was devised by Robert Banks Stewart, later to create the Jersey-based police show >*Bergerac*.

GUEST CAST: Daniel Day Lewis, Michael Elphick, Diana Dors, Toyah Wilcox.

SILK STALKINGS

USA 1991–9 Approx 170 x 60m, 1 x 120m col CBS/USA Network. Stephen J Cannell Productions/ Stu Segall Productions.
EXEC PR *David Peckinpah.* **PR** *Stu Segall.*
DR *Various, including Ron Satlof, John Paragon, Carl Weathers, Rob Estes, Chris Potter, Peter DeLuise, Mitzi Kapture, Stephen J Cannell, Brian Trenchard-Smith, Ralph Hemecker.* **WR** *Various, including Stephen J Cannell, Todd Trotter, David Peckinpah.* **MUS** *Mike Post, Danny Lux.*
CAST *Sgt Chris 'Sam' Lorenzo (Rob Estes) Sgt Rita Lee 'Sam' Lance (Mitzi Kapture) Capt Harry Lipschitz (Charlie Brill) Capt Hutchison (Ben Vereen) Asst DA George Donovan (William Anton) Det Michael Price (Nick Kokotahis) Det Holly Rawlins (Tyler Layton) Sgt Tom Ryan (Chris Potter) Sgt Cassandra 'Cassie' St John (Janet Gunn) Roy Conroy (Stephen J Cannell) Lt Lou Hudson (Robert Gossett) Eric Russell (Eric Pierpoint).*

Silk Stalkings first appeared in 1991 as part of CBS's 'Crime Time After Prime Time' slot, although – in an unusual TV industry deal – was jointly financed by CBS and cable channel USA Network. The setting was glamorous Palm Beach (though the show was actually filmed in San Diego), where PBPD detectives Sergeants Chris Lorenzo and Rita Lance investigated homicidal crimes of passion among the rich and infamous. These offings were, in Rita and Chris' parlance 'silk stalkings'. In the same would-be humorous parlance they nicknamed each other 'Sam'.

The show – shown exclusively on USA after CBS dumped 'Crime Time' to make way for *Letterman* – largely eschewed violent action in favour of perusing the motives of the villain and the sparkling relationship between Chris (handsome, witty) and Rita (pretty, witty). Astutely playing the old 'will they or won't they?' card, the producers kept Chris and Rita out of bed together until season five. (Not that sex was missing from the show; it was the main ingredient in the torrid murder cases Chris and Rita pursued.) The producers also played a wild joker card in giving Rita an inoperable brain aneurysm that might explode at any time. As it happened it never did, but Chris died stopping a bullet aimed at her ('The Last Goodbye'), and she quit the force because she wanted to care for their unborn child, which was all she had left of her old pardner. Apart from memories.

With Chris and Rita gone, Michael Price and Holly Rawlins, then Tom Ryan and Cassy St John took the lead roles, all of them mirrors of Chris and Rita. After all, if the formula ain't bust, don't fix it. *Silk Stalkings*, the longest-running and highest-rated original production on US cable, came to an end in April 1999.

GUEST CAST: Terri Treas, Tracy Scoggins, Kristen Cloke, Jared Martin, Robert Forster, Nicholas Ball.

SOFTLY, SOFTLY

UK 1966–76 264 x 60m bw/col BBC1. BBC TV.

CR *Elwyn Jones.* **PR** *David E Rose, Leonard Lewis, Geraint Morris.* **DR** *Various, including Philip Dudley, Vere Lorrimer.* **WR** *Various, including Alan Plater, Elwyn Jones, Robert Jones.*

CAST *Det Chief Supt Charlie Barlow (Stratford Johns) Det Chief Insp John Watt (Frank Windsor) Det Insp Harry Hawkins (Norman Bowler) Sgt Evans (David Lloyd Meredith) PC Henry Snow (Terence Rigby) Det Chief Insp Lewis (Garfield Morgan) Det Cons Stone (Alexis Kanner) Mr Blackitt (Robert Keegan) PC Henry Snow (Terence Rigby) Det Cons Box (Dan Meaden) Asst Chief Cons Gilbert (John Barron) P/W Det Sgt Allin (Peggy Sinclair).*

Spin-off from police show >*Z Cars*. Initially detectives Barlow and Watt were relocated to the fictitious West Country region of Wyvern, but in 1970 the title was changed to the cumbersome *Softly, Softly – Task Force*, and Barlow promoted to Head of Thamesford Constabulary CID's Task Force, Watt accompanying him as his soft cop alter ego. After brief service there, Stratford John's perennially popular bull-headed Detective Chief Superintendent character was seconded to the Home Office for *Barlow at Large* (1971–5, 30 x 50m, BBC1), in the latter seasons abbreviated to *Barlow*. Meanwhile, back at *Softly, Softly*, the cast plodded on until 1976, always with quality scripts (Alan Plater was among those in the writing room), but also with a disconcerting black hole in the screen where Barlow had once loomed. Realizing that it had wasted one of the great double acts of UK television, the BBC then teamed Barlow and Watt in a 1973 investigation of the real-life Jack the Ripper case, the format being continued in *Second Verdict* (1976, BBC1), in which the duo put their magnifying glass over six true-crime mysteries of yesteryear.

The title 'Softly, Softly' was derived from the slang saw, 'softly, softly, catchee monkey'.

SONNY SPOON

USA 1988 15 x 60m NBC. Stephen J Cannell Productions. UK tx 1990 BSB.

EXEC PR *Stephen J Cannell.* **PR** *Randall Wallace.* **MUS** *Mike Post.*
CAST *Sonny Spoon (Mario Van Peebles) Lucius DeLuce (Joe Shea) Asst DA Carolyn Gilder (Terry Donahoe) Monique (Jordana Capra) Johnny Skates (Bob Wieland) Mel (Melvin Van Peebles).*

'He's a scam, he's a sham, he's a flim-flam man.'

Thus ran the trailer for this off-centre PI show featuring jive-talkin' black shamus, Sonny Spoon. As if to underline Spoon's serious street credentials, he worked out of a phone both while his best contacts and helpers were happy hooker Monique, Skates, a paraplegic skateboarder, and newsvendor Lucius. A more respectable aide was Carolyn Gilder, the young assistant attorney at the DA's office, who admired Sonny's success rate in catching criminals but not his louche ways. Among which, smart tongue and scamming aside, there was a marked habit of resorting to disguises – anything from an old mama to a reverend.

Likeable stuff, which deserved better than its short run. It came via Stephen J Cannell, and owed much to the character of Tenspeed in Cannell's earlier >*Tenspeed* and *Brown Shoe.* Mario Van Peebles (one of the 50 Most Beautiful People in the World, according to *Time* magazine) starred as Sonny, while his famous director father Melvin occasionally popped up in *Sonny Spoon* as 'Mel'.

SPECIAL BRANCH

UK 1969–74 52 x 60m col Thames TV (seasons 1 & 2)/Euston Films (seasons 3 & 4). USA tx syndicated (season 4).

EXEC PR *Lloyd Shirley (seasons 3 & 4), George Taylor (season 4).* **PR** *Reginald Collin, Robert Love (seasons 1 & 2), Geoffrey Gilbert (season 3), Ted Childs (season 4).* **DR** *Dennis Vance, Mike Vardy, Peter Duguid, William G Stewart, Voytek, Jonathan Alwyn, Guy Verney, James Goddard, Tom Clegg, John Russell, William Brayne, Douglas Camfield, John Robbins, David Wickes, Don Leaver, Terry Green.* **WR** *Various, including George Markstein, Trevor Preston, C Scott Forbes, Emanuel Litvinoff, Roy Bottomley, Anthony Skene, Adele Rose, Robert Banks Stewart, Paul Wheeler, Michael Chapman, Peter Hill, Louis Marks, Roger Marshall, Alan Scott & Chris Bryant, Tony Williamson, David Butler, Ian Kennedy Martin,*

215

⊗ Special Branch *ushered in a slew of door-kicking actioners to the British screen.*

Ray Jenkins, Peter J Hammons. **MUS** *Robert Earley.* **CAST** *(seasons 1 & 2) Insp Jordan (Derren Nesbitt) Supt Eden (Wensley Pithey) Det Supt Inman (Fulton Mackay); (seasons 3 & 4) Det Chief Insp Craven (George Sewell) Det Chief Insp Haggerty (Patrick Mower) Det Sgt North (Roger Rowland) Commander Nicols (Richard Butler) Commander Fletcher (Frederick Jaeger) Strand (Paul Eddington).*

A new-style police series with a new breed of policemen. This being 1969, even a copper could feel the influence of fashion and along came Inspector Jordan, as tough as his sideburns were long and his tie was wide. Long before >The Sweeney (from the same stable, Thames/Euston, in 1975), these policemen were human enough to have faults and flares.

Inspector Jordan was a cop with some of the glamour of a special agent. He was a member of Scotland Yard's Special Branch, a cloak-and-dagger team of spy-hunters whose duties led them into situations that threatened national security. Storylines, though, were standard affairs – Russian VIPs in need of protection, strange thefts at British Embassies, bomb plots against oil sheikhs and the ever-present threat of the KGB (although a nod in the direction of contemporary concerns also brought in hippie encampments and German student revolutionaries).

After the success of its first two videotaped seasons, the series underwent a complete transformation and was revamped, recast and handed over to fledgeling production company Euston Films, to become their first ever filmed series. From then on, Euston Films would prove uniquely influential on British television drama with credits including *Minder, Selling Hitler, Capital City* and *Shrinks*.

Jordan disappeared in the third and fourth seasons, as did his boss Superintendent Eden. In their place came Detective Chief Inspector Alan Craven, played by the distinctive George Sewell (*UFO*), followed by Detective Chief Inspector Tom Haggerty, played by Patrick Mower (later the unscrupulous Detective Superintendent Steve Hackett in >*Target*). Mower, another modern copper with his own methods, quickly assumed the Nesbitt role of ladies' man and trendy dresser. Other Euston cast members included Paul Eddington as Strand, a high-powered, toffee-nosed civil servant who kept an unwelcome eye on the detectives and their budgets.

SPENSER: FOR HIRE
USA 1985–8 66 x 60m col ABC. John Wilder Productions/Warner Bros TV. UK tx 1989–91 BBC1.

EXEC PR *John Wilder.* ***PR*** *William Robert Yates, Dick Gallegy, Robert Hamilton.* ***DR*** *Various, including John Wilder, Richard Colla, William Wiard, Virgil Vogel, Cliff Bole, David M Whorf, Winrich Kolbe, Don Chaffey, Sutton Roley.*

WR *Various, including John Wilder, Robert B Parker, Joan H Parker, Alex Gansa, Howard Gordon, Daniel Freudenberger, William Robert Yates, Norma Safford Vela, Tom Chehak, Steven Hattman, Robert Hamilton.*

CAST *Spenser (Robert Urich) Susan Silverman (Barbara Stock) Hawk (Avery Brooks) Lt Martin Quick (Richard Jaeckel) Sgt Frank Belson (Ron McLarty).*

PI show featuring Robert Urich (>*Vega$*) as the eponymous Galahad-with-a-gun. The latter was aided in his principled quests – which were invariably set in Spenser's home burg of Boston – by psychologist girlfriend Susan and black Magnum-carrying associate, Hawk (Avery Brooks).

A curiously soft-sell version of Robert B Parker's novel cycle, almost entirely lacking its Chandleresque wit (note that Spenser was an hommage to Marlowe, signified not least by both characters being named after Tudor scribes) and dizzyingly intense violence – despite several

217

episodes being written by Parker himself. But watchable enough on its own MOR terms, and successful enough to generate a spin-off, *A Man Called Hawk*, featuring Brooks (who would eventually beam up to *Star Trek: DS9*). The producers also had a knack of spotting a telegenic face, and Rob Morrow, Giancarlo Esposito, Jimmy Smits and David Hyde Pierce all got early acting assignments on the show.

After Spenser's cancellation, the gumshoe came back in a quartet of 120-minute TVMs made in Canada and shown on the Lifetime cable channel. The TVMs were: *Spenser: Ceremony* (1993)/*Spenser: Pale Kings and Princes* (1994)/*Spenser: The Judas Goat* (1994)/*Spenser: A Savage Place* (1995).

GUEST CAST: Anthony Head, Giancarlo Esposito, Jimmy Smits, David Hyde Pierce, Rob Morrow, Charles Kimbrough, Eriq La Salle, Bobby Orr.

STARSKY AND HUTCH

USA 1975–9 88 x 60m col ABC. A Spelling-Goldberg Production for ABC. UK tx 1976–81 BBC1.

CR *William Blinn.* **EXEC PR** *Aaron Spelling, Leonard Goldberg.* **PR** *Joseph T Naar.* **DR** *Reza Badiyi, George W Brooks, William Crain, Rick Edelstein, Randal Kleiser, Earl Bellamy, Georg Stanford Brown, Ivan Dixon, Paul Michael Glaser, Robert Kelljan, Randal Kleiser, Fernando Lamas, Arthur Marks, George McCowan, Dick Moder, Ivan Nagy, Sutton Roley, Barry Shear, David Soul, Claude Starrett Jr, Virgil W Vogel, Don Weis, Peter Levin, Jack Starrett, Leo Penn, Gene Nelson, Charles Picerni, Michael Schultz.* **WR** *Tom Bagen, William T Blinn, Jeffrey Bloom, Ron Buck, Robert Earll, Rick Edelstein, Michael Fisher, Steve Fisher, Al Friedman, Fred Freiberger, David P Harmon, Robert E Swanson, Sal Green, David P Harmon, Jeff Kanter, Marshall Kauffman, Edward J Lasko, William Lansford, Tom Maschella, Michael Mann, Ben Masselink, Joe Reb Moffly, Steven Nalevansky, Don Patterson, Parker Perine, Sidney Ellis, Paul Michael Glaser, Richard Bluel, Anthony Yerkovich, Robert Dellinger.* **MUS** *Tom Scott, Mark Snow.*

CAST *Det Dave Starsky (Paul Michael Glaser) Det Ken Hutchinson (David Soul) Huggy Bear (Antonio Fargas) Capt Harold Dobey (Bernie Hamilton).*

Freeze!…Prototype squealing-tyres cop show, starring David Soul (originally Solberg, and later the crooner of the immortal 'Don't Give Up On Us Baby') as soft-spoken, yoga-loving undercover cop Ken Hutchinson, with Paul Michael Glaser as his cardigan-wearing, junk-food-eating partner, Dave Starsky. Together they sped around an unidentified US city (but presumed to be LA) in a red 1974 Ford Gran Torino with white speed stripes on a mission to put all lowlifes behind bars. While easily burlesqued for its 'buddyism' and incessant car chases,

⊙ *David Soul (left) and Paul Michael Glaser in buddy-buddy cop show* Starsky *and* Hutch.

Starsky and Hutch contained, for the time, some grittily realistic stories and settings. On transmission in the UK, the BBC refused to broadcast the drugs episode 'The Fix'. The show was also one of the first in the cop genre to introduce major black characters, in the shape of quick-tempered Captain Dobey and the jive-talking snitch Huggy Bear (played by Antonio Fargas, who later sent up the superfly *S & H* character in *I'm Gonna Git You Sucka!*).

Stylistically, too, the show had its moments, notably the episode 'Shootout', written by David P Harmon, in which the boys were holed up in a restaurant whilst blasting it out with da mob, which was filmed in real time. As the seasons progressed, however, such shootie-shootie action saw the show increasingly become the target of

American churches and the nation's Parent Teachers Association. (In Britain, Kenneth Oxford, Chief Constable of Merseyside, later complained that as a result of the show 'police on duty were adopting sunglasses and wearing their gloves with the cuffs turned down. They also started driving like bloody maniacs.') In consequence, the action was watered down for the 1977–8 season, the gap filled with romance and an emphasis on the buddies' friendship that took the show into the realm of handkerchief-wringing schmaltz; a final episode saw Starsky dying in hospital while Hutch swore revenge on the villain responsible. (To the relief of viewers Starsky made a miraculous recovery of biblical proportions.)

The series, created by Spelling and Goldberg (>*Charlie's Angels, Beverly Hills 90210*) was preceded by a 1975 TV movie, *Starsky and Hutch*. Both stars, who harboured ambitions to work behind the camera, directed episodes of the series, as did Fernando Lamas, better known for his on-screen movie roles as a high-roller, and Ivan Dixon, formerly Sergeant James Kinchloe in *Hogan's Heroes*. Among the boys in the writing room was was one Michael Mann, who would later create >*Miami Vice*.

SHOW TRIVIA: Several customized Ford Gran Torinos were used in the making of *Starsky and Hutch*, the number plates of which were 071 NCY, 026 PRZ, and 537 ONN.

GUEST CAST: Lynne Marta, Alex Rocco, Marki Bey, Melanie Griffiths, Roz Kelly, Suzanne Somers, Danny DeVito, Joan Collins ('Starsky and Hutch on Playboy Island'), Lynda Carter, Jeff Goldblum, Philip Michael Thomas, Rene Auberjonois, Scatman Crothers, Yvonne Craig.

STRANGERS

UK 1978–82 32 x 60m col ITV. Granada.
CR Murrary Smith, Richard Everitt. **PR** Richard Everitt. **DR** Various, including William Brayne, Tristan DeVere Cole, Jonathan Wright-Miller, Charles Sturridge, Ken Grieves, Laurence Moody, Ben Bolt, Baz Taylor. **WR** Various, including Murray Smith, Edward Boyd. **MUS** Mike Moran. **CAST** Det Sgt/Det Chief Insp George Bulman (Don Henderson) Det Cons Derek Willis (Dennis Blanch) WDC Linda Doran (Frances Tomelty) WDC Vanessa Bennett (Fiona Molison) Det Chief Supt Lambie (Mark McManus) William Dugdale (Thorley Walters) Det Insp Rainbow (David Hargreaves) Det Sgt Singer (John Ronane) Det Insp Casey (Bruce Bould).

A spin-off from the spy saga *The XYY Man*, in which glove-wearing Sergeant Bulman (Don Henderson) was moved – via a disciplinary transfer – from London to Manchester's C23 unit. Here Bulman joined with Detective Constable Derek Willis (another *XYY* character), WDC Linda Doran and Detective Sergeant Singer on undercover jobs where local police might be spotted; as outsiders ('strangers') Bulman and Co, so the premise went, would not. Bulman, however, returned to a base in the capital city in the third season as part of a peripatetic 'Inner City Squad' – designed to bust crimes the land o'er – under the command of grim Scottish Detective Chief Superintendent Lambie (played by Mark McManus in a virtual try-out for his later role as >Taggart).

Although Bulman's novelty as hardcase but jazz loving, hamster-owning, Shakespeare-quoting detective was already palling, he was retired from HM Constabulary to go into a solo show, *Bulman* (1985–7, 20 x 30m col, ITV), in which his plan for a quiet life mending clocks on Shanghai Road was interrupted by the arrival of Lucy McGinty (Siobhan Redmond, later >*Between the Lines*), who persuaded him to become a PI.

GUEST CAST: Hywel Bennett, Maurice Colbourne, Kenneth Cope, David Daker, Colm Meaney, Nigel Stock.

THE STREETS OF SAN FRANCISCO

USA 1972–80 120 x 60m col ABC. A Quinn Martin Production/Warner Bros. UK tx 1973–80 ITV.

CR *Quinn Martin.* **EXEC PR** *Quinn Martin.* **PR** *John Wilder, Cliff Gould, William Yates.* **DR** *Various, including Walter Grauman, William Hale, Barry Crane, Virgil W Vogel, Barry Shear, Theodore J Flicker, Seymour Robbie, Arthur Nadel, Michael Douglas, Allen Reisner, Richard Donner, William Wiard, Bernard L Kowalski, Harry Falk, George McCowan, Arthur H Nadel, Michael O'Herlihy.* **WR** *Various, including Walter Black, Rick Husky.* **MUS** *Pat William (theme), John Elizade, Robert Prince.* **CAST** *Det Lt Mike Stone (Karl Malden) Det Insp Steve Keller (Michael Douglas) Det Insp Dan Robbins (Richard Hatch) Jean Stone (Darleen Carr) Lt Lessing (Lee Harris).*

As actor Karl Malden once pointed out, '*The Streets of San Francisco* had three stars – Mike Douglas, me and San Francisco.' Filmed on location with much panache, the series used hilly 'Frisco in the way that >*The Naked City* had used New York. The city was more than a backdrop; it was a character, moody and dangerous beneath its urbane charm.

The show's teleplays were frequently suspenseful – perhaps the best was the William Hale-directed siege story 'Labyrinth' – and the lead performances outstanding. The series, of course, was of some career-launching importance. Although Michael (eldest son of Kirk) Douglas had appeared on the small and big screens before, he had never achieved real notice. Playing young college graduate SFPD Inspector Steve Keller opposite veteran Lieutenant Mike Stone changed all that in one short TV

222

season. But Hollywood soon beckoned and Douglas left in 1975 (his character was said to have 'entered teaching', being replaced as rookie detective by Inspector Dan Robbins) to produce *One Flew Over the Cuckoo's Nest*. He has stayed in film land ever since. One of his best cinema performances was in *Basic Instinct*, in which he played ... a San Francisco cop.

And yet, no matter how good Douglas or San Franscisco was in *Streets*, it was the wonderful bulbous-nosed, granite-like Malden (real name Mladen Sekulovich) who stole the show as Mike

⊗ The Streets of San Francisco *was based on a novel by Carolyn Weston. Karl Malden (left) and Michael Douglas starred.*

Stone, with a performance every bit as good as his Academy Award-winning performance in *A Streetcar Named Desire*.

Those on the guest cast included a legion of upcoming talent, Arnold Schwarzenegger, Tom Selleck (>*Rockford Files*, >*Magnum PI*) and Don Johnson (>*Miami Vice*, >*Nash Bridges*) among them. The series was based on the novel *Poor, Poor Orphan*, by Carolyn Weston.

GUEST CAST: Arnold Schwarzenegger, Don Johnson ('Hot Dog' 1977), Tom Selleck, James Hong, Tom Bosley, Sharon Acker, George Dzundza, Johnny Weissmuller, Bill Bixby, Mark Hamill, Harry Rhodes, Cheryl Ladd, Tyne Daly, Joseph Cotton, Michael Ansara, David Soul, Paul Michael Glaser, Nicholas Colasanto, James B Sikking, Lew Ayres, Joe Don Baker, Leif Erickson, John Saxon, Stefanie Powers, Ida Lupino, Edward Mulhare, Nick Nolte.

S . W . A . T .

USA 1975–6 1 x 120m, 36 x 60m col ABC. Spelling-Goldberg. UK tx 1976 ITV.

CR *Robert Hamner.* **EXEC PR** *Aaron Spelling, Leonard Goldberg.* **PR** *Robert Hamner.*
DR *Various, including Reza Badiyi, George McCowan, Richard Benedict.* **MUS** *Barry De Vorzon.*
CAST *Lt Dan 'Hondo' Harrelson (Steve Forrest) Off Jim Street (Robert Urich) Sgt David Kay (Rod Perry) Off Dominic Luca (Mark Shera) Off T J McCabe (James Coleman) Betty Harrelson (Ellen Weston) Matt Harrelson (Michael Harland) Kevin Harrelson (David Adams).*

This Spelling-Goldberg series featured the work of the West California Special Weapons and Tactics team (hence 'SWAT'). The élite unit was composed of five Vietnam vets, whose training and equipment enabled them to negotiate the crimes of the urban-jungle, particularly those 'holed up' with an arsenal to hand. The members of SWAT were: team leader 'Hondo' Harrelson (Steve Forrest from >*The Baron*), Street the scout (Robert Urich, later >*Vega$* and >*Spenser: For Hire*), Kay the communications expert, and Luca and McCabe the snipers.

It was highly popular, but was cancelled after 36 episodes because of fears over its violence quotient. *S.W.A.T.* was spun off from an episode of *The Rookies* (1972–3, 68 x 60m col), another Spelling-Goldberg crime show for ABC network.

The episodes were: *S.W.A.T. (TVM)/The Killing Ground/A Coven of Killers/The Bravo Enigma/Pressure Cooker/Hit Men/Jungle War/ Death Score/Death Carrier/The Steel-Plated Security Blanket/Omega One/Blind Man's Bluff/ Sole Survivor/Deadly Tide I/Deadly Tide II/Kill S.W.A.T./Dealers in Death/Time Bomb/The Vendetta/Criss-Cross/Courthouse/Vigilante/ Ordeal/Dangerous Memories/The Swinger/ Terror Ship/Murder by Fire/Silent Night – Deadly Night/The Running Man I/The Running Man II/ Lessons in Fear/Deadly Weapons/The Chinese Connection/Dragons and Owls/Any Second Now/Soldier on the Hill/Officer Luca, You're Dead.*

GUEST CAST: Farrah Fawcett, Leslie Nielsen, Georg Stanford Brown, James Keach, Elisha Cook Jr, Lesley Ann Warren, James Darren, James Hong.

223

THE SWEENEY

UK 1975–82 52 x 60m col ITV. Euston Films/Thames TV.

CR Ian Kennedy Martin. **PR** Ted Childs.
DR Various, including Terry Green, Tom Clegg, Jim Goddard, David Wickes, Douglas Camfield, Mike Vardy, Viktor Ritelis, William Brayne.
WR Various, including Trevor Preston, Troy Kennedy Martin, Roger Marshall, Robert Banks Stewart, Allan Prior, Ronald Graham, Tony Hoare, P J Hammond. **MUS** Harry South.
CAST Det Insp Jack Regan (John Thaw) Det Sgt George Carter (Dennis Waterman) Chief Insp Frank Haskins (Garfield Morgan).

'We're the Sweeney, son, and we haven't had any dinner...'

Developed from a 1974 pilot, *Regan*, aired as part of ITV's *Armchair Theatre*, Euston Films' landmark police series eschewed the cosiness of the standard British cop show (notably, the paradigmatic >*Dixon of Dock Green*) in favour of hard-edged realism and visceral action. Its portrait of the police was far from flattering: the series' chief characters, Detective Inspector Jack Regan (played by John Thaw, *Redcap*, >*Z Cars*, *Thick as Thieves*, >*Inspector Morse*) and his young sidekick, East Ender George Carter (Dennis Waterman), routinely ignored the rule-book, hit suspects, associated with villains, swore and drank to excess. In one episode, Jack Regan burgled the office of Chief Inspector Haskins – the man with the unenviable job of keeping the surly Regan under control – in search of his annual report.

Made on a shoestring budget of £40,000 per episode, *The Sweeney* – the title was derived from 'Sweeney Todd', Cockney rhyming slang for Scotland Yard's Flying Squad – was shot on film, with outstanding, often witty writing. Muscular though the action was, the series' success rested in large part on the matey relationship between Regan and Carter. To enhance this, the scriptwriters killed off Carter's wife (played by Stephanie Turner, later >*Juliet Bravo*) so that the detective sergeant could spend his rest hours, as well as his working hours, drinking Scotch with his kipper tie-wearing 'guvnor' (Regan being already divorced).

Among the more notable of the large guest cast was George Cole in the episode 'The Tomorrow Man' (also with John Hurt). Cole would later co-star with Dennis Waterman in the hit series *Minder*. The instalment 'Hearts and Minds' featured the English comic duo Morecambe and Wise.

Although the show attracted criticism for its violence and swearing (in the latter department 'bastard' was a show staple, although the line 'Look slag, I don't give a toss who you have in your bed' raised many phones), in retrospect there

⊗ *Shut it! Dennis Waterman as George Carter in 70s actioner* The Sweeney.

was an innocence under its bruiser exterior. Storylines invariably concerned the apprehension of professional villains (preceded by spectacular car chases and ended by the line, 'Yer nicked!'), security van robbers, lorry hijackers and the like – all bad boys but not murdering psychopaths. Yet even if *The Sweeney* was not as dangerous as supposed, no other British police series has come close on the excitement gauge. There were two cinema spin-offs, *Sweeney!* (1976) and *Sweeney 2* (1978).

SHOW TRIVIA: Regan's car was a Ford Granada V6 Mark I / The villains usually drove a Jaguar 'S-type' / The show's enduring catchphrase was 'Get yer trousers on – yer nicked!' / Another was 'SHUT IT!'

GUEST CAST: John Hurt, George Cole, Eric Morecambe, Ernie Wise, Hywel Bennett, Brian Blessed, Diana Dors, Lesley Anne Down, Patrick Mower, Peter Vaughan.

SWITCH

USA 1975–8 1 x 90m, 70 x 60m col CBS. Universal TV/Glen A Larson Productions. UK tx 1983–4 C4.

CR *Glen A Larson.* **EXEC PR** *Glen A Larson, Jon H Epstein, Matthew Rapf.* **PR** *Jack Laird, Gene R Kearney, Paul Playdon, Leigh Vance, John Peyser.* **DR** *Various, including Bruce Kessler, Paul Krasny, Leon Penn, Sutton Roley, Sigmund Neufeld Jr, Edward M Abroms, Jerry London, Glen A Larson, Phil Bondeli, E W Swackhamer.* **MUS** *Glen A Larson (theme), Stu Phillips.*

CAST *Peterson 'Pete' Ryan (Robert Wagner) Frank McBride (Eddie Albert) Malcolm Argos (Charlie Callas) Maggie Philbin (Sharon Gless) Lt Modeer (Richard X Slattery) Wang (cook) (James Hong) Revel (waitress) (Mindi Miller) Lt Griffin (Ken Swofford) Lt Shilton (William Bryant).*

Private eye caper with comedy touches, modelled on the hit movie *The Sting*. Robert Wagner played reformed con man Pete Ryan, and Eddie Albert retired cop Frank McBride. Together Ryan and McBride formed a PI agency which specialised in pulling elaborate 'switches' – on those cons who were not reformed. Although based in LA, the twosome wheeled the land o'er, leaving trusty secretary Maggie (Sharon Gless, later >*Cagney and Lacey*) to mind the office. Restaurateur Malcolm Argos, another ex-thief, occasionally gave a hand in the stings. The show enjoyed a three-year run, with later episodes somewhat dropping the 'switch' element of the format in favour of straight sleuthing. After the close of the show, Wagner continued to find that crime TV does pay with the success of >*Hart to Hart*.

GUEST CAST: Natalie Wood, Anne Archer, Allen G Norman.

TAGGART

UK 1983– 63+ x 60m, 4 x 90m col ITV. STV.
CR *Glenn Chandler.* **PR** *Various, including Murray Ferguson.* **DR** *Various, including Haldane Duncan, Peter Barber-Fleming, Laurence Moody, Marcus D F White.* **WR** *Various, including Glenn Chandler, Julian Jones, Stuart Hepburn.* **MUS** *Mike Moran.* **CAST** *Det Chief Insp Jim Taggart (Mark McManus) Det Sgt/Det Insp Mike Jardine (James MacPherson) WDC/WDS Jackie Reid (Blythe Duff) Det Sgt Peter Livingstone (Neil Duncan) Jean Taggart (Harriet Buchan) Alison Taggart (Geraldine Alexander) Supt McVitie (Iain Anders) Det Cons Stuart Fraser (Colin McGredie) Dr Andrews (Robert Robertson).*

Police drama starring former boxer Mark McManus (>*Strangers*) as a bolshie working-class detective in an ultra-urban Glasgow. First met in a three-parter, *Killer*, anti-hero *Taggart* survived initially poor production values to become an enormously popular screen fixture, with some *Taggart* specials achieving viewing figures of over 18 million. He was helped to such heights by creator Glenn Chandler's drily complex plots. When McManus died prematurely in 1994, the series continued with Taggart's middle-class sidekick Detective Inspector Jardine (a Christian tee-totaller, to Taggart's dismay) and WDC Reid leading the murder investigations. *Taggart* without Taggart worked better than it had a right to, partly because McManus's performance had left such an indelible impression on the screen that he still seemed to be there, back at the station in Northern Division glumly issuing orders.

The episodes to date: *Killer/Dead Ringer/ Murder in Season/Knife Edge/Death Call/The Killing Philosophy/Funeral Rites/Cold Blood/ Dead Giveaway/Root of Evil/Double Jeopardy/ Flesh and Blood/Love Knot/Hostile Witness/Evil Eye/Death Comes Softly/Rogues Gallery/Nest of Vipers/Double Exposure/The Hit Man/Ring of Deceit/Death Benefit/Gingerbread/Death with Dishonour/Instrument of Justice/Forbidden Fruit.*

GUEST CAST: John Hannah, Amanda Redman, Barbara Dickinson.

T. AND T.

USA 1988-90 20 x 30m col. Syndicated and The Family Channel.

DR *Ken Girotti, Don McCutcheon*

CAST *T. S. Turner (Mr T.) Amanda 'Amy' Taler (1988-89) (Alex Amini) Terri Taler (1990) (Kristina Nicoll) Danforth (Dick) Decker (David Nerman) Det. Jones (1988) (Ken James) Aunt Martha Robinson (1988) (Jackie Richardson) Renee (1988) (Rachael Crawford) Sophie (1988) (Catherine Disher) Joe Casper (1988-9) (Sean Roberge) Det. Dick Hargrove (1990) (David Hemblen).*

A blatant vehicle for >A-Team muscleman Mr T., T. S. Turner was a tough former boxer who worked as a detective/investigator for attorney Amanda Taler. Still adorned with his trademark Mohawk haircut, this time Mr T. wore smooth suits over his bulging muscles. Although, when the need arose – as it did in every episode – T. S. would hot-foot off to his locker, change into a street-wise leather outfit and hunt down the bad guys. Supporting players for series one were Decker, a pal who ran the gym where T. S. went to work out, Det. Jones the cop who had come to have something like respect for T. S. and Sophie the secretary who worked for Amy. A bachelor, T. S. lived with his Aunt Martha and her pretty teenage daughter Renee. By the time it ran for season two in 1988, *T. and T.* had undergone a number of changes: The suits, and thus also the locker routine, were no more, and the same went for many of the co-stars. T. S. now worked out of an office in Decker's gym, dressed casually and found fewer reasons to fight. Young Joe Casper, who lived with Decker and worked part time at the gym, was added to the cast. In January 1990 *T. and T.* returned for a third season on cable's The Family Channel. By now T. S. had a new partner, Amanda Taler's younger sister Terri, a new contact on the police force, Detective Hargrove, and a return to more violent criminal cases.

Mr T., real name Lawrence Tero, was born Laurence Tureaud on 21 May 1952 in the ghetto area of Chicago. The second youngest of twelve, he was raised by his mother on welfare. He wrestled and played football while in high school and later worked as a gym instructor, bouncer and bodyguard for the likes of Michael Jackson, Leon Spinks and Muhammad Ali ('I am the best bodyguard because I'll take a bullet, I'll take a stab wound, I'll take a hit upside the head. I'm like a kamikaze pilot.', *Playboy*, September 1983). In 1980 Sylvester Stallone spotted him on NBC's *Games People Play* and cast him as the foul-mouthed Clubber Lang in *Rocky III* (1982). From there he went on to star as Sgt Bosco 'B.A.' (for Bad Attitude) Baracus in *The A Team* (1983). Tero's other works include an autobiography *Mr T: The Man with the Gold*, 1984, a TV ad for TR3 car polish, and *Mr T.'s Commandments,* a full length LP album released in 1984 by Columbia Records. He was nominated in 1983 for a Razzie Award as Worst New Star for *Zlocin u Skoli,* 1982. In 1985 he entered the world of pro wrestling as Hulk Hogan's tag team partner at the first wrestlemania.

TARGET

UK 1977–8 17 x 50m col BBC1. BBC TV. US tx 1982–3 TEC.

PR *Philip Hinchcliffe.* **DR** *Various, including Douglas Camfield, Chris Menaul, David Wickes, Ben Bolt, Mike Vardy, Gordon Flemyng.*
WR *Various, including Ken Follett, David Wickes, Philip Hinchcliffe, David Agnew, P J Hammond, Tony Hoare.* **MUS** *Dudley Simpson.*
CAST *Det Supt Steve Hackett (Patrick Mower) Det Chief Supt Tate (Philip Madoc) Det Sgt Louise Colbert (Vivien Heilbron) Det Sgt Frank Bonney (Brendan Price).*

Fifty-minute actioner featuring the cases of Detective Superintendent Steve Hackett (Patrick Mower, >*Special Branch*), the head honcho with a Regional Crime Squad working the South Coast ports of Britain.

Intended as the BBC's answer to >*The Sweeney,* its violence allotment and depiction of the police as door-kicking face-smashers caused a squall of protest which cut short the first season,

toned down the second, and resulted in a third not being commissioned.

The episodes were: *Shipment/Blow Out/Big Elephant/Hunting Parties/Vandraggers/Lady Luck/Set Up/Roadrunner/Carve Up/Rogue's Gallery/A Good and Faithful Woman/Queen's Pardon/Fringe Banking/Promises/The Trouble with Charlie/Figures of Importance/The Run.*

GUEST CAST: Pamela Stephenson, Carl Rigg (as Detective Constable Duke), David Daker, Lance Percival, Patricia Hodge, Ronald Lacey, Christopher Ryan, Prunella Scales, Stephen Greif.

TENAFLY

USA 1973–4 5 x 90m NBC. A Universal Television Production. UK tx 1974 ITV.

EXEC PR *Richard Levinson, William Link.* **PR** *Jon Epstein.* **DR** *Richard A Colla, Robert Day, Bernard Kowalski, Jud Taylor, Gene Levitt.* **WR** *Richard Levinson, William Link.*
CAST *Harry Tenafly (James McEachin) Ruth Tenafly (Lillian Lehman) Herb Tenafly (Paul Jackson) Lorrie (Rosanna Huffman) Lt Sam Church (David Huddleston).*

Harry Tenafly was a rarity among television's private detectives: not only was he black, he was also a dedicated and happy family man, living in Los Angeles with his conventional, pretty wife Ruth and their son Herb.

Black private eyes on television enjoyed a brief

⊘ Jeff Goldblum (left) and Ben 'Roots' Vereen were the stars of the semi-forgotten Tenspeed and Brown Shoe.

vogue in the early Seventies. In the same week in which *Tenafly* featured as a segment of NBC's *Wednesday Mystery Movie* – alternating every four weeks with >*Banacek, Faraday and Company* and *The Snoop Sisters* – >*Shaft* was beginning on CBS, again as part of an alternating series. But Tenafly was a less romanticised detective than Roundtree's Shaft. An ordinary, hard-working man, without Roundtree's

movie-star looks and sex appeal, he neither chased nor was chased by beautiful women.

Action in the series was divided between Tenafly's home and his office life (he worked for High Tower Investigations Inc). His friend and confidant at the Los Angeles Police Department, Lieutenant Sam Church, was regularly called upon to get Harry out of jams. But unfortunately *Tenafly's* very lack of thrills or glamour proved to be its downfall. Television audiences never took to the show, and it was taken off the air after six months and only five episodes – just two weeks before *Shaft* too was cancelled.

TENSPEED AND BROWN SHOE

USA 1980 1 x 100m, 12 x 60m col ABC. Paramount TV. UK tx 1981 ITV.
CR Stephen J Cannell. **PR** Stephen J Cannell, Alex Beaton, Chuck Bowman, Juanita Bartlett.
DR Various, including Stephen J Cannell, Rod Holcomb, Harry Winer. **WR** Various, including Stephen J Cannell. **MUS** Mike Post and Pete Carpenter.
CAST E L 'Tenspeed' Turner (Ben Vereen) Lionel 'Brown Shoe' Whitney (Jeff Goldblum).

👁 Or what Jeff Goldblum did before fame came knockin'. Goldblum played a demure Los Angeles stockbroker (thus 'a brownshoe' or square) who teamed up with a streetwise con-

229

artist, Tenspeed (Ben Vereen from *Roots*) to form an unlikely PI agency. They tended to find that Brownshoe's qualifications as a karate black belt and Olympic pistoleer came in useful when Tenspeed's mouth and guile did not.

Slickly made and acted, it also played witty homage to the PI genre, in a remake of Hammett's *Maltese Falcon* – twice. Something of a Stephen J. Cannell special (he created, produced, directed and wrote it) it deserved to do better than a thirteen-episode run and has rarely seen the light of a cathode ray tube since. A lost classic.

The episodes were: *Tenspeed and Brown Shoe/Robin Tucker's Roseland Roof and Ballroom Murders/Savage Says: There's No Free Lunch/ Savage Says: What Are Friends For?/The Sixteen Byte Data Chip and the Brown-Eyed Fox/The Millionaire's Life/Savage Says: The Most Dangerous Bird is the Jailbird/It's Easier to Pass an Elephant through the Eye of a Needle than a Bad Check in Bel Air/Loose Larry's List of Losers/ This One's Gonna Kill Ya/No title/The Treasure of Sierra Madre Street/Diamonds Aren't Forever.* **GUEST CAST:** Stephen J Cannell, Rene Auberjonois, Red West, Lewis Arquette.

THE THIN MAN

USA 1957–8 78 x 25m bw NBC. MGM. UK tx 1957–8 BBC.
PR Samuel Marx, Edmund Beloin.
CAST Nick Charles (Peter Lawford) Nora Charles (Phyllis Kirk) Lt Ralph Raines (Stafford Repp) Lt Steve King (Tol Avery) Lt Harry Evans (Jack Albertson) Beatrice Davies (Nita Talbot).

A wealthy New York husband and wife (plus dog, Asta) are amateur sleuths investigating murder cases in between exchanging witty repartee.

TV take on Dashiell Hammett's famed *Thin Man* novels. It suffered in comparison with the movie versions (which began with *The Thin Man* itself in 1934 and were blessed with the heavenly casting of William Powell and Myrna Loy), being their inferior in plotting, pace and banter. But it was pleasant enough to last 78 episodes, and was notable for the casting of 'Rat Pack' actor Peter Lawford (who was also J F Kennedy's brother-in-law) as Nick. Moreover, the 'Thin Man' format of a mystery-comedy with married (or at least partnered-up) 'tecs would come back to the small screen again and again, not least with >*Hart to Hart*, >*McMillan and Wife* and >*Remington Steele*.

T J HOOKER

USA 1982–6 1 x 90m, 91 x 60m col ABC/CBS. Spelling-Goldberg/Columbia Pictures TV. UK tx 1983–5 ITV.
CR Rick Husky. **EXEC PR** Aaron Spelling, Leonard Goldberg. **PR** Various, including Chuck Bowman, Jack V Fogarty, Don Ingalls, Ed Waters, Bernie

Kukoff, Jeffrey M Hayes, Rick Husky, Simon Muntner, Kenneth R Koch, Stephen Downing, Steve Kline, Mark Rodgers. **DR** Various, including William Shatner, Leonard Nimoy, Sigmund Neufeld, Charlie Picerni, Ric Rondell, Bruce Seth Green, Vincent J McEveety, Paul Krasny, Don Chaffey, Reza Badiyi, James Darren, Bruce Kessler, Don Weis, Michael Langer, Cliff Bole. **WR** Various. **MUS** Mark Snow.

⊗ *William Shatner (right) in a publicity pose for the hypnotically bad* TJ Hooker.

CAST *Sgt T J Hooker (William Shatner) Off Stacy Sheridan (Heather Locklear) Off Jim Corrigan (James Darren) Off Vince Romano (Adrian Zmed) Capt Sheridan (Richard Herd) Fran Hooker (Lee Bryant) Vicki Taylor (April Clough).*

👁 In which William Shatner played a veteran cop, T J Hooker, who rode around in a patrol car chasing criminals before moseying back to the Police Academy to teach the young something of his wisdom. Ever desirous of bringing the bad guys to justice, Hooker had

232

consistently refused promotion – and all the paperwork that that brung – in order to keep working the villain-infested streets. Officer Vince Romano was Hooker's headstrong rookie partner, and sexy Officer Stacy Sheridan (Heather Locklear, a clothes-horse in *Dynasty*) was the daughter of Hooker's commanding officer. Also seen was Sheridan's time-toughened partner, Officer James Corrigan (played by James Darren from sci-fi classic *The Time Tunnel*).

T J Hooker wasn't so much made as committed – like a crime. Shatner was kitted out with a toupee that looked as though a groundhog was squatting on his head, while the writing was cliché rich, sensitivity poor. Even a cameo from Leonard Nimoy (who also directed on the show, as did Shatner himself) only served to divert the mind upwards to *Star Trek*.

GUEST CAST: David Hedison, George Murdock, Tori Spelling, Delta Burke, James Hong, Sharon Stone.

TOMA

USA 1973–4 1 x 90m, 22 x 60m col ABC. Roy Huggins Public Arts/Universal TV.
CR Edward Hume. **EXEC PR** Roy Huggins, Jo Swerling. **PR** Stephen J Cannell. **DR** Various, including Nicholas Colasanto, Richard Bennett, Charles S Dubin, Marc Daniels, Jeannot Swarc Alex Grasshof, Daniel Haller. **WR** Various, including Stephen J Cannell, Edward Hume,

Juanita Bartlett, John Thomas James (aka Roy Huggins), Dave Toma, Tony Musante, Gerald DiPego.
CAST Det Dave Toma (Tony Musante) Insp Spooner (Simon Oakland) Patty Toma (Susan Strasberg).

Like >*Serpico*, a policier based on the maverick exploits of a real-life undercover cop, here Dave Toma of the Newark Police Department. Although a ratings success, the show closed after one season because actor Tony Musante found the production schedule a grind. ABC hired in a new lead, Robert Blake, tinkered with the format slightly, and issued >*Baretta* in its stead.

Susan Strasberg (d.1999), who played Toma's wife, was the daughter of Lee Strasberg, the famous acting coach at the Actors' Studio in New York. Meanwhile, the real Toma guested in every episode, as well as serving as show consultant.

GUEST CAST: Dave Toma, Philip Michael Thomas, Martin Sheen.

A TOUCH OF FROST

UK 1992– 24+ x 120m col ITV. Yorkshire Television.
EXEC PR Richard Bates, David Reynolds, Philip Burley, David Jason. **PR** Various, including Martyn Auty. **DR** Various, including David Reynolds, Paul Seed, Graham Theakston, Sandy Johnson, Roger Bamford, Roy Battersby, John Glenister, Alan

Dossor, Adrian Shergold. **WR** Various, including Malcolm Bradbury, Michael Russell, Sian Orrels, R D Wingfield, Richard Harris, Russell Gascoigne. **MUS** John Hiseman, Barbara Thompson.
CAST DI Jack Frost (David Jason) Supt Mullett (Bruce Alexander) DS Toolan (John Lyons) DS Barnard (Matt Baredock) DC Ernie Trigg (Arthur White) DCI Peters (Nigel Harrison) Shirley Fisher (Lindy Whiteford) WPC/DS Hazel Wallace (Caroline Harker) Sgt Wells (Paul Moriarty) PC Jordan (Ian Driver) PC Austin (Colin Buchanan) DCI Allen (Neil Phillips).

👁 Popular police procedural starring David Jason, who overcame the accumulated typecasting of comic roles to successfully portray downbeat Detective Inspector Frost in these adaptations of R D Wingfield's stories. Set in the fictional town of Denton, the TV cases of the irascible and bacon sandwich-loving copper were penned by writers of the first rank (Malcolm Bradbury among them), but it was Jason – in a virtual masterclass of acting, drawing out every nuance of his character – who caused most to reach for the 'on' button. At the end of the fifth season, Frost's protégé Detective Sergeant Barnard was killed, and Frost – who had once won the George Cross for bravery – left the force in disgust and grief. He came back, however, in 1999 for more murder, mystery and maverick coppering.

Episodes to date: Care and Protection/Not with Kindness/Conclusions/A Minority of One/ Widows and Orphans/Nothing to Hide/ Strangers in the House/Appropriate Adults/ Quarry/Dead Male One/No Refuge/Paying the Price/Unknown Soldiers/The Things We Do for Love/Fun Times for Swingers/Deep Waters/ Penny for the Guy/House Calls/True Confessions/No Other Love/Appendix Man/ One Man's Meat/Private Lives/Keys to the Car.

TREASURY MEN IN ACTION

USA 1950–5 Approx 80 x 30m bw ABC/NBC. An ABC Production.
PR Everett Rosenthal, Robert Sloane.
CAST The Chief (Walter Greaza) Announcer (Carl Frank/Murray Golden).

👁 Live half-hour action series based on real cases drawn from the files of the US Treasury Department. Walter Greaza played 'The Chief', with a fresh weekly cast pursuing counterfeiters, smugglers, tax evaders (of course), moonshiners and other law-defying types. Episodes ended with a stern reminder to the audience that crime doesn't pay.

The show provided screen work for a legion of tyro actors, among them James Dean.
GUEST CAST: James Dean, Charles Bronson, Lee Marvin, Jason Robards Jr.

21 JUMP STREET

USA 1987–90 103 x 60m col Fox/syndicated.
A Stephen J Cannell Production/Columbia
Pictures Television/20th Century Fox TV. UK tx
1989– Sky 1.

CR *Stephen J Cannell, Patrick Hasburgh.*
EXEC PR *Stephen J Cannell, Patrick Hasburgh,
David Levinson, Bill Nuss.* **DR** *Various, including
Rob Bowman, Daniel Attias, James Whitmore Jr,
Kim Manners, Jefferson Kibbee, Steve Beers,
Kevin Hooks, Mario Van Peebles, Tucker Gates,
Bill Corcoran, Peter DeLuise, Pete D Marshall.*
WR *Various, including Bill Nuss, Clifton
Campbell, Jonathan Lemkin, Patrick Hasburgh,
Glen Morgan, James Wong, Thania St John,
Michelle Ashford.* **MUS** *Liam Strasberg (theme),
Holly Robinson (theme vocals).*
CAST *Off Tom Hanson (Jeff Yagher (pilot)/Johnny
Depp) Off Doug Penhall (Peter DeLuise) Off Judy
Hoffs (Holly Robinson) Off Harry Truman Ioki
(Dustin Nguyen) Capt Richard Jenko (Frederic
Forrest) Capt Adam Fuller (Steven Williams) Off
Dennis Booker (Richard Grieco) Sal 'Blowfish'
Banducci (Sal Jenco) Jackie Garrett (Yvette Nipar)
Off Anthony 'Mac' McCann (Michael Bendetti)
Clavo (Tony Dakota) Off Joey Penhall (Michael
DeLuise) Dorothy Pezzino (Gina Nico) Kati Rocky
(Alexandra Powers).*

Like >*The Mod Squad* and >*Renegades*
before it, a police drama in which a group
of youthful crime-busters went undercover in the
local teen scene. Here the featured young cops
were members of a special unit of a big-city
police department (no exact location was ever
specified) which battled crime in high schools.
Thus each week officers Tom Hanson, Judy Hoffs,
Harry Ioki and Doug Penhall – all of whom were
selected for the unit because they could pass
muster as students – went back to school to
infiltrate the drug/auto-theft/prostitution/extortion
rings which periodically grip the US education
system on the home screen. The team's base was
a disused chapel at 21 Jump Street, where their
laid-back, Sixties leftover boss Captain Jenko kept
a wise eye on his charges. When Jenko was
killed by a hit-and-run drunk driver, the by-the-book
Adam Fuller became the unit's leader.

Pacy and, like >*Miami Vice*, laced with
Eighties music, *21 Jump Street* was fledgeling
network Fox's hottest early hit, but they dropped
the show in 1990 when it cooled. It continued,
however, for a fifth season in first-run syndication.
By this time, cast changes were speeding up.
Johnny Depp, no less, who played Hanson, quit
in 1990 (he apparently wanted out almost from
the start, but was constrained by his contract),
and departing in the same year were Peter
DeLuise and Dustin Nguyen. Richard Grieco, who
played Officer Booker (much disliked by Penhall
and Hanson), was spun off to his own short-run
Booker series in which he became that TV trusty,

a private investigator. Brought in as replacements were Michael Bendetti as 'Mac' McCann and Michael DeLuise as Doug Penhall's younger brother, Joey. The show achieved 21 episodes in syndication before its final termination.

SHOW TRIVIA: Although set in a nameless US city, *21JS* was filmed in Vancouver, Canada / Actress Holly Robinson's father was the voice of 'Roosevelt Franklin' on *The Muppets* / Although called Harry Ioki by one and all, Nguyen's character's real name was Vinh Van Tran / Nguyen himself was a Vietnamese refugee, whose real-life experience provided the story for the 'Christmas in Saigon' episode / The show's theme was penned by Liam Strasberg, who also wrote 'Like an Egyptian' for the Bangles / Among the writers were Glen Morgan and James Wong, later to become mainstays of *The X-Files* and >*Millennium* / Actors Peter and Michael DeLuise are sons of veteran actor Dom DeLuise – who guested on the show.

GUEST CAST: Jason Priestley, Brad Pitt, Dom DeLuise, Bridget Fonda, Rob Estes, Shannen Doherty, Sherilynn Fenn, John Waters.

TWIN PEAKS

USA 1990–1 2 x 120m, 28 x 60m col ABC. A Lynch/Frost Production/Spelling Entertainment. UK tx 1990–1 BBC2.

CR *David Lynch, Mark Frost.* **EXEC PR** *David Lynch, Mark Frost.* **PR** *Hayley Payton, Gregg Fienberg, David J Latt.* **DR** *Graeme Clifford, Caleb Deschanel, Mark Frost, Ulrich Edel, Duwayne Dunham, Diane Keaton, Tina Rathbone, James Foley, Lesli Linka Glatter, Stephen Gyllenhaal, Todd Hunter, Jonathan Sanger.* **WR** *Various, including David Lynch, Mark Frost, Harley Peyton, Robert Engels, Barry Pullman, Jerry Stahl, Tricia Brock, Scott Frost.* **MUS** *Angelo Badalamenti, David Lynch.*

CAST *Agent Dale Cooper (Kyle MacLachlan) Sheriff Harry S Truman (Michael Ontkean) Leland Palmer (Ray Wise) Audrey Horne (Sherilynn Fenn) Jocelyn 'Josie' Packard (Joan Chen) Laura Palmer/Madelaine Ferguson (Sheryl Lee) Donna Hayward (Lara Flynn Boyle) Catherine Martell (Piper Laurie) Peter Martell (Jack Nance) Big Ed Hurley (Everett McGill) Nadine Hurley (Wendy Robie) Benjamin Horne (Richard Beymer) Shelly Johnson (Madchen Amick) Leo Johnson (Eric Da Re) Dr Lawrence Jacoby (Russ Tamblyn) Deputy Andy Brennan (Harry Goaz) Norma Jennings (Peggy Lipton) Hank Jennings (Chris Mulkey) Lucy Moran (Kimmy Robertson) Gordon Cole (David Lynch) Margaret, the Log Lady (Catherine E Coulson) Deputy Tommy 'The Hawk' Hill (Michael Horse).* **VIDEO** *Screen Entertainment.*

An eerie and bizarre murder mystery set in the verdant US Pacific Northwest, which became an obsession in America and Britain in 1990. The mastermind behind the project was

avant-garde film-maker David Lynch, the show continuing his fascination with the dark life behind the white picket fences of small-town America, as already evidenced in the movie *Blue Velvet*.

The TV series, co-developed with >*Hill Street Blues* luminary Mark Frost and set in the lumber town of the title, hinged around the question: 'Who killed Laura Palmer?', a beautiful High School student. The main investigator was obsessive FBI agent Dale Cooper, a man prone to ecstasy when drinking coffee and eating cherry pie, and whose detecting methods included

⊙ *Who killed Laura Palmer? Agent Cooper (right) and assorted residents of eerie Twin Peaks.*

Tibetan mysticism, dreams and ESP. (It was an open secret that Cooper was a Lynch self-portrait.) Gradually, Cooper's hunting for the murderer revealed that Palmer was not the innocent she seemed, and that Twin Peaks, behind the picture postcard image, was a mired pool of drugs, adultery, avarice, pornography and satanism (with some of these evils explored through running sub-plots). The finger of suspicion pointed at most of the inhabitants before the culprit was revealed as Palmer's own father, possessed by the demonic 'Killer BOB'.

There was an almost surreal, dream-like mood to the show – especially in the segments directed by Lynch – enhanced by the famously weird minor characters and touches: the Log Lady, the fish in the percolator at the diner, Cooper's delivery of his own narrative into a micro-recorder for the unseen Diane ('Diane, I'm holding in my hands a small box of chocolate bunnies'). Meanwhile Cooper's one-liners – 'This is where pies go when they die' and 'Damn fine coffee – and hot' (actually a steal from Deputy Chester in *Gunsmoke*) – became virtual mantras among TV watchers.

The large cast featured two of Lynch's stock movie rep, Kyle MacLachlan *(Dune)* and Jack Nance *(Fraserhead)*, with Lynch himself occasionally appearing as FBI Chief Cole. The show also introduced a gallery of new faces, including Sherilynn Fenn (who later starred in Jennifer Lynch's *Boxing Helena*). David Duchovny, later of *The X-Files*, played a transvestite FBI agent.

Although ratings dipped dramatically towards the end of the opening season (largely because of lightweight, directionless scripts, not redeemed by gimmicks for gimmicks' sake), the show staggered through to its conclusion, even spinning off a movie, *Fire Walk With Me*, in 1992. It also left a

heavy imprint on such subsequent off-beat TV shows as *Northern Exposure* and *Eerie Indiana*.
GUEST CAST: Ted Raimi, David Duchovny, Alicia DeWitt.

THE UNTOUCHABLES
USA 1959–63 117 x 60m bw ABC.
Desilu/Langford Productions. UK tx 1966–9
ATV.
EXEC PR Jerry Thorpe, Leonard Freeman, Quinn Martin. *PR* Howard Hoffman, Alan A Armer, Alvin Cooperman, Lloyd Richards, Fred Freiberger, Charles Russell. *DR* Various, including Walter Grauman, Tay Garnett, Phil Karlson, Howard Koch, Stuart Rosenberg, Paul Stanley, John Peyser, Abner Biberman, Richard Whorf, Leonard Horn, Ida Lupino, Bernard McEveety, Alen Reisner, Robert Butler, Lazlo Benedek, Robert Florey. *WR* Various. *MUS* Wilbur Hatch, Nelson Riddle.
CAST Eliot Ness (Robert Stack) Agent Martin Flaherty (Jerry Paris) Agent William Longfellow (Abel Fernandez) Agent Enrico Rossi (Nick Georgiade) Agent Cam Allison (Anthony George) Agent Lee Hobson (Paul Picerni) Agent Rossmann (Steve London) Frank Nitti (Bruce Gordon) Al Capone (Neville Brand) Narrator (Walter Winchell).

In 1960 a television monitoring group based in Los Angeles reported that in one week alone television had shown 144 murders,

237

143 attempted murders, four attempted lynchings, two massacres or mass murders, 52 other killings and eleven planned murders. A ratings war between the major US networks was responsible for this escalating violence in TV crime series, and most notorious among the offenders was Quinn Martin's *The Untouchables*. With an eye on the competition, Martin had told his writers early on, 'More action, or we are going to get clobbered.' The writers obliged and *The Untouchables*, a fast-action classic among crime dramas, soon became known as 'the weekly bloodbath', with the palookas getting mown down in up to three machine-gun shoot-outs per instalment.

The series was based on the autobiography of Eliot Ness, a Treasury Department crime-buster based in Chicago in Prohibition days. Ness had played a major part in breaking the power of notorious gangster Al Capone in 1931, a story dramatised in a two-part TV show *The Scarface Mob*, aired on Desilu Playhouse in 1959. The special prompted ABC to run a series – which almost reeked of speakeasy authenticity – with Robert Stack, an accomplished movie actor, starring as Ness. With Capone safely behind bars, the action focused on the battle between the gangster's two top lieutenants, Jake 'Greasy Thumb' Guzik and Frank 'The Enforcer' Nitti for control of the empire he had left behind, and Ness's attempts to bring the mobsters to justice. The real-life Ness had in fact disbanded his

famous band of agents, the Untouchables (so-called by a Chicago newspaper because of their incorruptibility), after the Capone case, but on the small screen *The Untouchables* went after famous gang bosses from Bugs Moran (in whose garage the St Valentine's Day Massacre took place) to Ma Baker, East Coast hoods such as Mad Dog Coll, Dutch Schultz and Philadelphia crime boss Walter Legenza.

The series was a massive hit. Apart from the satisfaction of seeing the Mob get it every week, there was the music and the stars – it guest-featured some of the medium's heaviest of heavies: William Bendix, Lloyd Nolan, Neville Brand and Neremiah Persoff. The period props and costumes were part of the appeal: *The Untouchables* was all double-breasted suits, flash cars and violin cases. It also had a different, quasi-documentary feel, with a staccato voice-over provided by old-style columnist Walter Winchell. The show's departures from reality attracted complaints from the FBI, Italian-American groups and prison officers, but the producers simply added a disclaimer to the end of each episode and carried on.

Yet success was short-lived. The programme went from number 43 in the charts in its first season to number eight in its second, then back to number 41 in the third. In its fourth and final season there was an attempt to win back audiences by making Ness more human and the

The Untouchables a guaranteed cert, and this
duly arrived on the airwaves in 1993, under the
title *The Untouchables*, with Tom Amandes as Eliot
Ness and William Forsythe as Ness's arch-enemy,
Al Capone. It was eased into being by the
success of Brian De Palma's 1987 movie version
starring Kevin Costner.

The episodes were: *The Empty Chair/The
George 'Bugs' Moran Story/Noise of Death/Ma
Barker and Her Boys/You Can't Pick a Number/
The Jake Lingle Story/Ain't We Got Fun/The
Vincent 'Mad Dog' Coll Story/Mexican
Stakeout/The Artichoke King/The Ten-State Gang
/The Dutch Schultz Story/Underground Railway/
Syndicate Sanctuary/Star Witness/One Armed
Bandit/The St Louis Story/The Big Squeeze/
Little Egypt/Unhired Assassin/The White Slavers/
Three Thousand Suspects/The Doreen Maney
Story/Portrait of a Thief/The Underworld Bank/
Head of Fire, Feet of Clay/The Frank Nitti Story/
A Seat on the Fence/The Jack 'Legs' Diamond
Story/The Rusty Helier Story/The Waxey Gordon
Story/The Mark of Cain/The Otto Frick Story/
Nicky/The Big Train/The Purple Gang/The Kiss
of Death Girl/The Larry Fay Story/The Tommy
Karpeles Story/The Masterpiece/Augie 'The
Banker' Clamino/The Organization/Jamaica
Ginger/The Underground Court/The Nick Moses
Story/The Antidote/The Lily Dallas Story/Murder
Under Glass/Testimony of Evil/Ring of Terror/Mr
Moon/Death for Sale/Stranglehold/The Seventh*

*Robert Stack as Eliot Ness in The Untouchables,
dubbed 'the weekly bloodbath' for its violence
quotient.*

killings more motivated. New investigators from
other government bureaus were brought in,
including Barbara Stanwyck as a lieutenant from
the Bureau of Missing Persons. But production
ended in 1963 after 117 episodes, and
organised crime didn't feature again on the small
screen until J Edgar Hoover gave permission for
the series >*The FBI* (another Quinn Martin
production) to be made in 1965.

The recidivist tendency of TV made a remake of

239

Vote/The Nero Rankin Story/The King of
Champagne/The Nick Acropolis Story/90 Proof
Dame/Tunnel of Horrors/Power Play/The Matt
Bass Scheme/Loophole/The Troubleshooters/The
Genna Brothers/Hammerlock/Jigsaw/Mankiller
City/Without a Name/Canada Run/Fall Guy/
The Silent Partner/The Gang War/The Whitey
Steele Story/Takeover/The Death Tree/The
Stryker Brothers/Element of Danger/The Maggie
Storm Story/Man in the Middle/Downfall/The
Case Against Eliot Ness/The Ginnie Littlesmith
Story/The Contract/Pressure/The Monkey
Wrench/Arsenal/The Chess Game/The Night
They Shot Santa Claus/The Pea/Cooker In the
Sky/The Economist/A Taste of Pineapple/The
Snowball/Elegy/Bird in the Hand/Come and Kill
Me/The Eddie O'Hara Story/An Eye for an Eye/
Search for a Dead Man/A Fist of Five/The Floyd
Gibbons Story/Doublecross/The Speculator/Jake
Dance/Blues for a Gone Goose/Globe of
Death/Junk Man/Man in the Cooler/The
Butcher's Boy/The Spoiler/One Last Killing/The
Giant Killer/The Charlie Argos Story/The Jazz
Man/The Torpedo/Line of Fire.
GUEST CAST: Jack Lord, Telly Savalas, Herb
Vigran, Lee Marvin, Edward Asner, Sondra Blake,
Carroll O'Connor, Roy Thinnes, Ricardo
Montalban, Telly Savalas, James MacArthur,
Harry Dean Stanton, Joan Blondell, Brian Keith,
Rip Torn, Louise Fletcher, Martin Landau, William
Bendix, Alan Hale Jr, J Carrol Naish, Lee Van
Cleef, Vic Morrow, Peter Falk, Elizabeth
Montgomery, Jack Elam, Marion Ross, Robert
Duvall, Robert Vaughn, Robert Redford, Jack
Kugman, Clu Gulager, Robert Loggia, Charles
Bronson, Barbara Stanwyck, Lloyd Nolan.

VAN DER VALK
UK 1972–7 / 1991–2 25 x 60m, 4 x 120m
col ITV. Thames TV/Euston Films/Elmgate.
EXEC PR Lloyd Shirley, George Taylor, Brian
Walcroft. **PR** Michael Chapman, Robert Love,
Geoffrey Gilbert, Chris Burt. **DR** Various, including
Douglas Camfield, Mike Vardy, Anthony
Simmons. **WR** Various, including Arden Winch,
Philip Broadley.
CAST Piet Van der Valk (Barry Foster) Arlette Van
der Valk (Susan Travers/Joanna Dunham/Meg
Davies) Commissaris Samson (Nigel
Stock/Ronald Hines) Wim Van der Valk (Richard
Huw).

Languid 60-minute series following the
cases of a moody blond detective with the
Amsterdam CID. Eminently watchable police
procedural show, helped by the unusual setting
and location filming. Adapted from the novels of
Nicholas Freeling, it generated a British number
one hit single in the Jack Tombey (aka Jan
Stoeckhart) 'Eye Level' theme as recorded by the
Simon Park Orchestra. A 1991–2 revival in a
120-minute format failed to take.

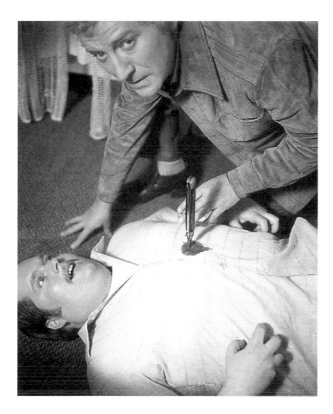

CAST Dan Tanna (Robert Urich) Beatrice Travis (Phyllis Davis) Angie Turner (Judy Landers) Bobby Borso ('Binzer') (Bart Braverman) Chief Eli Two Leaf (Will Sampson) Lt David Nelson (Greg Morris) Philip Roth (Tony Curtis) Sgt Bella Archer (Naomi Stevens).

Superior private eye actioner featuring Las Vegas-based 'tec Dan Tanna. Helping the handsome shamus on his weekly murder cases were his red Thunderbird car, sexy receptionist Angie, sexy secretary Beatrice, legman Binzer and Sergeant Archer of the (Vegas) police. Philip 'Slick' Roth (Tony Curtis) was the millionaire casino-owner who had Tanna on a retainer.

Vega$ was dreamed up by Michael Mann (later to be a prime mover and shaker on >Miami Vice and >Crime Story), and had a sure-fire hit setting in the fleshpots and cashpots of Arizona gambling capital, which it exploited to the nth degree. It made a star out of former TV weatherman and >S.W.A.T. regular Robert Urich (who had, incidentally, been persuaded to Hollywood by friend Burt Reynolds, >BL Stryker, >Dan August). Urich later donned gumshoes again when he became >Spenser: For Hire.

Vega$ was preceded by a two-hour TVM (1978) directed by Richard Lang.

GUEST CAST: Tori Spelling, Kim Basinger, Richard Basehart, Melanie Griffith, Leslie Nielsen, James MacArthur, Victor Buono (as Diamond Jim).

⊗ Barry Foster as Van der Valk. The show spun-off a number one record.

GUEST CAST: Lisa Daniely, Ian Hendry, Bob Hoskins, Lalla Ward, Christopher Timothy.

VEGA$

USA 1978–81 69 x 60m col ABC. Spelling-Cramer. UK tx 1978–81 ITV.
CR Michael Mann. EXEC PR Aaron Spelling, Douglas S Cramer. PR Alan Godfrey, E Duke Vincent. DR Various, including Richard Lang.
MUS Dominic Frontiere, John Beal.

WALKER, TEXAS RANGER

USA 1993– 32+ x 60m col CBS. CBS Television/Amadea Film. UK tx 1993– Sky 1.

EXEC PR Chuck Norris, Aaron Norris, Leonard Katzman. **PR** Rick Husky, Gordon Dawson. **DR** Various, including Tony Mordente, Michael Preece, Eric Norris. **MUS** Christopher Franke, Jerrold Immel.

CAST Cordell 'Cord' Walker (Chuck Norris) Jimmy Trivette (Clarence Gilyard Jr) Alex Cahill (Sheree J Wilson) C D Parker (Noble Willingham) Uncle Ray Firewalker Floyd (Red Crow Westerman) Det Carlos Sandoval (Marco Sanchez).

Hour-long action drama series starring Chuck 'MIA' Norris as Cordell Walker, a Vietnam vet turned modern-day Texas Ranger. To get his bad man 'Cord' tended to use intuition (he had Native American ancestors) and he-man martial arts skills. This contrasted sharply with the methods of his rookie partner Trivette, a black from Baltimore who liked to use such modern accessories as a computer and cellular phone. C D Parker, a retired Ranger who ran a saloon, was often on hand to give sage advice, while county Assistant DA Alex Cahill (Sheree J Wilson, formerly April Stevens in Dallas) was Walker's mutual attraction – although she often disagreed with his methods. It was old-fashioned TV – your basic guys in the white hats beating the guys in the black hats – but struck a chord among people who needed an unambiguous hero, and became a big and lasting ratings runner. The show was filmed on location in Dallas. Supervising producer was J Michael Straczynski, the man behind the classic space saga Babylon 5.

SHOW TRIVIA: Norris, a former karate world champion, had American Indian blood himself – his father was a Cherokee / Norris's real name was Carlos Ray / Clarence Gilyard Jr, who played Trivette, had performed in a long-running crime show before; he had played Conrad McMaster in >Matlock.

GUEST CAST: L Q Jones, Roy Thinnes, Clu Gulager, Robert Vaughn, Richard Herd, Lee Majors, Barbara Bain, Rick Aiello, Ken Kercheval.

WISEGUY

USA 1987–90 1 x 120m, 71 x 60m col CBS. Stephen J Cannell Productions.

CR Stephen J Cannell, Frank Lupo. **EXEC PR** Stephen J Cannell. **DR** Rod Holcomb, Robert Iscove, Charles Correll, Aaron Lipstadt, Dennis Dugan, Kim Manners, James Whitmore, William Fraker, Ken Wahl, Peter D Marshall, Guy Trikonis. **WR** Stephen J Cannell, Frank Lupo, Eric Blakeney, Stephen Kronish, David J Burke, John Schulian, Ken Wahl, Alfonse Ruggiero, Clifton Campbell. **MUS** Mike Post.

CAST Vinnie Terranova (Ken Wahl) Frank McPike (Jonathan Banks) Dan Burroughs ('Lifeguard') (Jim

Byrnes) Michael Santana (Steven Bauer) Father Pete Terranova (Vinnie's brother) (Gerald Anthony) Carlotta Terranova/Aiuppo (Elsa Raven) Mark Cermak (Dwight Koss) Sonny Steelgrave (Ray Sharkey) Pat 'The Cat' Patrice (Joe Dellasandro) Sid Royce (Dennis Lipscomb) Herb Ketcher (David Spielberg) Roger LoCocco (William Russ) Susan Profitt (Joan Severance) Mel Profitt (Kevin Spacey) Eli Sternberg (Jerry Lewis) David Sternberg (Ron Silver) Carole Sternberg (Patricia Charbonneau) Rick Pinzolo (Stanley Tucci) Isaac Twine (Paul Winfield) Amber Twine (Patti D'Arbanville) Winston Newquay (Tim Curry) Don Rudy Aiuppo (George O Petrie) Mark Volchek (Steve Ryan) Amado Guzman (Maximilian Schell) Rafael Santana (Manolo Villaverde) Dahlia (Mendez Martika).

The crime TV watcher's crime show. *Wiseguy* came via ever busy Stephen J Cannell Productions, debuting first in 1987, and used – to a degree unprecedented even by >*Hill Street Blues* – polysemic plots and storyline arcs (of up to ten episodes). Ken Wahl played savvy Organised Crime Bureau agent Vinnie Terranova, sent deep undercover to infiltrate the Mob in Atlantic City. Frank McPike was Terranova's boss at OCB, and Daniel Burroughs ('Lifeguard') his only channel of communication when he was on the case. Sophisticated and suspenseful, *Wiseguy* continued its intoxicating course after Terranova brought down palooka Sonny Steelgrave, following Terranova as he fingered big-time smuggler Mel Profitt (Kevin Spacey), who was also aiding a Caribbean dictator in a coup attempt. Alas, this assignment went to bloody bits when Terranova discovered that the coup had been illegally set up by the CIA, and another 'wiseguy' undercover agent Roger LoCocco was assassinated. At this, Terranova quit the OCB in disgust to work at a gas station in Brooklyn. However, the activities of the local racists and mobsters persuaded him back to work at the OCB (the better to bring the bad guys down), and subsequent cases saw him working undercover in the clothing industry, the rock music biz, and out in the sticks at Lynchboro, where the town was run by a mad oldster, Mark Volchek. Meanwhile, his mother Carlotta had married Rudy Aiuppo, New York's biggest crime boss – who soon discovered that his stepson was a government fink. After negotiating all this, Terranova once again quit the OCB.

When Ken Wahl left *Wiseguy* in 1990, the action centred on the Cuban-American Michael Santana, a disbarred federal prosecutor, played by Steven Bauer. At McPike's request Santana went undercover to expose the corrupt practices of businessman Amado Guzman.

GUEST CAST: Joan Chen, John Santucci, Debbie Harry, Mick Fleetwood, Jon Polito, Chazz Palminteri, Robert Davi, James Stacy.

Z CARS

UK 1962–78 667 x 25/50m bw/col BBC1. BBC TV.

CR Troy Kennedy Martin. **PR** David E Rose, Richard Beynon, Ronald Travers, Ron Craddock. **DR** Various, including John McGrath, Terence Dudley, Paddy Russell, Vivian Matalon, Philip Dudley, Richard Harding, Eric Taylor, Eric Hills, Christopher Barry, Shaun Sutton, Robin Midgeley, Alan Bromly, Michael Hayes, Ken Loach. **WR** Various, including Troy Kennedy Martin, John Hopkins, Robert Barr, Alan Plater, Bill Barron, Allan Prior, Keith Dewhurst, John McGrath, Bill Lyons, Elwyn Jones. **MUS** 'Johnny Todd' theme played by Johnny Keating.

CAST Det Insp Charlie Barlow (Stratford Johns) PC Jock Weir (Joseph Brady) PC Bert Lynch (James Ellis) PC David Graham (Colin Welland) Desk Sgt Twentyman (Leonard Williams) Det Supt Miller (Leslie Sands) Det Insp Goss (Derek Waring) Det Cons Scatliff (Geoffrey Hayes) PC Quilley (Douglas Fielding) Det Insp Witty (John Woodvine) Det Sgt John Watt (Frank Windsor) PC 'Fancy' Smith (Brian Blessed) PC Bob Steele (Jeremy Kemp) PC Sweet (Terence Edmond) Desk Sgt Blackitt (Robert Keegan) Det Sgt Stone (John Slater) Det Insp Bamber (Leonard Rossiter) PC Newcombe (Bernard Holley) Det Con Skinner (Ian Cullen) Det Insp Hudson (John Barrie) Det Insp Todd (Joss Ackland) Det Insp Brogan (George Sewell) WPB Bayliss (Alison Steadman) PC Owen Culshaw (David Daker) PC Alec May (Stephen Yardley) Det Insp Moffet (Ray Lonnen) Det Sgt Bowker (Brian Gethin). **VIDEO** BBC.

Over in the States audiences were thrilling to machine-gun operas of TV violence, but it took writer Troy Kennedy Martin to notice (while listening to police radio during a bout of mumps) that Britain's >Dixon of Dock Green was out of date. With the backing of new BBC Director General Hugh Green and his head of drama Sidney Lawrence, and with help from respected documentarists Elwyn Jones and Robert Barr, Martin set out to create a lifelike, new-style police series for the Sixties. The result was Z Cars.

The location was the tough Liverpool docklands – Kirby became overspill estate Newtown for the series, and Seaforth became Seaport – and the four young recruits driving around in Ford Zephyr patrol cars Z-Victor-One and Z-Victor-Two, call-sign 'Zulu', encountered harsh urban realities very different from those in Dixon's manor. Newtown was a mixed community, displaced by slum clearance, brought together on an estate without amenities or community feeling. The series – heralded by the flute-and-drum theme 'Johnny Todd' – opened on the grave of PC Farrow, shot down in the execution of his duty. The answer was to bring in patrol cars, and the first job was to find the 'crew'. Z-Victor-One was soon in the hands of Northcountryman PC Fancy Smith and

⊗ *Jeremy Kemp (left) and James Ellis in BBC's land-mark police series* Z Cars.

Scots PC Jock Weir. Z-Victor-Two held Irishman PC Herbert Lynch and red-haired PC Bob Steele. And in *Z Cars* Liverpool Docklands got the policemen it deserved – these cops were no angels. Constable Lynch was not above a flutter on the horses, Constable Bob Steele was revealed in episode one as a wife-beater, and violence on the beat was met by violence from the men in the patrol cars. The Police Federation, viewers and even Jack Warner complained, but within two months of the show's first episode in 1962 it was attracting an audience of 14 million.

Z Cars ran for sixteen years until 1978, when it in turn began to look dated next to new shows like >*The Sweeney*. The two characters who created the most impact were hard and soft men Detective Inspector Charlie Barlow and Detective Sergeant John Watt. Barlow, a huge man not above verbal or physical violence, and the gentler

246

Watt, his ideal foil, were so successful that they departed for the Regional Crime Squad and their own spin-off series, >Softly, Softly.

Another early departure was creator Troy Kennedy Martin, who left Z Cars three months after its first transmission, unhappy with the way the series was going. He had wanted a true-to-life series where the police would lose some of the time, but the BBC made sure that the criminal got arrested at the end of every episode.

Even so, the series moved British television police drama on to a new realism. Its all-round high-quality production was the result of a combination of BBC drama-documentary expertise, superb casting – Stratford Johns, Frank Windsor, Leonard Rossiter, Brian Blessed, Colin Welland, who all became household names – and scripts from leading writers such as John Hopkins, Robert Barr, Alan Plater and Allan Prior. A young Ken Loach was among those trying his hand at directing. Guest stars included such young talents as Judi Dench, and among the production team were Julia Smith and Tony Holland, who many years later were to be the creators of the BBC's EastEnders. Actor Brian Blessed's later roles included Caesar Augustus in I Claudius; actor and writer Colin Welland starred in Dennis Potter's Blue Remembered Hills and wrote the award-winning feature film Chariots of Fire; and Stratford Johns fast outgrew his part in Softly, Softly to be given his own series Barlow at Large (1971–3) and Barlow (1974–6), in which he was elevated to Detective Chief Superintendent. Geoffrey Hayes, meanwhile, who played DC Scatliff, became the presenter of TV programme Rainbow.

Creator Troy Kennedy Martin later wrote the multiple BAFTA Award-winning nuclear political thriller Edge of Darkness (1985) for BBC2.

GUEST CAST: Judi Dench, Kenneth Cope, Ralph Bates, Stephanie Turner, John Thaw.

ZERO ONE

UK 1962–5 39 x 25m bw BBC1. BBC TV/MGM. US tx 1962 syndicated.

PR Lawrence P Bachmann.
CAST Alan Garnett (Nigel Patrick) Maya (Katya Douglas) Jimmy Delaney (Bill Smith).

Smartly made action drama show, following the cases of airline detective Alan Garnett, chief London op of the International Air Security Board (call-sign 'Zero One'). Aiding Garnett was the obligatory beautiful secretary, Maya, and legman Jimmy Delaney. Although co-produced with US company MGM, the show crashed – as it were – Stateside, where sponsors shied away from the subject-matter of its storylines, such as sky-jacks, trafficking and sabotage. In Canada the show found willing sponsors in General Motors, the car manufacturer.

INDEX

Note: Page references in **bold type** indicate main references.

254

PICTURE ACKNOWLEDGEMENTS

The publishers would like to thank the following agencies for supplying images. Every effort has been made to acknowledge all copyright holders. However, should any photographs not be correctly attributed, the publisher will undertake any appropriate changes in future editions of the book. The images listed below are protected by copyright.

10, 22, 36, 39, 51, 68, 71, 76, 81, 82, 87 105, 132, 137, 179, 182, 192, 199, 210, 222, 225, 239, 245 Pictorial Press
11 Pictorial Press/© Granada
24, 103, 121, 194, 208 Pictorial Press/© Polygram
133 Pictorial Press/Combi Press
163 Pictorial Press/© Sky One
189 Pictorial Press/© Columbia Pictures Industries
130 Pictorial Press/© Universal Pictures
236 Pictorial Press/© Photo PS

29, 44, 49, 55, 70, 75, 92, 95, 117, 125, 143, 145, 147, 149, 154, 219 Kobal Collection
38 Kobal Collection/© 20th Century Fox Television

41 Kobal Collection/© CBS Entertainment
59 Kobal Collection/© NBC Television Network
119 Kobal Collection/© CBG Communications Photography
152 Kobal Collection/© CBS TV Network Photo Division
160 Kobal Collection/© ABC Visual Communications

20, 45, 63, 73, 85, 97, 111, 115, 157, 201, 229, 231 Ronald Grant Archive
58 Ronald Grant Archive/© Granada Television
173 Ronald Grant Archive/© Photos from Four
197, 205 Ronald Grant Archive/© NBC Photo
212 Ronald Grant Archive/© BBC Picture Publicity

17, 26, 83, 142, 155, 168, 176 Aquarius

16 Corbis/Everett

28, 77 BBC Photographic Library

65, 100, 109, 185, 216, 241 Pearsons TV Stills Library